American Politics Since 1945

American Politics Since 1945

Edited with an Introduction by
Richard M. Dalfiume

❦ a New York Times Book

Quadrangle Books
CHICAGO

Library of Congress Catalog Card Number: 69-20160

The publishers are grateful to the contributors herein
for permission to reprint their articles.

Contents

3. The Kennedy Administration

4. The Johnson Administration

5. The New Nixon

American Politics Since 1945

Introduction

Truman and the Roosevelt Coalition

ANY SUMMARY of American politics since 1945 must begin with an understanding of the "Roosevelt Revolution," the process which changed the Democratic party from the minority into the majority party of the nation. In large part, this phenomenon was the result of changing political allegiances in the nation's cities, the fastest growing segment of an increasingly industrialized country.

From 1920 to 1964, here is the record of net party plurality in the nation's twelve largest cities:

1920	1,540,000	Republican
1924	1,308,000	Republican
1928	210,000	Democratic
1932	1,791,000	Democratic
1936	3,479,000	Democratic
1940	2,112,000	Democratic
1944	2,230,000	Democratic
1948	1,481,000	Democratic
1952	1,081,000	Democratic
1956	391,000	Democratic
1960	2,711,000	Democratic
1964	4,357,000	Democratic

(Source: Samuel Lubell, *The Future of American Politics,* 1965 edition)

Historian Carl Degler writes that ". . . it was the political activity of urban voters which raised the Republican party to a position of dominance in American politics for a third of a century, just as it has been the cities which have been largely responsible for the Democratic party's leading place in the nation's political life for the most recent third of this century."

The urban trend away from the Republicans began in 1928 with the Herbert Hoover–Al Smith campaign. Smith, a Catholic, a descendant of Irish immigrants, and a product of big-city streets, politicized the nation's immigrants and their children, a part of the population that was rapidly becoming the majority in most American cities. The depression and the New Deal consolidated these voters under the Democratic banner. The Democratic hold on the cities was further strengthened by appeals to Negroes and organized labor. The black voter's traditional loyalty to the party of Lincoln was broken by Republican neglect, the relief programs of the New Deal, and the political recognition offered by the Roosevelt administration. In a similar way, the worker was brought into the Roosevelt coalition through relief and recovery programs and federal intervention in collective bargaining on behalf of organized labor.

FDR's coalition was not simply an urban affair, however. It also included the "Solid South," whose politics would show more unpredictability as the years passed and disenchantment increased over the growing influence of Northern Negroes, labor, and liberal intellectuals in the party, but whose power in Congress earned deference from Roosevelt in the 1930's and from every President since. And there were the farmers of the Midwest who, having suffered depression throughout most of the twenties, rallied behind New Deal farm programs.

It was the very diversity of this Roosevelt coalition, one wing rural and conservative, the other wing urban and liberal, that gave it the character of a highly volatile substance, ready to explode at any moment and shatter its container, the Democratic party, into tiny pieces. Roosevelt's success in making the coalition work was partly the result of his being a master political broker with the various interest groups. Moreover, depression politics generally allowed the Roosevelt administration to court interest groups by conferring economic benefits, a strategy that also helped to improve the country's economic well-being. The sense of crisis during the first years of the New Deal was pervasive enough that many normally conservative members of Congress went along with the Roosevelt program, biding their time.

In assessing the political legacy FDR bequeathed to Harry Truman as President in 1945, it is important to remember that Roosevelt lost his magic touch with Congress long before his death. Beginning with the Supreme Court "packing" bill in 1937, conservatives in Congress from both parties became bolder and joined informally to block liberal measures. The failure of the New Deal to end the depression, the reassertion of congressional authority, and the rejuvenation of the Republican party after years of wandering in the wilderness were also factors which slowed Roosevelt's programs. Finally, with the coming of World War II, foreign affairs took precedence over domestic reform.

It is difficult to recapture the anxiety of many Americans as World War II came to an end. Because the full employment of World War II had ended the depression, most ordinary Americans, as well as economists, thought the coming of peace would mean a return to depression conditions. Many liberals were concerned that, without another round of domestic reforms, bad economic conditions would bring domestic fascism. Conservatives viewed any resurgence of New Deal–type reform as a disaster, and they were prepared to fight to erase as much of the New Deal as possible. Consumers were interested in ending rationing as soon as possible in order to purchase the good things of life with savings of the prosperous war years; at the same time they were irritated by a continuing shortage of consumer goods and alarmed by galloping inflation which raised the prices of everything they bought. Organized labor argued for continued government price controls, but an end to wage controls. Industry favored continued wage controls, but thought the return of free enterprise demanded an end to price controls. Farmers were concerned about the inflation that raised the cost of goods they had to buy, but they demanded that the government guarantee continued wartime prosperity through high agricultural price supports.

Inflation rather than deflation turned out to be the primary concern for Americans in the postwar years. Unlike the politics of depression that enable a President to parcel out favors to major economic blocs and at the same time contribute to economic recovery, the politics of inflation called for holding the line against the demands of major pressure groups. But the latter approach was alien to Harry Truman's philosophy of politics. He was a man of the middle, committed to what today is called "consensus politics." The descendant of rural, Protestant, Southern Democrats, he had risen in local, state, and national politics with the help of the Catholic, Negro, urban machine of Tom Pendergast in Kansas City, Missouri. As a Senator he had staunchly supported the New Deal and President Roosevelt, yet he remained on excellent terms with the conservatives and Southern Democrats in the Senate. Indeed, Roosevelt was persuaded to dump Vice-President Henry Wallace in 1944 and choose Truman as his running mate because Truman had ties with both the liberal and conservative wings of the party.

In dealing with the problems of reconversion from a wartime economy, Truman followed his instinct for the middle. But his efforts to conciliate all of the interest groups ended by alienating them. While Truman defended continued government price controls as necessary to stem inflation, the administration weakened controls or allowed them to become ineffective; the defense of controls angered those, like businessmen, who wanted them abolished, while their discontinuance angered consumers and labor. With price controls ineffective, organized labor was more determined than ever to win wage increases. When the country was rocked by a wave of strikes in late 1945 and 1946, the administration supported compromises which granted wage increases to labor and price increases to employers, a course of action that did nothing to halt inflation. When the railway brotherhoods brought the country to the verge of paralysis with a strike in May 1946, the President pulled out all stops and in a special message to Congress asked for the power to draft the strikers into the military so that the government could operate the railroads. Although the strike was settled before the President finished his message, labor, along with consumers, had been alienated.

The Democratic coalition was also weakened in other areas. Truman had long had the support of Missouri Negroes when running for state offices, but his national image among black Americans was that of a Southerner. They remained suspicious despite Truman's strong civil rights record as a Senator and despite his support for a permanent Fair Employment Practices Commission during his first two years as President. New Deal liberals, in general, found it hard to identify with the twangy-voiced, blunt-talking Midwesterner, and to consider him the appropriate successor to Franklin Roosevelt. Yet by the end of 1945, Truman had advocated a raise in the minimum wage, extension of social security, a permanent FEPC, a government full-employment program, an extensive slum clearance and public housing program, a series of flood control and hydroelectric projects, and national health insurance and federal aid to education programs. Liberals preferred to look beyond the rhetoric, where they saw an evil specter in the men around the President. They saw Texan Tom Clark appointed as Attorney General and James F. Byrnes of South Carolina as Secretary of State. There was John W. Snyder, conservative Missouri banker and long-time friend of the President, who, as head of the Office of War Mobilization and Reconversion and then as Secretary of the Treasury, exerted a strong influence on the administration's economic policies. Babbitt-like figures such as oilman Edwin W. Pauley, businessman George Allen, and influence-peddler Harry Vaughn had access to the President's ear, while the incorruptible Secretary of the Interior Harold Ickes left the administration in a dispute over patronage, and Henry Wallace, whom many New Dealers considered the true heir to Roosevelt, was fired from his post as Secretary of Commerce when he broke with the Truman position on foreign policy. In the lower levels of the federal government, the exodus of New Dealers was even more marked.

With the alienation of major parts of the Democratic coalition, the Republicans won their first national victory since 1928 in the elections of 1946, capturing control of both houses of Congress. Over the protest of a small group of Republican moderates in Congress, the conservative leadership of the GOP, Senator Robert Taft of Ohio and Representative Joseph Martin of Massachusetts, read the election results as a mandate to roll back the New Deal. Party leaders were convinced that a Republican President in 1948 would be the inevitable result of the GOP's return to power—despite the facts that the Republican party was still a minority party, and that many voters still blamed Republicans for the depression. Nor did the Republican leadership consider Harry Truman, who still had two more years in office before the election.

Truman's popularity continued to fall and reached its low point before the Democratic convention in 1948. While many Democrats were seeking to dump the President in favor of General Dwight D. Eisenhower, others were deserting the party to support Henry Wallace and the Progressive party. In the South, forces were at work which would result in the defection of the Dixiecrats and the formation of the States' Rights party. Yet Truman overcame apparently insurmountable odds to win a remarkable victory in 1948.

The basic reason lay in the still potent Democratic coalition and the short-term political forces that allowed it to function again.

The task of putting Humpty Dumpty together again was partly the result of conscious planning. A group of administration liberals began meeting soon after the election of the Republican 80th Congress to plot strategy for Truman's campaign in 1948. This palace guard, composed of Oscar R. Ewing, director of the Federal Security Agency, Clark Clifford, Special Counsel to the President, and Leon Keyserling, member of the Council of Economic Advisers, among others, was determined to counteract the conservative advice of the Cabinet and Democratic leaders in Congress. They wanted to build a distinctive liberal domestic program which would appeal to the most important blocs of voters—the farmers, the consumers, and the ethnic and labor vote in the cities. According to these strategists, Truman should stop trying to reconcile the irreconcilables and adopt a bold program that abandoned consensus. To a remarkable degree, these men succeeded in getting the President to follow their program. And Truman apparently was inclined toward a new direction. His situation was different. He was now in the role of the opposition, no longer having to lead a Democratic Congress.

The 80th Congress did its share to heal the fractured Democratic party. While Truman bombarded the Republican Congress with proposals for liberal domestic legislation—continued high price supports for farmers, public housing projects, urban redevelopment, national health insurance, increased minimum wage and social security benefits, anti-inflation legislation, a strong civil rights program—Congress either ignored or watered down these proposals. Instead the Republicans gave overwhelming support to a Displaced Persons Act that discriminated against Catholics and Jews, and passed the Taft-Hartley Act (designed to reduce organized labor's power in collective bargaining) over Truman's strong veto and labor's charges that it was a "slave labor law."

The anti–New Deal stance of the 80th Congress made Truman's campaign charges against the "do-nothing" Republicans credible to many voters. According to the President, the GOP had "flouted the will of the people," had passed a labor relations law that could eventually "enslave totally the workingman," had "stuck a pitchfork in the backs of farmers," and had passed an "anti-Semitic, anti-Catholic" immigration bill. (Truman's charges ignored congressional legislation that supported the administration's foreign and military policies.)

In addition, Truman frequently warned the voters that a Republican President was likely to bring a depression into office with him, a specter that remained real to an electorate that still remembered the hard times of the thirties. While the GOP presidential candidate, Governor Thomas E. Dewey of New York, took the high road, conducting an aloof campaign which skirted the issues, Truman crisscrossed the country, stirring his audiences with "give-'em-hell" speeches. Assured by the opinion pollsters, his campaign strategists, and newsmen that he was a sure winner, Dewey fiddled while Truman burned the Republican bridges to the White House. Many Republicans shared Senator Taft's lament when the returns were in: "It defies all common sense for the country to send that roughneck ward politician back to the White House."

When a self-confident President Truman delivered his annual message to Congress in 1949, urging a "Fair Deal" program of domestic reform, he and liberals had high hopes that this Democratic 81st Congress would enact such a program. Except for the Housing Act of 1949, however, the Fair Deal made little progress. The forces of deadlock in Congress that had appeared in the last days of the New Deal were institutionalized by 1949. Republican legislators, frustrated by Truman's victory in 1948, were determined to build a winning case against the Democrats by 1952. Southern Democrats, entrenched in important committee chairmanships because of the seniority system, were prepared to join forces with Republicans to thwart the urban, liberal, Northern Fair Deal. Indeed, the Democratic majorities in Congress during most of the years after 1945 proved to be only paper majorities whenever Republicans and Southern Democrats decided to get together on an issue.

This was more than a conservative coalition. It was also largely a rural coalition. All across the country, because of the failure of state legislatures to reapportion their legislative districts over the years, the urban population was underrepresented in both the state and national legislatures. Since the President is elected by the popular vote of city dwellers who make up the great majority of the electorate, malapportionment contributed to political statemate by giving disproportionate power to rural representatives in Congress. The result has been described by political scientists as four-party politics: Republican and Democratic liberal, urban presidential parties, and Republican and Democratic rural, conservative congressional parties. Not until the *Baker v. Carr* decision of the Supreme Court in 1962 could urban voters look forward to having an equal voice in government and to removing this obstacle to the popular will.

Truman's domestic reform program was also made more difficult by the fact that he was the first President forced to conduct a "dual presidency." Because of the developing Cold War, new directions in foreign policy competed with peacetime domestic programs for the attention of most Americans. In Congress, the same conservative coalition that worked to thwart domestic reform was an integral part of the internationalist coalition that supported the administration's foreign policy; so the President could not push a reform program without alienating support for his foreign policy. With the outbreak of the Korean War in June 1950, the chances for domestic reform were further reduced. The major concern became the military containment of communism.

Anti-communism had become a staple of the American political diet long before Senator Joseph McCarthy of Wisconsin charged in early 1950 that Communists honeycombed the State Department. From the first days of the New Deal, conservatives of both parties had charged that social legislation was communism in the disguise of democracy. The Republican frustration with Truman's narrow victory in 1948 was translated into an ever-increasing barrage of charges about communist influence in government. The hardening lines of the Cold War, symbolized by the Communist coup in Czechoslovakia in 1948, "our loss of China" in 1949, and the invasion of South Korea, plus the spectacular spy trials of the Rosenbergs and Alger Hiss, contributed to the public's concern and gave many wild charges an influence out of proportion to their credibility.

By the 1952 election, many voters were once again alienated from the administration. The public had moved from a position of overwhelming support of intervention in the Korean conflict to one of frustration as the war bogged down in a stalemate that seemed to characterize the indecisiveness of a foreign policy of containment. This frustration and a dissatisfaction with Truman were vented in an emotional reception for General Douglas MacArthur when he returned home after being relieved as United Nations commander in Korea. And to the issues of communism and Korea, the Republicans were able to add corruption when a series of influence-peddling scandals were disclosed in the administration.

The Eisenhower Administration

The decade of the 1950's was dominated by the personality of Dwight D. Eisenhower. He won the Republican nomination in 1952 as the representative of the moderate, internationalist, Eastern wing of the party, but only after a bitter fight with Senator Robert Taft, the spokesman for the powerful conservative, neo-isolationist wing of the party. The internal conflict forced Eisenhower to struggle to maintain an uneasy truce with this element throughout his two terms in office. He twice defeated the articulate and inspiring former governor of Illinois, Adlai Stevenson, a man whose intellectual qualities seemed to alienate more voters than they attracted.

Eisenhower's immense popularity cut across party, class, and occupational lines to an unusual degree, pulling support from normally Democratic voters, as the decline in the Democratic urban plurality indicates. Many of these voters had been the poor of the New Deal period for whom the battles of social justice had been fought. But those battles had been largely won. Now these voters had become a new middle class—homeowners who had to pay taxes to support social welfare programs and who were concerned that inflation would cut their purchasing power. Eisenhower's pledges to balance the budget and halt the growth of government had a definite appeal. For the many concerned about the threat of communism, both internal and external, Republican pledges to get rid of the alleged communists in government and to replace the frustrating policy of containment with a new one of "liberation" of those under Soviet domination sounded appealing. Eisenhower's pledge during the 1952 campaign to go to Korea, and the subsequent peace he achieved, convinced many voters that a Republican President was better able to assure peace.

While these specific issues were important to those who voted for Eisenhower, opinion surveys indicated that his personality was of paramount importance. The response to his personal qualities—his sincerity, integrity, sense of duty, religious nature, and his extreme likability—ranked above and overshadowed his performance as President in the minds of the voters.

Why did this man, one of the century's most popular leaders, have so little impact on the future? Looking back from the turbulent and conflict-filled 1960's, one is inclined to agree with William V. Shannon's 1958 assessment that the Eisenhower era was a time of "the great postponement." "He has not shaped the future nor tried to repeal the past," Shannon wrote. "He has not politically organized nor intellectually defined a new consensus. When he leaves office ... the foreign policies and the domestic policies of the past generation will be about where he found them in 1953." Part of the answer to our question lies in the mood of the American people during the fifties. Middle-class prosperity obscured those who remained in poverty; the problem of race seemed remote to Northern suburbanites, and in any case it was a Southern problem that the Supreme Court was handling; the plight of the cities was not unendurable for those who worked in clean, air-conditioned offices and returned home above or below it all on the commuter trains. Most Americans seemed content with things the way they were, and they supported a President who largely agreed.

Historians and journalists have generally concluded that President Eisenhower was a weak and indecisive leader. Most of those critics, however, have failed to appreciate the extent to which many of Eisenhower's actions were determined by deliberate choice based on an explicit theory of leadership and philosophy of the presidency. Unlike the strong Presidents of American history, Eisenhower disdained the latent power of his office. He believed that Franklin D. Roosevelt had "usurped" the power of Congress, for example, and that it was his duty to restore this power to the national legislature. This view ignored the growth of a conservative coalition in Congress since Roosevelt's second term and implied an unrealistic separation of the executive and legislative branches of government. Moreover, Eisenhower viewed the use of patronage to gather support in Congress for administration programs as an unethical use of force which demeaned the office of the President. This attitude prevailed despite Eisenhower's frequent private blasts at the GOP's conservative leaders on Capitol Hill who often failed to support their own President. Eisenhower also refused to use his enormous popularity in a direct appeal to the people, or to participate in the give and take of personal attack in politics. These characteristics were displayed perfectly in his handling of Senator Joseph McCarthy.

In 1952 Eisenhower deleted a paragraph from a Wisconsin campaign speech praising his old friend General George Marshall, then the target of vehement attacks by McCarthy. When the Wisconsin Senator continued his attacks on government agencies and personnel under a Republican regime, Eisenhower adopted the attitude that McCarthy was a matter for the Senate to deal with, that any rebuke from the White House would only enhance the Senator's publicity value. The President's loathing and contempt for McCarthy was expressed in his private remark, "I refuse to get into the gutter with that guy." Thus Eisenhower's inaction was the result of deliberate choice, not indecision. But to many people, contemporaries and historians, the price of restraint was too high in terms of the damaged reputations and careers of dedicated public servants, the loss of civil liberties, and the tarnished image of the United States abroad.

Civil rights is another area of concern where Eisenhower's convictions were strongly evident, although critics claim to see indecisiveness. While it is true that he took action against discrimination in the armed forces, in government employment, and in the District of Columbia, these were areas where the President had a direct responsibility. Similarly, the Civil Rights Act of 1957 was designed to enforce the constitutional right to vote, and the sending of federal troops to Little Rock to enforce a federal court order to desegregate was action to meet a challenge to the constitutional authority of the President and the federal courts. While Eisenhower readily affirmed his resolve to uphold the law as set forth in the Supreme Court's desegregation decision, he refused even to hint publicly that he personally agreed with the decision. Actually, he disagreed with the very core of it, that integration was the only way to achieve equality. He warned in private that "social disintegration" might result if the beliefs of white Southerners were not respected in this matter. Social equality did not mean "that a Negro should court my daughter." The nation thus found little guidance from the White House at the opening of a new era in race relations.

Eisenhower has been accused of weak leadership for caving in to the traditional Republican conservatives on several key issues. This argument apparently accepts at face value the administration's claim that it represented "Modern Republicanism." Despite the real friction and name-calling between Eisenhower and the conservative wing of the GOP, the fact is that in domestic affairs their ideas tended to converge, even if the gap in foreign affairs remained wide. Not long after Robert Taft's death, the President compared himself with the former Senator: "Taft was really more liberal than me in domestic matters. Taft was extremely liberal on housing and on social security. . . . He was very liberal on [federal aid to] education. I would not go along with him on any of these."

The administration's essential conservatism is best illustrated by its fiscal and economic policies. Throughout Eisenhower's eight years in office, no commitment was stronger than that to a balanced budget, reduced taxes, and a "sound dollar." These three goals could be achieved only by a "free economy," one with little or no federal interference or participation. President Eisenhower's own economic predisposition was strengthened by the businessmen who surrounded him in his Cabinet and throughout the federal government, and who were his closest advisers and friends in private life. The obsession with the budget found expression in the adoption of a defense policy of nuclear deterrence ("a bigger bang for the buck"), in an agriculture policy that sought to lower the cost of government price supports, in a refusal to support general federal aid to education (both because of the cost and a conviction that education was a state and local responsibility), and in a rejection of support for medical care for the aged under social security. In 1957 the country witnessed the spectacle of the administration waging war against itself over the budget for fiscal 1958. A few days after the President submitted his budget to Congress, Secretary of the Treasury George Humphrey publicly attacked it for being too big. Eisenhower followed by congratulating Humphrey and inviting Congress to attack his own proposals. Congress had never seen anything like it. Finally, the administration's tight economic policies contributed to three economic recessions during eight years.

Eisenhower was basically a conservative on domestic matters, and any tribute to him for consolidating the New Deal–Fair Deal seems unrealistic. Major exceptions were the several amendments to the Social Security Act extending coverage and broadening benefits, all of which received strong support from the President in an effort to demonstrate that the Republican party was concerned with the average man. The fact that eight years of Republican leadership left intact the New Deal–Fair Deal reform structure, however, does not demonstrate liberalism or choice. There was no public demand that these reforms be overturned, and political necessity demanded their acceptance. In the broad area of public power and natural resources, Eisenhower did manage to move away from the liberal policies of the immediate past, although not as far as he would have liked. He made no secret of his feelings about the Tennessee Valley Authority, for example. "By God, if ever we could do it, before we leave here, I'd like to see us sell the whole thing, but I suppose we can't go that far," he told one Cabinet meeting. Nevertheless, Eisenhower did attempt to stifle the growth of TVA by encouraging private utilities to meet increased demands for electrical power in the TVA area. He also fought successfully to turn over to the states the tidelands oil deposits, extremely valuable properties which Presidents Roosevelt and Truman, with support from the Supreme Court, had claimed for the federal government.

Stalemate continued to characterize national politics in the fifties. The American people, the President, and the Congress believed there was no need for rapid moves in any direction. The Supreme Court was the only element of government that appeared ready to prick the conscience of the American people and address itself to the future. Despite the overwhelming popularity of Eisenhower with the voters and his own frequently stated desire to rebuild the Republican party, no new majority coalition of voters appeared. While the voters were electing a Republican President by large margins in 1952 and 1956, they elected a Republican Congress only in 1952. Democratic majorities in Congress grew from 1954 on, and the 1958 elections produced a Senate of 64 Democrats and 34 Republicans, and a new House of Representatives of 282 Democrats and 154 Republicans. Throughout the eight Eisenhower years the Democratic party maintained a 2-to-1 edge in registered voters over the Republicans, demonstrating that a weakened Roosevelt coalition was still operating and potentially able to elect a Democratic President.

The Kennedy Administration

Political scientists called the 1960 election a "reinstating" one: the Democrats' position as the majority party was reasserted in the election of a President, unlike the "deviating" elections of 1952 and 1956 in which the minority party had won the presidency. For Catholics and religious liberals, the election of John F. Kennedy erased once and for all the old taboo, vivid in the minds of many who remembered Al Smith's campaign in 1928, that a Catholic could never be elected President. Those with an intense dislike of Richard M. Nixon rejoiced over his defeat, convinced that he was finished as a national political figure. Even Nixon's supporters thought he had failed to convince the voters that there was a "new Nixon," despite an image-building campaign throughout the Eisenhower years designed to overshadow an early record of illiberalism and questionable political tactics. For friend and foe alike, Nixon's defeat in the California governor's race of 1962 was taken as the final step along the road to political obscurity. Finally, the liberals who had suffered through the Eisenhower years with a sense of impotence viewed the 1960 election as the resurgence of a virile reform leadership.

The promise of new leadership had not always seemed so great. Elected to Congress in 1946 as a young war hero, John Kennedy was as conservative as his Irish Catholic constituency. In these years he seemed to support the conservative line in foreign policy, making speeches about the "betrayal" of Poland at Yalta and the Truman administration's responsibility for the "loss" of Nationalist China. Further, the young Congressman had an intense dislike for what he called the "real liberals" and took no interest in liberal causes such as civil rights and civil liberties. "I never joined the Americans for Democratic Action or the American Veterans Committee," he told a journalist in 1953. "I'm not comfortable with those people." Liberals reciprocated with a growing distrust when Kennedy, who was elected to the Senate in 1952, failed to speak out in public against McCarthy.

After the fall of McCarthy, Kennedy's liberal image improved, thanks to the exposure he achieved as a candidate for the Democratic vice-presidential nomination in 1956, his special efforts to identify with the cause of civil liberties, and his promotion by two leading Harvard liberal intellectuals, Arthur M. Schlesinger, Jr., and John Kenneth Galbraith. His political development and intellectual growth made it possible for liberals who supported Hubert Humphrey or Adlai Stevenson in 1960 to fall in line when their men were defeated. Moreover, Kennedy campaigned on one of the most liberal platforms in American history, including federal action to stimulate the nation's economic growth, legislation to eliminate all forms of racial discrimination and to protect civil rights, medical care for the aged under social security, and federal aid to education.

Throughout the campaign the Democratic candidate promised "to get America moving again." Kennedy emphasized repeatedly that the nation needed a strong chief executive, a role he fully intended to play. He quoted Woodrow Wilson to the effect that "the President is at liberty, both in law and conscience, to be as big a man as he can. . . . His office is anything he has the sagacity and the force to make it. . . . His capacity will set the limit." These words were music to the ears of those who felt an urgency to remedy the defects of President Eisenhower's passive leadership.

But who was demanding great change? Kennedy's 113,057 popular vote margin over Nixon was the smallest for a President in seventy-two years—hardly a mandate. He had carried only twenty-four states to Nixon's twenty-six, and while winning the presidency the Democrats had lost two seats in the Senate and twenty-two in the House. Though Congress still had large Democratic majorities, the old malady of Southern and conservative defection made the division much closer. President Kennedy was to learn a lesson taught to every President since the middle of Franklin D. Roosevelt's second term. From quoting Woodrow Wilson on the unlimited powers of the presidency in 1960, a much wiser man would write in 1963 that "the President . . . is rightly described as a man of extraordinary powers. Yet it is also true that he must wield those powers under extraordinary limitations . . ."

The potential for stalemate was not immediately evident. For a time the chord of idealism and leadership struck by Kennedy's inaugural address—"Let the word go forth from this time and place, to friend and foe alike, that the torch has passed to a new generation of Americans"—obscured the obstacles. The administration won an early victory by enlarging the House Rules Committee, the graveyard of liberal legislation under the supervision of its Democratic chairman, Howard W. Smith of Virginia. While legislation might now get past this committee, however, there was no guarantee it would be approved by a majority in the House of Representatives. The new President's appeal had been in the industrial Northeast and in other urban areas. Liberal and moderate Democratic Congressmen numbered about 150 members in the 87th Congress, almost seventy members short of a majority. With about twenty Republicans liberal enough to be lured across party lines, the President needed to attract about fifty Southern Democrats for an absolute majority on any vote. He decided to do what Presidents before him had done: buy the Southern votes with patronage and compromises in his programs. The strategy disappointed and alienated many of the urban liberals he had to count upon as the strongest supporters of his program.

This decision to defer to the Southerners was most noticeable in the area of civil rights. The 1960 Democratic platform pledges were the most far-reaching in the party's history, and candidate Kennedy had announced in 1960 that he had instructed Democratic legislators to draw up an omnibus civil rights bill embodying all of the platform commitments to be introduced in the new Congress. He had also criticized President Eisenhower's failure to end racial discrimination in federally assisted housing, an act that required only "a stroke of his pen." Once in office and confronted by the need to attract Southern votes for his broad economic program, Kennedy's promise to issue the executive order on housing was delayed for two years. When the omnibus civil rights bill was introduced in Congress, the White House press secretary declared that it was not an administration-backed bill, and "the President does not consider it necessary at this time to enact new civil rights legislation." The President's ready appointment of federal judges nominated by Southern Senators was also an attempt to sway these potential opponents of his program. The behavior and opinions of many of these appointees did little to increase respect for law and much to obstruct implementation of civil rights statutes.

The administration did move with a kind of vigor lacking during the sluggish Eisenhower years. Corporation executives, union and community leaders were called to the White House for pep talks on the need for action to end discrimination. The Washington Redskins professional football team was persuaded to recruit black football players, a move that immediately improved its won-lost record. Kennedy took more substantive action in creating the President's Committee on Equal Employment Opportunity to combat racial discrimination in the employment policies of government agencies and private firms holding government contracts. While the committee could cancel contracts of companies that discriminated, it never did so, and the success of voluntary compliance agreements is debatable. The Justice Department moved more firmly than the preceding administration to enforce the voting rights provisions of the 1957 and 1960 Civil Rights Acts, but as contemporary observers noted, the department's action did not meet the problem. Only when the 1961 "Freedom Riders" were greeted with violent attacks did Attorney General Robert Kennedy intervene with the Interstate Commerce Commission to issue regulations banning segregation in bus terminals and other interstate transportation facilities. Not until June 1963, after the 1962 rebellion over integration at the University of Missis-

sippi, the unleashing of Police Chief "Bull" Connor's dogs and clu
against nonviolent demonstrators in Birmingham, Alabama, in April
1963, and many other less publicized confrontations, did the President send to Congress the most comprehensive civil rights bill ever
proposed. This legislation would eventually become the Civil Rights
Act of 1964, but the black man was already impatient and disillusioned with white America. "Black power" was waiting in the wings
even as the March on Washington of 1963 came to its glorious conclusion with Martin Luther King's "I Have a Dream" speech.

The irony of the President's consensus strategy lay in the fact
that all his efforts failed to win necessary congressional support for
the administration's major goals. Kennedy's one outstanding legislative achievement was the Trade Expansion Act of 1962. His other
major aims—farm legislation, tax reform, a civil rights law, medicare, federal aid to schools—bogged down in Congress. Despite
the contention of Kennedy apologists that after the President's re-
election in 1964 he would have been in a position to press more
boldly for legislation, the fact is that he came to the office with the
determination and promise to be a "strong President" when he really
had little opportunity to be such a President without a new political
tack. The congressional deadlock that had plagued Harry Truman
persisted and reached crisis-like proportions. Perhaps it was beyond
any President to change, but there is no evidence that Kennedy
explored the problem intellectually.

There is a curious quality to the Kennedy performance. The same
man who appointed narrow-minded, mediocre segregationists as
federal judges outdid any administration in history in staffing the
executive departments and the White House offices with competent,
dedicated, brilliant men. The same President who addressed himself so eloquently to the problems of the present and future—the
cities, poverty, inhibiting economic myths, the quality of American
life—sought change through the political methods of the past. The
same individual who sought to adapt American foreign policy to a
changing world, who proposed the Alliance for Progress, who so
carefully weighed the alternatives in the Cuban missile crisis, who
saw the danger in committing American troops and prestige in
Laos, condoned the Cuban invasion and the increasing commitment
of American military power in Vietnam. Perhaps the President who
deplored Eisenhower's defense policies and who called for a "flexible
response" missed a vital point: decisions regarding the nature of

the nation's defense establishment and military equipment are inextricably linked to political decisions about what kind of wars a nation is willing to fight. Many people look back longingly to the Eisenhower years of peace and wonder if the flexibility and training for brushfire and guerrilla wars, Kennedy innovations, did not make it all too easy for the United States to get bogged down in Vietnam. However history interprets John F. Kennedy—and there is still much about his administration that is not known—it must consider the lift he gave the nation. Members of the younger generation identified with the first President born in this century, with his young wife and small children. They believed the torch had been passed to their generation, and they responded to the call by joining the Peace Corps, the Negro Revolution, and by leading massive criticism of the society they had inherited from their elders. Perhaps the Kennedy years were not Camelot, but the period since the young President's assassination indicates that success in the presidency cannot be measured only by the amount of legislation pushed through Congress.

The Johnson Administration

Few men ever came to the White House better acquainted with the ways of government and politics than Lyndon B. Johnson. Johnson's family had long been involved in the politics of Texas; despite what journalists have written about his Populist lineage, the Johnson family was in fact part of the local Democratic establishment that dominated county politics. Influential Texans liked the young teacher, and they made it possible for him to come to Washington in 1932 as secretary to a Congressman, a wealthy Texas rancher. At the age of twenty-four Johnson attracted attention in the early days of the New Deal; Sam Rayburn took him under his wing and President Roosevelt selected him as Texas State Director of the National Youth Administration. From this position he was elected to the House of Representatives in 1936 and to the Senate in 1948. Within four years he was Democratic floor leader of the Senate, displaying an ability to dominate that individualistic body which amazed his friends and overwhelmed his potential opponents.

The long experience in government, the reputation for wizardry in Congress, and the natural sympathy for a man who succeeded a fallen leader were among the advantages the new President enjoyed.

But few men ever assumed the office of the presidency with so little political or public enthusiasm. Johnson was not a polished speaker or a popular national personality. He was a Southerner, the first to occupy the White House since Woodrow Wilson. His past record was neither liberal nor conservative, and in fact contained much that antagonized liberals. Johnson had opposed Truman's civil rights program and then supported the 1957 and 1960 Civil Rights Acts as his ambition for national office grew. He had supported the Taft-Hartley and Landrum-Griffin acts, both of which were anathema to organized labor. His alleged one-man rule of the Senate, close cooperation with President Eisenhower in the fifties, and frequent lack of concern for liberal attempts to build a staunch opposition to that Republican administration alienated many who considered themselves the true inheritors of the New Deal and Fair Deal. In addition, there were charges of servitude to the oil and gas interests of Texas and a reputation in Washington as a trickster-opportunist-manipulator who bullied his staff, had an exaggerated sense of personal vanity, and delighted in petty revenge against those who crossed him. When he became President, Johnson was immediately embarrassed by the Senate investigation of the affairs of his protégé, Robert G. ("Bobby") Baker, who had been secretary to the Senate Democrats.

President Johnson's first priority was to unite the country and demonstrate this unity to the world. The goal was not only in the national interest but in his personal interest. He had less than a year to convince the party that had denied him its nomination for the presidency in 1960 that he should have it in 1964. He was aware that although he had been President Kennedy's personal choice as a running mate, most of the dead President's supporters, including his brother Robert, had opposed the selection. Labor and liberals were hostile, and black Americans did not trust this man from the South.

The new President's first move seemed obvious: drape himself with the mantle of Kennedy as soon as possible. The Kennedy staff and Cabinet were asked to stay on under the new chief. The themes of continuity and unity were evident in Johnson's first address to Congress. He pledged himself to continue pushing for New Frontier programs that Congress had failed to pass. He called for Congress, as its first order of business, to pass the civil rights bill, then pending, in memory of the slain leader. This plea was coupled with an emotional call for sectional reconciliation and a reuniting of the

South with the rest of the nation. For the fiscal conservatives, Johnson pledged that "the expenditures of your government will be administered with the utmost thrift and frugality"; then, for the liberals, he indicated that "this does not mean that we will not meet our unfilled needs or that we will not honor our commitments. We will do both." Aware that Congress had largely rejected Kennedy's strong executive leadership, Johnson sought to reassure the legislators by recalling his own years of congressional service, praising Congress' past record, and proclaiming his intention always to respect that body's independence. That said, he asked Congress to act without delay on a variety of problems confronting the nation.

This was the beginning of Lyndon Johnson's consensus, the building of a Democratic tent large enough to hold all but the most alienated of Americans. For the President, consensus was both a tactic and an ideology. In Texas Democratic politics he had fought to prevent the emergence of a dominant faction because it would be easier to unite disparate elements around the kind of consensus he chose. As Senate Majority Leader, much of his reputation rested upon his ability to reconcile the apparently irreconcilable. As President, a desire to be loved by all the people became an end, obscuring for the time being the reality of conflict in society. For a while, because of short-run political forces and a willing Congress, the vision of a Great Society—something for black people, something for the poor, something for labor, something for business, something for the consumer—seemed a reality. Johnson broke the congressional deadlock, and out of the legislature flowed more reform legislation than the nation had seen since the New Deal. Ironically, the President's consensus and the Great Society legislation were in large part made possible by the capture of the Republican party by the followers of Senator Barry Goldwater of Arizona.

Senator Goldwater's nomination by the Republican party in 1964 reflected the rapid growth of the right wing in America since the late 1950's. More important for the 1964 presidential election, however, Goldwater was seen by the vast majority of the electorate, including the moderates and liberals of his own party, as a radical factional leader with ideological notions about major changes in the national government. He became *the* issue. Lyndon Johnson skillfully developed the image of himself as the safe, conservative candidate who would lead in a known direction. For the purpose of building a consensus, an opponent like the Arizona Senator was almost too good to be true. Goldwater advocated the sale of the TVA, attacked social security before an audience of old folks, told farmers of his opposition to federal farm subsidy programs, and frightened everyone with his ideas about decentralizing control of nuclear weapons. In addition, his support of right-to-work laws and opposition to the Civil Rights Act of 1964 moved organized labor and black Americans in even greater numbers to the Democratic party. With a massive defection of normally Republican voters, including corporation leaders and moderates who had been read out of their party, President Johnson achieved one of the largest pluralities in American history—61.4 per cent of the two-party vote. He seemed well on the way to achieving his consensus.

Before the 1964 election Johnson had several legislative victories that foreshadowed what was to come. Two pieces of legislation sought by President Kennedy, a big income tax reduction to stimulate the economy and the Civil Rights Act of 1964, were passed. The President's most important independent initiative was his "war on poverty," which he declared in his first State of the Union Message and which became a cornerstone of the "Great Society." The basic anti-poverty legislation, the Economic Opportunity Act of 1964, established ten programs, among which were Head Start, the Job Corps, and VISTA. Despite increasing opposition, Congress extended the anti-poverty programs in 1965, 1966, and 1967. The pace of reform was stepped up when the huge Democratic majorities in Congress, the largest since New Deal days, arrived on the President's coattails as a result of the smashing victory in 1964. In 1965 came Medicare for the aged, a broad program of federal aid to education, an Appalachian Development Act, a Voting Rights Act, a program of rent supplements for low-income families, and a new Department of Housing and Urban Development. The year 1966 saw the enactment of a Demonstration Cities program, a Partnership for Health program of grants to the states for health services, and the creation of a Department of Transportation.

Now, however, the President began to lose his momentum. The Democrats lost three Senate seats and forty-seven House seats in the 1966 elections, resulting in a more conservative Congress. Although Congress passed a strong meat inspection bill in 1967, and a truth-in-lending bill and a Civil Rights Act in 1968, the White House had to devote greater efforts to funding those programs already in existence rather than initiating new proposals. From a high degree of personal popularity in 1964, the President sank so low in the public eye that he withdrew from the 1968 presidential race on March 31, 1968. Although he said he was refusing to seek re-election in order to have a better chance of ending the war in Vietnam, many in his own party believed that the administration, intent on achieving a military victory, had missed many opportunities for peace.

The increasing commitment of men and money in Vietnam heightened the natural tensions inherent in the Johnsonian consensus and led to its dissolution. The cost of pursuing the war compelled reductions in what critics had already labeled an inadequate War on Poverty. This only sharpened the sense of exclusion in black ghettos, where uprisings had occurred in 1964, 1965, 1966, culminating in the summer of 1967, the most violent in the nation's history, with outbreaks in a hundred cities. The impatience of black Americans and white youth with the country's inability—or lack of will—to end violence at home and abroad exacerbated an ever-present white backlash and generation gap, and led to demands for "law and order." Attempts by the administration to deny a civil war existed in Vietnam and to claim that the war was being won, despite facts to the contrary on both these points, led to a "credibility gap" and a loss of confidence in the government. With over 500,000 troops committed to the war by 1968, President Johnson's assurances in the 1964 campaign that the conflict was one for Asian boys to win or lose came back to haunt him. For many the Great Society had become a sick society, and they looked forward to the 1968 presidential election for an alternative.

All during the early months of 1968 the hopes for a meaningful choice looked bright. For those most concerned about building a wall around the country's black ghettos under the guise of "law and order," there was former Governor George C. Wallace of Alabama. He had already demonstrated that his appeal extended beyond the South in some surprisingly large votes in the primaries of Northern industrial states in 1964. Now pollsters predicted he would get 20 per cent of the nation's votes and could conceivably accomplish his goal of preventing either major party candidate from achieving a majority in the electoral college. For a while, liberal Republicans rested their hopes for change with Governor Nelson Rockefeller of New York. But Richard M. Nixon, through hard work on the Republican banquet circuit and devotion to party unity after the disaster of 1964, proved to most of the party regulars that he had gained a new maturity and overcome his image as a loser.

The battle for a new alternative was most intense in the party in power. Senator Eugene McCarthy of Minnesota, with little money, no encouragement even from those colleagues who agreed with him, and no organization except for a group of college youth, announced in November 1967 that he would seek the Democratic nomination for President to offer an alternative to President Johnson's Vietnam policy. Specifically, he sought a de-escalation of the war and a negotiated settlement. Before his campaign was over, McCarthy articulated two more themes that were relevant for many critics of American government: a call for "a new kind of political action, a new kind of citizens' concern, and a new kind of participation in politics"; and a demand for a President different from the "strong" ones of the past who personalized their office and used their power arbitrarily, a new President who would see his primary role as a kind of combination philosopher, statesman, and moral leader. McCarthy's strong showing in the New Hampshire primary, and the Tet offensive in Vietnam that proved the war was far from being won, encouraged Senator Robert Kennedy to enter the campaign for the nomination. Taken together, these events forced Lyndon Johnson's withdrawal from the presidential race, which in turn led to a de-escalation of the bombing of North Vietnam and the Paris peace negotiations. For a brief moment Senator Kennedy, inheritor of his brother's legacy of an unfinished stewardship, appeared to be the best hope of stopping the party regulars' choice for the nomination, Vice-President Hubert H. Humphrey. For millions of disillusioned Americans—the poor, the blacks, many of the blue-collar workers George Wallace considered his supporters—Kennedy's voice of moral protest meant hope for the future. His death by an assassin's bullet in June 1968, and Humphrey's defeat of McCarthy at the bloody Democratic convention, dashed the hopes of many who had looked upon 1968 as a year that promised alternatives.

An awareness of the difference between the reality and the promise of American life set McCarthy and Kennedy apart from Nixon and Humphrey. Although Humphrey, aided by a total bombing halt in North Vietnam in the last week of the campaign and his belated movement away from the Johnson war policy, managed to make a close race, he seemed to cling to the idea that America's troubles could be remedied by the same liberal reforms that had failed in the past. Despite Humphrey's defeat, the election results demonstrated that there was still some life in the Democratic coalition. Congress remained under Democratic control; not since 1876 had a first-term President failed to carry into office with him a House of Representatives of his own political party.

President Nixon's campaign implied that the status quo—with a dash of new leadership—promoted by private enterprise and protected by fiscal responsibility and the police, was all that was needed to set America on the right course. For those who found hope in his campaign pledge to end the Vietnam conflict, there was also the harsh reality of his promise to use the money thus released to step up the missile race. For those who looked upon George Wallace's poor showing in the election as a sign that the racial division in American society was not so deep after all, it is useful to recall that the new President had his own racial appeal—an emphasis on strict law and order aimed at black militants, and promises to appoint conservatives to the Supreme Court and to slow down federal efforts supporting integration. The question is, can President Nixon govern any more effectively than his predecessor, especially since his appeal is not directed to those—the disenchanted youth and the disillusioned blacks—who demand major change?

Part 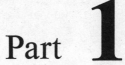 1

THE TRUMAN ADMINISTRATION

The President:
A New Portrait

by Arthur Krock

WHEN THE BOYS in Independence, Mo., half a century ago chose sides in their games they disputed over the division of the recognized champions but they always agreed on the umpire. Often it was necessary to hunt him down in the Public Library where, by the time he was 20 years old, the local legend was that he had "read every book in it." The nearsightedness that kept him off the teams, for any of which his physical and mental prowess otherwise equipped him, was no handicap there.

In a very few days Harry S. Truman, the former official umpire of games of Independence, will have finished his first year in the White House, where every day he is called to serve in a related capacity on the sterner fields of the nation and the world. In disputes of inestimable moment he must make decisions that direct the course of history and the fate of mankind. And also, when the role of umpire must be discarded for that of leader of the greatest power on the planet, his duty is to be that.

One of the most renowned of men whose destiny it was to judge dissentient claims and lead a people was Solomon, son of David. Therefore it is significant, and perhaps it may prove to have been a benevolent decree of fate, that Mr. Truman has long cherished Solomon as his model of a public man. A sentence from the prayer of the King of Israel upon his accession appeared in the President's

From the *New York Times Magazine*, April 7, 1946.

inaugural address. But because he reads, muses on and endeavors constantly to govern his public conduct by the whole passage in I Kings iii:5-14, it should be set down in full in any study of Mr. Truman. Accordingly it follows:

> In Gibeon the Lord appeared to Solomon in a dream by night: and God said, Ask what I shall give thee.
>
> And Solomon said, Thou hast shewed unto thy servant David my father great mercy, according as he walked before Thee in truth, and in righteousness, and in uprightness of heart with Thee; and thou hast kept for him this great kindness, that Thou hast given him a son to sit on his throne, as it is this day.
>
> And now, O Lord my God, Thou hast made thy servant king instead of David my father: and I am but a little child: I know not how to go out or come in.
>
> And thy servant is in the midst of thy people which Thou hast chosen, a great people, that cannot be numbered nor counted for multitude.
>
> Give therefore thy servant an understanding heart to judge thy people, that I may discern between good and bad: for who is able to judge this thy so great a people?
>
> And the speech pleased the Lord, that Solomon had asked this thing.
>
> And God said unto him, Because thou hast asked this thing, and hast not asked for thyself long life; neither hast asked riches for thyself, nor hast asked the life of thine enemies; but hast asked for thyself understanding to discern judgment;
>
> Behold, I have done according to thy words: lo, I have given thee a wise and an understanding heart; so that there was none like thee before thee, neither after thee shall any arise like unto thee.
>
> And I have also given thee that which thou hast not asked, both riches, and honour: so that there shall not be any among the kings like unto thee all thy days.
>
> And if thou wilt walk in my ways, to keep my statutes and my commandments, as thy father David did walk, then I will lengthen thy days.

The President, in my opinion, has never wallowed in the "humility" that was widely attributed to him when he took office. At no time has he been as humble as Solomon represented himself to be in his address to Jehovah (and I don't believe the King was either). Yet conversely Mr. Truman has never thought, and does not think now, that none before or after him did or can surpass him. The application of the passage should be read with moderation. But he has sought, and he believes he has, "a wise and understanding heart." He holds that to be the most desirable and necessary quality in a President of the United States. Though modest rather than humble, Mr. Truman is reasonably sure he shares this blessing with the great King.

The Bible is so much in the President's mind, and its literature so implanted in his thought, that something more must be said of the Scriptures as his reading and resource before coming to a survey of the other traits and characteristics. Note must be made of his approval of St. Luke, vi:26, as another sure guide of a public man: "Woe unto you, when all men shall speak well of you! for so did their fathers to the false prophets." A kindly, companionable person, anxious to be liked by the people of good-will, the President nevertheless knows the price of certain kinds of popularity, is not willing to pay it and holds it self-evident that to acquire this would be at the expense of duty:

But he is not pious in speech, and I do not believe he is in thought, as the devout would define that word. His philosophy is worldly. He is a politician who holds to rugged rules of the game, and he is the product of a big city machine with an evil history. He is a strict party man who thinks party disputes are family fights which should be conducted within the walls and the result accepted by the loser. Many of these battles he inherited from Franklin D. Roosevelt because that President gained and held office by making a coalition of normally antagonistic groups—the Southern Democrats and the radicals and union laborites of the North and the large cities; the lily-whites and the Negroes; the agrarian and the urban blocs, contending each for its separate economy. Other party battles have arisen in his own time because Mr. Truman is a post-war President, and when the shooting ends, wartime combinations for political action fall apart.

Hence the President must lead the nation and try to lead the Democratic party in an era of factions. The junction in Congress of some Democrats and most of the Republicans to amend drastically or reject what he calls "fundamental" legislation, carrying out the pledges of his predecessor or the party platform, is typical of the post-war legacy of incumbents of the White House. But, typical or not, Mr. Truman as a party man, as a believer in the two-party system and as the head of the one in power, pledged to carry out its platform pledges, sees no virtue in a coalition, mass or individual.

His friends come away from conversations with him absolutely certain that his views on this subject are these:

(1) The two-party system is indispensable to our form of government, and it is the best ever devised. That system is broken down by coalitions and there is no use talking to Mr. Truman about the right and duty of a public man to "assert his convictions" after he has accepted the convention or caucus process and the majority of his fellow-partisans have responded to an opposite conviction. A man should fight for his ideas as hard as he knows how within the party, within the caucus, within the convention and among his electors. But, losing, he should follow the majority or join another party. Otherwise, he should bear the brand of political renegade.

(2) Both major parties, it is true, are made up of unrelated and warring elements. But the cure for that, and the means to re-establish definite and responsible two-party government, is a realignment of the parties with those of like mind reassembled in harmonious groups. The refusal of Southern politicians to abandon the Democratic label while effacing every letter written upon it makes it impossible to suggest a way to attain this realignment, and it will probably not occur in Mr. Truman's time. But, perhaps, if Southern Democracy establishes in office more men like Governor Arnall of Georgia, the miracle may come to pass.

These views his intimates attribute to the President, and I believe the ascription to be reasonably accurate. In due course he may be obliged by party dissension to speak for himself and then any divergencies can be noted. Whatever these may be, my opinion is firm, however, that Mr. Truman will never fall in with the recent proposal of Henry A. Wallace—that a party committee, composed of the President, the majority leaders in Congress, etc.—shall decide whether a recalcitrant is to be "read out of the party" in power. He knows this is legally and politically impossible. And he knows also that purges must be self-operating to be effective, that if they are compulsory a party falls to pieces.

If his party breaks up, as well it may, centrifugal force will be the reason. The President intends that nothing in his own handling of the problem shall justify the charge that the destructive force was centripetal, set in motion by an act of his.

A politician by profession, the President thinks and talks often of his trade. These talks assure listeners that, while Mr. Truman agrees that the trend of political action is currently away from encouragement of the old-fashioned virtues of thrift, truth-telling and equitable government, he believes these virtues to be so fundamental in the American make-up that politics is obliged to reverse the trend. Persons who have discussed with him other matters in this category quote him also as a stanch believer in the convention system by which Presidential candidates are chosen.

This has been criticized as permitting professional politicians to present the people every four years with two candidates between whom they must choose, although they had small part in their selection and often have other preferences. Mr. Truman has impressed his friends as convinced that nevertheless no better procedure could be devised, because (a) no man has the physical stamina to campaign twice throughout the nation for the Presidency, first in a primary and then before the election; (b) any political process will surely be taken over by the leaders and the professionals: when the primary was superimposed on the convention system these soon took it over; (c) conventions and primaries as now established afford an excellent screening process that produces good candidates; (d) even in convention deadlocks, when a few leaders in "smoke-filled rooms" make the choices, interest requires them to put the party's best foot foremost, and that excludes poor material; (e) a first-rate demagogue could sweep a nation-wide Presidential primary.

As he sits at his post of command in the Oval Room of the White House office, he is inclined to think often of demagogues and remark to visitors that here, more than any other place, they could debase our heritage. The President of the United States can announce his intention to address the nation and soon afterward his words will be attended by the American people and millions elsewhere in the world. That power and the responsibility that attend it are much in Mr. Truman's mind, and this has increased his determination to resist any temptation that might nibble at any man in his place to employ what he considers to be demagogy.

History will in time write its estimate of Harry S. Truman, and even now—before he has been President a year—it is being offered a depreciating estimate of his capacity to lead and to understand. It is being advised by critics that, though his model be Solomon or another, this man who grew up in the narrow limits of state politics has not been sufficiently broadened by his subsequent experience, and probably could not have been by any, to breast the surging tides of this tempestuous age. "His time," says one appraiser, "should have been the era of James Monroe."

I shall not attempt in this study of the President as an individual to express an opinion of the merits of this or other criticisms. The man himself is interesting enough to fill the bounds of one article. With his stocky frame, his wholesome countenance, his pleasant voice and manner, his ready laugh, his alert, sinewy movements that proclaim a sound mind in a healthy body, his undeniable possession of what must be expressed by the effete word "charm," Harry Truman has been favored by nature.

He does not worry. He sleeps soundly at night, even if night intervenes in his wrestling with a great problem on which he has reached no decision. He does not worry because he tries to do his best, and his philosophy is that a man's best is all he can do. Also, the knowledge that worry detracts from efficiency is all the further persuasion he requires not to yield to it; he is a pragmatist. He sleeps soundly because he is healthy, though he does not always drop off when he goes to bed. Generally the President reads himself to sleep—that rarely takes long, and whodunits are not excluded by any means. Generally also he eats a light snack or drinks milk or orange juice.

But throughout the day his reading is ponderous, such being essential to the conduct of his office—reports, memoranda, legislative drafts, books to the purpose—until his eyes ache and his brain is weary. Mr. Truman is a good administrator and he knows how to delegate power and diffuse duties. Yet he cannot deputize the chore of reading certain official documents and related writings, more numerous and more complicated now than at any time in our history.

However, of the reading that Bacon said maketh a full man the President has done much. After "all the books in the Public Library of Independence" were devoured the young man fed his appetite on more: at nights in the Jackson County farmstead ere his political career widened before him; in barracks and in bivouac during the First World War in France; in his Kansas City days as a shopkeeper and officeholder; and during his years in the Senate prior to the formation of his special committee that checked the conduct of the war and consumed all his waking hours in that enterprise.

But over and over in those days, and now as well, it was always the Bible—not only the passages mentioned previously, but the resounding prose of Isaiah and the Gospels according to St. Luke and St. Matthew. The President is a walking index to the Scriptures, knows (and is delighted that so often his friends do not) that Exodus 20 is the Ten Commandments and that Luke vi:20-49 is the Sermon on the Mount. His interest in religion has led him to read every word in the Koran and the Book of Mormon. But a special lure in the latter can be traced to the fact that Independence was the Mormon Garden of Eden and the President's ancestors helped to drive the Mormon colony there to the Far West.

The President is familiar, too, with the standard secular literatures: Chaucer and Shakespeare and the poets represented in a dog-eared book he owns called "Anglo-Saxon Poetry," the novels of the great Victorians, among which he finds outstanding George Eliot's "Silas Marner." He has read Trollope's parliamentary series and remembers it as the best collection of novels about political life. But history and biography attract him most, and in these categories he has deeply immersed his mind. In biography he finds the lamp that best illuminates history, remarking that the way to understand the world is to know the people who have lived greatly in it.

He intently read "Mein Kampf," which I doubt can be said of more than a few members of Congress. And when he had finished it he was certain the preparedness of this nation for war must be as thorough and rapid as Congressional prodding could make it. That was the function to which he held the Truman committee, which was formed in March, 1941, too late to prevent the delays in preparedness in the spring and summer of 1940 that were produced by third-term politics pivoting on the nonintervention pledges, but very useful in the actual period of the war.

Of history the military sections are his favorites. Mr. Truman has an intimate acquaintance with the maneuvers of the great captains from the days of Alexander and enjoys discussing their technical faults and glories. He holds that the greatest maneuvers are to be found in non-decisive battles like Arbela, Cannae, Austerlitz and Chancellorsville, and that decisive engagements can be drawn battles, his illustration being Gettysburg. The President is at least a lay authority on the technique of the battles of the War Between the

States and the First World War, and he relaxes visibly at bull sessions with experts in which he can discuss his theories.

Political and social philosophy were opened to him in the Independence library—Plato, from whom he still likes to quote, and Prescott on the government and social-economics of the Incas. It has not escaped the President that this ancient civilization of Peru was the perfect Communist state and the only one. He does not find parallels to the pure Inca communism in police states like those of the Czars, of Hitler and the Kremlin. And he inclines to the view that pure communism such as preceded the arrival of Pizarro in Peru was the finest government man has ever achieved—though he agrees that modern science and invention make an academic exercise now of any efforts at duplication.

The President, as has been said, does not worry. And he does not scare. His physical courage has repeatedly been proved, and his intimates are sure he has never been terrified by a dark intruding thought or a problem that seems to defy solution and is heavy with menace. He is disposed to speak lightly of this quality and attribute it to the Kentucky feudist blood that flows in his veins. But a personal philosophy enters also. Mr. Truman thinks of himself as an instrument for the public welfare; fear would blunt the instrument; hence fear must never be admitted to his consciousness. Pragmatism again.

Inspecting history's exhibit of such instruments he believes that Jefferson was the best, and, though many acquainted with the career and writings of that statesman contend that modern Democrats are at most ugly stepchildren of Jefferson's principles, the President thinks his own descent real and legitimate. Like Jefferson (and like Brandeis) he abhors bigness. He would rather see 100 small insurance companies than four big ones, 100 industrial corporations and labor unions where a few now dominate the scene. Bigness, in the President's view, gives too much power to groups and to individuals and tends to thwart true democracy. His advocacy of a combined Army and Navy is inconsistent with this conviction. But in this general attitude Mr. Truman's lineal political descent from Cleveland and Bryan and Wilson is plainly revealed.

This political ancestry is more direct and complete than Mr. Roosevelt's was. To form his winning coalition in 1932 that President abetted popular concentrations of mass groups, like those in the labor unions. And to maintain the coalition it was necessary to encourage bigness in this quarter. He eluded some of the domination of this bigness through the circumstance that labor divided into two wings which he could balance against each other. But the result was still magnitude. And, though Mr. Roosevelt followed the doctrine of Jefferson, Jackson, Cleveland, Bryan and Wilson against industrial and financial bigness, the war in Europe and our subsequent participation obliged him to dilute his activities against monopoly.

Mr. Truman looks forward to the day when conditions will favor the break-up of all large combinations. But to attain this end requires support from Congress, which he has not acquired. He has been heard to observe that if members would work and study harder and dig into the great problems with the ardor and industry of the Truman committee, a better day would dawn sooner and more surely. But that is only one of the complaints he has against Congress, all of them drawn from personal experience.

These complaints he realizes, however, arise from more sources than the inaptitude of Congress for hard labor. He knows well the history of the post-war Presidents—Monroe, Taylor and Fillmore, Johnson, McKinley and T. Roosevelt, and Harding. Of all these he thinks he has inherited the heaviest burdens; he does not except even Johnson. And trouble in Congress has always been a load for post-war Presidents to carry.

The piano keys under his own fingers and the standard classics of music can always turn his thoughts from these gloomy reflections. So can any writing by Mark Twain, fellow-Missourian and the President's favorite humorist. He is as ready to relax and laugh as any man could be, and this also explains his choice of companions and the influence of some of them over him. This native geniality and love of company find their happiest expression in card games and exchanges of tall tales and anecdotes. His taste in the latter is that of the country American of the Border—standard as are so many other things about him.

What is published in the press is a politician's business statement and the prospectus of his material future as well. Mr. Truman is as acutely conscious of this as any President has been, and he is a peruser of many newspapers and close reader of a few. But unlike many of his predecessors he has little fault to find with the press. He thinks that Washington reporting is fair and excellent, especially that of his press conferences. And of reporters in general he has no complaints. His quarrel, although the word is too strong, is with publishers and editors.

The President would not if he could restrict the expression of any opinion on the editorial page which an editor or publisher is willing to stand behind. It is the editorial columnists of whom he disapproves, and that heartily. A newspaper, in his view, should confine all opinion to the unsigned article under the masthead of the management, which thereby assumes responsibility in the name of the paper. He thinks it must be laziness that induces editors in many instances to let columnists do their research for them—and consequently their thundering. And he cannot understand why publishers permit these privileged outsiders to form the opinion of their readers.

But Mr. Truman, nevertheless, enjoys the editorial columns of the syndicated oracles. And he enjoys the gossip columns also (though he disapproves of them as beneath what should be the journalistic standard), whether he finds them in the daily press or in the news magazines, which to him are gossip columns in booklet form. So long as the news columns show fair reporting—and he believes in the great majority they do—he does not trouble himself about the editorials of the newspaper management. Give him a fair break on page one, says Mr. Truman, and the editorial page can carry what it will.

These are some of the aspects—truthfully presented, I think—of the man who will next week complete his first year as President of the United States. The portrait is not thrilling, but there is much of comfort and reassurance in it, and much to admire. Here is to be seen no flaming leadership, little of what could be called scholarship and no more that is profound. But it is very good and human and courageous. Common sense shines out of it, and political experience, the lack of which has been the downfall of Presidents.

Intellectuals, noting his reading, will not call him one of them. But the bases of a liberal education, self-acquired, will be found there, together with special historical knowledge not often encountered in the White House.

Those with more advanced tastes in music may also find limitations in the President's which will disappoint them. He thinks Lhevinne was the greatest of all pianists. His preference is to hear the standard classics of Beethoven, Chopin and Mozart. He especially delights in the antiphonies of the Pilgrims' Chorus from Wagner's

"Tannhaeuser" and the Andalusian melodies of Bizet. While he can listen to modern music without fidgeting, he also can leave it alone.

The President plays the piano in a fashion that can be called "acceptable." This ability was not self-taught. In Independence, when he was a boy, there lived a Mrs. E. C. White, graduate of the Boston Union Conservatory. She was engaged to instruct him and found him facile and eager. He is very grateful to Mrs. White for opening to him those Western islands "which bards in fealty to Apollo hold."

The usual fee for piano lessons in those days and places was 50 or 75 cents an hour. But it cost the family $2 an hour for Mrs. White.

A wish to learn how to do things well has always been characteristic of the Trumans.

The Republican "Mandate" and '48

by Louis H. Bean

POLITICAL OBSERVERS are asking a pertinent question as the Eightieth Congress gets into its stride: Did the Republicans, who now control both Houses, receive a mandate from the voters last November? Undoubtedly many Republicans believe they have a mandate, and their course as legislators will be influenced by their convictions. Moreover, they are looking forward to 1948 as the year in which they hope to score both a Presidential and a Congressional victory.

As a rule, so-called mandates are not clearly given in Congressional elections. Fifteen to 20 per cent of the voters in Presidential elections do not vote in off-year Congressional elections. Issues in Congressional campaigns are often confused, or sometimes lacking. It is in Presidential elections that Congress may get anything like a clear mandate, provided the issues are sharply differentiated by the platforms of the candidates. One must therefore be careful not to read into the 1946 election mandates that the voters did not intend.

For these reasons it is worth while to examine the basic facts of that election and determine what, if any, was the nature of the mandate, and to judge what prophetic meaning the Eightieth Congress has for 1948.

First, let us see what it was that influenced the voters. Probably the most common explanations of the Republican victory are the

From the *New York Times Magazine*, January 19, 1947.

GOP slogan, "Had Enough? Vote Republican"; the Administration's handling of strikes; the Wallace affair, and "that man in the White House." But there are two facts, insufficiently emphasized, that are of greater significance—the reduction in consumer purchasing power because of the marked rise in living costs in 1946, and an unusually large number of voters who failed to take part in the election.

There are two more interpretations of the Republican gains. One is that 1944 Democratic voters either voted Republican in 1946 or stayed away from the polls because the Republicans did such a good campaign job of tying up the CIO, the Communists and Administration officials into one neat bundle.

The other interpretation, particularly of the small vote, is suggested in a recent release by the Bureau of the Census showing that several million people had migrated from their voting residences during the year before the election. They may not have been politically settled by the fall of 1946.

Pre-election tests of what was bothering voters in 1946 revealed no general revulsion against the social, economic and international programs promoted by the New Deal Administration before the war. The surveys did reveal that the public was much concerned over relatively temporary reconversion problems. When the investigators of the American Institute of Public Opinion asked about the outstanding problems facing the country after the election, voters and others listed control of inflation as of prime importance. They then listed food and other shortages, peace, and strikes and labor troubles, in descending order. For every person who listed peace as a problem, there was one who listed strikes and labor troubles, there were two who listed food and other shortages, but there were five who listed control of inflation. Two-thirds who had opinions were concerned over prices and food.

The election results tend to corroborate the central showing of these pre-election surveys—namely, that the voters must have been influenced primarily by the shrinkage in their purchasing power which took place after the middle of 1946 as food prices shot up sharply. The Republicans gained most where living costs hurt most. Rising food prices normally take greatest toll among the dollars in the workers' weekly wage and salary envelopes. On the other hand, farmers gain, or at least do not lose, in that kind of a situation. By October, 1946, factory workers' real purchasing power was nearly 20 per cent below what it had been in early 1945, and among workers in durable, heavy-goods industries, the losses amounted to more than 20 per cent.

Consequently we find that in ten predominating agricultural States the Republicans gained on the average less than three percentage points in the popular vote. On the other hand, their gains in the industrial States, such as Rhode Island, Connecticut, New York, Delaware, Pennsylvania, Ohio, Illinois and Michigan, ranged between four and ten points, with the greatest gains in States in which heavy-goods industries are situated. The Republicans picked up about thirty seats in the metropolitan areas in excess of the twenty or twenty-five they might normally have won.

The other major feature which contributed to the Republican victory was the small turnout. Contrary to common belief, the registrations were light and the votes cast in the various States were far below normal. In fact, next to the voting apathy in 1942, the number of voters who stayed away was probably the largest, absolutely and relatively, since World War I. As has happened in practically every off-year Congressional election, the party in power lost ground with a light vote.

The extent to which a light vote affects the Democratic proportion in Congress is shown in the accompanying chart. Here the total

TOTAL VOTE FOR THE HOUSE

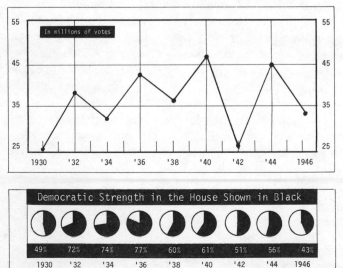

In millions of votes

Democratic Strength in the House Shown in Black

| 49% | 72% | 74% | 77% | 60% | 61% | 51% | 56% | 43% |
| 1930 | '32 | '34 | '36 | '38 | '40 | '42 | '44 | 1946 |

votes cast for Congressmen in off-year elections are contrasted with the votes cast in Presidential years. The record also shows the Democratic proportion of the total number of Congressmen elected in off-years and in Presidential years. It is clear that Democratic strength in Congress had been on the decline since 1934 and that the Democrats finally lost control as a result of three Congressional elections.

The one in 1938, a year of depression and light vote, cost them 71 seats. The one in 1942, a year of very light voting, cost them 45 seats; the 1946 election, still another year of light voting, cost them 55 seats and control, for this final loss reduced their percentage from 55 in 1944 to 43 in 1946.

Undoubtedly, many who voted Democratic in 1944 voted Republican in 1946, but neither the size of the Republican vote nor the size of the Democratic vote shows any large number of 1944 Democrats shifting to the Republican side. A normal total Congressional vote for 1946 would have been about 43 million and, according to the 1944 results, it should have divided about 22.5 million Democratic and 20.5 million Republican. The 1946 total vote was probably only about 34.5 million and divided about 15 Democratic, 18 Republican and 1 million of other parties. Thus the 9 million who stayed away appear to have been 7 million Democrats and 2 million Republicans.

This large stay-away vote shows abnormal apathy or general discontent with the reconversion behavior of the Democratic Administration. It does not, however, show that the discontent caused many Democrats to take on the Republican label. In fact, the total Republican vote appears to have been about 2 million short of a normal vote for 1946. This does not mean that there wasn't any shifting between parties, but the number couldn't have been large unless many 1944 Republicans stayed away. But this can hardly be the case. If, for example, it were argued that 3 million Democrats shifted, then there could have been only 15 million regular Republican votes, and the other 5.5 million regular Republicans must have stayed away.

This hardly fits in with the notion of a landslide and mass movement from the Democratic to the Republican side. It looks more like the voting in the 1938 Congressional elections, as shown in the accompanying chart. Then, too, practically all of the stay-away voters were Democrats, or independents voting Democratic.

THE PARTY VOTE FOR CONGRESS

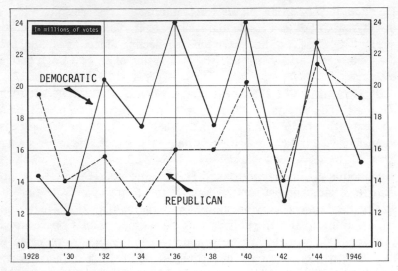

The 1938 stay-away vote was an expression of discontent because of a loss of income associated with unemployment, and one suspects the 1946 election was affected in the same way by the reduction in purchasing power.

Those who talk about a mandate for the Eightieth Congress usually speak in terms of changing labor laws and cutting the Federal budget. But since there is no clear evidence in the 1946 election of specific mandates on these or other items, erroneously conceived Congressional action on such fronts in 1947 could easily modify the present prospects for the 1948 election. What are those prospects?

What does the make-up of the Eightieth Congress mean for 1948 in the light of the record of American political tides? That record is shown in the chart which follows. It portrays the Republican and Democratic tides for the ninety-two-year life of these two major parties. It is a measure of the ups and downs of Democratic strength in the House of Representatives since 1854. The record is sufficiently varied and irregular to permit both Republicans and Democrats to glean support for their particular hopes.

Does the decline in the New Deal political tide from 79 per cent Democratic in 1936 to only 43 per cent in 1946 mean a prolonged

DEMOCRATIC TIDES IN THE HOUSE, 1852-1946

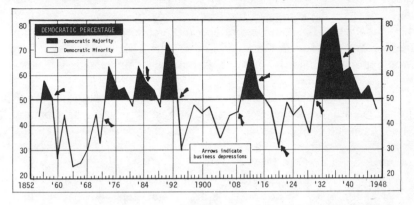

Republican Administration as we had in the Eighteen Sixties, Eighteen Nineties and Nineteen Twenties? That is, of course, one possible and not unreasonable conclusion, but not the only one. The 1936-46 Democratic decline has already covered about half the period it has taken in the past between the peaks of Democratic control (1856-74, 1890-1912 and 1912-36).

This could suggest that the decline in Democratic strength from the unusually high level attained in 1936 is about as low as it is likely to go and that the process of regaining Democratic Congressional seats recently lost may start with the 1948 election. It could mean that the Republicans would lose control after the Eightieth Congress or after several Congresses, but not after as many as in the Nineteen Twenties. In that case one would have to assume that the Democrats will succeed in getting the independent vote to participate again and in bringing into their fold some of the groups they have lost in recent elections, and also winning a substantial part of the emerging veteran vote.

Another comparison may be made. The record shows that business depressions, which mean loss of purchasing power, have usually produced changes in Administration. On this basis, the 1946 election may be compared with that of 1920, when the Democrats lost heavily. But with substantial recovery in 1922, the Democrats regained more seats than they lost in 1920 and came within a few seats of recapturing control. A similar pick-up in Democratic strength in 1948 would restore the Democrats to their 1944 position.

Republicans will, of course, not fail to observe in this record the six cases where the incoming party gained control in an off-year election. These instances were 1858, 1874, 1890, 1894, 1910 and 1918. In five of these cases the incoming party elected its Presidential candidate. The one exception, the Presidential election after 1874, actually proved the rule. Tilden, the Democratic candidate, won a popular majority, but the Republican Congress cast the deciding electoral vote for Hayes.

There is one observation to be made with regard to the 1948 prospects for the Senate. During the past ten years Democratic strength in the Senate has declined about as much as in the House, from 80 per cent in 1936 to 47 per cent in 1946. But it may be of some cheer for the Democrats that in 1948 Republicans cannot gain much more in the Senate, for all but four of the Democratic Senators up for re-election in 1948 are Southerners whose re-election is usually a certainty.

The results of the 1948 election will, of course, be determined, in part, by the record the minority Democrats and their President will make in contrast to what the Republicans do. It will be determined also by the character and voting record of the candidates, by the domestic business situation, by the international situation, and by the efforts each party puts into the campaign.

Meantime, it is worth noting that the cost of living and other reconversion problems of 1946 will recede in the voters' memory and be replaced by new problems in 1948, just as the depression problems of 1920 gave way to recovery psychology in 1922 and made possible marked Democratic gains. It is also worth considering what the voters' reaction is likely to be if in 1948, as many predict, we are in the midst of a depression. In that case, whom will voters blame, the Republican majority in Congress or the Democratic President and the Democratic minority?

That Baffling Personality, Mr. Wallace

by Cabell Phillips

THE EVALUATION of Henry Agard Wallace has been a continuing preoccupation of editorial writers and political analysts for the last fifteen years. He has been variously assayed as a harmless mystic, an inspired prophet, a ruthlessly practical politician and a dangerous radical. On only one verdict has there been universal agreement, by friends and enemies alike: that his is the most bafflingly complex personality in American public life today.

He can be, and has been, at one and the same time, a defender of Adam Smith capitalism and of Marxian collectivism; of the philosophy of abundance and of the policy of "plowing under every third row." He has been the shining champion of the Common Man, yet on conspicuous occasions has abandoned him to predatory enemies. He has been a business man-scientist and a religious ascetic. He has been an earnest and soaring idealist and a political demagogue.

In 1932 he was a registered Republican who voted the Democratic ticket and contributed $25 to the campaign fund of Socialist Norman Thomas. He is capable of such magnificent inconsistencies as, "I don't see how anybody nominated by a third party could realize any ambition" (January, 1947), and, "I announce tonight I shall run as an independent candidate for President of the United States in 1948" (December, 1947).

No man can say with certainty that he knows Henry Wallace or can predict today what he will do tomorrow. He lives deeply cloistered

From the *New York Times Magazine*, February 8, 1948.

within his own mind, preoccupied by inner conflicts and passions, and gives only so much of himself to external stimuli as will meet the minimal requirements of the moment. Yet it is in a way a brilliant, far-reaching mind, well endowed by heredity and training, and it has carried him to conspicuous heights in the life of the nation, unaided by wealth or other influences.

Today he is the patron and candidate of a new third-party movement which, while it will not carry him into the White House in 1949, unquestionably will have a profound effect in determining who the tenant will be. It is a movement embracing the most dissident elements of the Far Left and here received unqualified Communist support. Its principal component is the Progressive Citizens of America, which is composed in about equal parts of militant trade unionists, political intellectuals from the arts and sciences and a heterogeneous collection of Left-Wingers. The organization claims approximately 100,000 members with chapters in twenty-four states. Its essential doctrine calls for the abandonment of the Marshall Plan and a rapprochement with Russia, and the installation of a series of domestic reforms considerably more ambitious than anything ever attempted by the New Deal.

There are many political observers who believe that the net effect of the Wallace candidacy will be to lure away enough independent voters from the Democratic ranks to obtain the defeat of President Truman (or whoever the party's candidate may be) and to make certain the victory of a Republican such as Senator Robert A. Taft of Ohio or Gov. Thomas E. Dewey of New York.

Recently in Chicago I asked Mr. Wallace how, in view of that political prediction, he rationalized his candidacy in terms of procuring even a relatively liberal administration for the country during what he himself has termed "the four fateful years after 1948."

He gave me the quick, nervous smile that has become a Wallace hallmark, and ran his fingers through his hair.

"That's quite a question," he said, "but of course I don't agree that the principal effect of my candidacy will be Truman's defeat.

"As for getting a liberal administration after 1948, I don't believe a Truman Administration would be even 'relatively liberal,' as you chose to put it. There is nothing 'relatively liberal' about supporting kings and dictators and reactionaries. There is nothing liberal about loyalty orders and purges.

"I think the people of the country are tired of having nothing but a choice between evils; they want a chance to vote for the greatest good, not the lesser evil."

Whatever its logic, Mr. Wallace has chosen a thesis of indisputable popularity. And he is capable of offering it with a contagious evangelism that gives his following the flavor of a crusade.

I talked to a couple of young Midwestern college students recently who are the leaders of a Wallace-for-President club on their campus. I asked them how they accounted for Wallace's wide popularity among younger voters—a phenomenon which they previously had assured me was indisputable.

"It's because Wallace is the one leader in the country with the guts to preach the only kind of liberalism that means a damn today —an affirmative, dynamic liberalism," the younger of the two, a precocious 18-year-old, said. He sported a large blue-and-white Wallace button on his lapel.

"American youth is fed up with the timidity and the compromises of the old-line political bosses. It's the same old crowd and the same sort of thinking that gave us the depression and the Second World War.

"Henry Wallace represents a clean break from that outmoded mentality. He's as far ahead of his time in 1948 as Roosevelt was in 1932. And that's the only sort of leadership that will save the country from fascism and a war with Russia."

The Wallaces of Iowa are among the bedrock families of America. They emigrated from Ireland and settled on the western slopes of the Alleghenies, near Pittsburgh, in 1823. The first American-born Henry Wallace grew up to be a lusty, strong-willed man who found the narrow dogmatism of his day intolerable. As a young man he moved West to put his roots down in the comparatively frontier territory of Iowa. From a rugged, free-wheeling neighborhood oracle he evolved over the years into a sort of provincial patriarch, the publisher of a mighty paper and a power in the political and agricultural life of the whole Middle West. The name "Uncle Henry" still bears a magic connotation in the folklore of the American Corn Belt.

Henry Agard Wallace, a grandson of "Uncle Henry," was born on a farm in Adair County, Iowa, on Oct. 12, 1888. He grew up a shy, reticent boy, but the neighbors agreed that of all the Wallace progeny, he most favored "Uncle Henry" in astuteness and strong-headedness. He had a deep mind and a resolute will, they said, which would get him places.

Their conviction was largely borne out. The family paper, Wallace's Farmer, prospered under his editorship in the decade following the First World War. His inquisitive and inventive mind led to the development of a seed corn business that made him comparatively wealthy. His eminence as an agricultural philosopher brought him national renown.

Henry Wallace was Franklin Roosevelt's third choice for Secretary of Agriculture in the first New Deal Administration. But the two men soon discovered a kinship in their idealism which has tinted, if it has not colored, much of national history since. When the first clamor of public acclaim for the New Deal began to subside, Wallace became—as he has remained until this day—its most passionate advocate and its most docile sacrificial goat. He has been by turns its hero, its martyr and its fall-guy.

His constancy was rewarded with the Vice Presidency in 1940. Four years later he was coldly jettisoned in favor of Senator Harry S. Truman of Missouri. Then, in an astonishing act of atonement, he was installed as Secretary of Commerce, where he was a barn-size target for the growing Congressional rancor against Roosevelt and the New Deal.

The death of FDR left Henry Wallace, as it did many other liberals, a spiritual and political orphan. Reconversion and the course of world reconstruction under the Truman Administration are as a chill wind to the aspirations of these prophets of the Century of the Common Man. The great goals, as they see them, have been abandoned in an obscene race for "normalcy" at home and for the old balance of power politics throughout the world. Alienated, they have coalesced in diminishing numbers farther and farther to the Left—a position not totally unoccupied to begin with, of course. Wallace found a hospitable sanctuary in their midst.

The dénouement came in October, 1946, with his famous speech at Madison Square Garden denouncing the Truman-Byrnes policy toward Russia. Within a week his forced resignation from the Cabinet occurred, and he set forth on the trail of a free-lance Messiah which has now culminated in his third-party candidacy.

Henry Wallace is a large, disheveled man with shaggy eyebrows and an unruly thatch of iron-gray hair. His steel-gray eyes, questing and penetrating, seem somehow dissociated from his perpetual expression of shy friendliness; they, not the spoken words or the nervous smile, are the index of what he is thinking. There is an overpowering earnestness about him, and you feel that he would not tell you the time of day without first searching his soul to see if it agreed with the clock. Most interviewers are disconcerted upon encountering so much moral austerity and intellectual detachment in one man.

In mid-January he made a triumphal appearance at the PCA national convention in Chicago—which was, to all intents and purposes, the third-party nominating convention.

To a number of Washington correspondents who covered the meeting, his new obligation as a party leader seemed to have worked one notable change in his character. There was missing some of the directness of manner, the disarming forthrightness that one remembered. In press conferences and private conversations with reporters he seemed to calculate the effect of each remark and to indulge in strategic evasions when the questions looked troublesome.

He had "not read" recent columns of Mrs. Eleanor Roosevelt chiding him for his political apostasy. He was "not familiar with the record" of Illinois Republican Senator C. Wayland Brooks, one of the country's most notable isolationists. He repeatedly refused to come to grips with the most persistent question of all—the implications of the Communist support of his candidacy. When reminded that FDR had openly rejected the Communists in 1940, he hedged on the question of whether he would do likewise by saying that he would "have to look up the record to see what Roosevelt did."

It was pretty apparent that Henry Wallace had decided to become "cagey." It fitted him no better than such artificial accouterments of the personality usually do.

For a brief period between his platform appearances I sat in his hotel room with him and asked him to talk about his decision to break with the orthodox parties and to start one of his own. Would he, for example, be inclined to go along with Truman's domestic program as set forth in the State of the Union message if the issue of foreign policy were not involved?

"Yes, I think I would," he said, settling into a chair and declining my offer of a cigarette. "The real cleavage is on foreign policy. I've said all along that that is the principal cause of my break with the Democratic party.

"By that I don't mean I have very much faith in President Truman putting across any substantial part of his domestic program. Truman never fights for his good intentions. He had almost the same program in 1945 and in 1946. And what did he do with it?"

I asked him why he appeared so consistently silent on Russia's political imperialism in Poland and the Balkan countries while condemning this country's "dollar imperialism," as in the Greek-Turkish loan and the Marshall Plan. The question seemed to strike a sensitive spot for he answered with some vehemence.

"Why does the American press keep on talking about 'Russian imperialism' and 'Russian aggression'? It isn't that, any more than our efforts in Mexico and South America are imperialism.

"American newspapers have greatly distorted what is going on in Europe. I have a number of friends who know those countries well. I have visited some of them myself. From all these sources I get a very different picture of what is going on.

"I think a better phrase is Russia's drive for security. We've known ever since the Yalta conference that Russia would insist on friendly nations on her borders. She has a right to that protection. That's what this 'imperialism' everyone talks about amounts to."

"All right," I said, "let's call it a drive for security instead of imperialism. Won't you agree that Russia is pursuing it by rather high-handed and aggressive means?"

"Well, yes," he replied after a momentary hesitation. "It's a totalitarian approach. Russia is a totalitarian country. I don't believe in totalitarianism.

"But you have to remember that the Russian people are afraid of us. When they see us project plans like the Truman Doctrine and the Marshall Plan they interpret them as warlike moves—as the preliminary to outright warfare and invasion. That increases their anxiety to safeguard themselves. It makes them more belligerent and hostile. We retaliate. And the tensions are built up and up on both sides."

The only way to relieve those tensions, he went on, was for the United States to change its attitude, to demonstrate conclusively its good-will toward the Russian Government.

"What, specifically, do you think our policy toward Russia ought to be?" I asked.

"We need a complete reorientation of our attitude toward the Soviet nations," he replied. "We have to recapture the spirit of trust and cooperation that existed between Roosevelt and Stalin in 1945.

"Our foreign policy today is in the hands of a soldier who has a typically militaristic point of view toward international affairs. I have the greatest respect for Secretary Marshall as a soldier and as a man. But I happen to know that he detests Russia. He has eliminated from his counsel the one general who understands and is sympathetic toward the Russian point of view. He is completely surrounded by anti-Russians. What can you expect our Russian policy to be under the circumstances?

"If I were to become President I would immediately arrange a personal meeting with Stalin. Beforehand, I would have every branch of the Government search out all the policies and practices that are causing friction between the two countries. I would hope that he would do the same thing. Then we could sit around a table and discuss those frictions one by one and come to mutual understanding."

"And you think Stalin is amenable to this sort of settlement of differences?"

"Why, yes, I am sure he is. He would have to be."

The interview was ended by his secretary before he could elaborate the point.

The "Wallace myth" which has persisted for many years has depicted the former Vice President as a chaste vessel of all the standard virtues of humility, honesty, sincerity and loyalty. "Fuzziness" and "wrong-headedness" were the epithets most commonly used by his detractors. But of late even the ranks of the Wallace worshipers have been assailed by doubts. There has been a positive, rather than a negative, compulsion visible in many of his more recent vagaries. Things have been done and said that are not explainable by innocent "wrong-headedness."

Why did he persist a year ago in his criticism of the Administration's proposal for international control of atomic energy after confessing to Bernard M. Baruch, the plan's architect, that his criticisms were erroneous and invalid? What impelled him last summer to stump the tense capitals of Europe denouncing the "war aims" of his Government? What frantic zeal has constrained him to become the oracle for Communist and Left-Wing demagogy?

For the people around Wallace today are not the ones who followed him a year or ten years ago. He has been abandoned by virtually every recognized spokesman for organized labor, by most of his New Deal colleagues, such as Mrs. Eleanor Roosevelt, Wilson Wyatt and Leon Henderson, and even by some of the mainstays of the PCA, such as Dr. Frank Kingdon and Bartley Crum. He has been forced to retreat into the desolate company of the most radical fringe of the Far Left. And there is a pervasive Communist coloration to this new "Gideon's Army," which Henry Wallace now leads.

At the Chicago convention there were many symptoms of this condition: the overslick parliamentary procedure that smothered any incipient opposition; the prearranged slate of candidates, including a number of generally acknowledged Communist disciples, swept into office by acclamation; such casual acknowledgments as that of the great Negro baritone, Paul Robeson, who said: "I want to destroy fascism; and to do it I'm prepared to accept the opposite form of dictatorship"; the brittle sophistry of the official pronouncements that highlighted all the weaknesses of American democracy and ascribed their existence to such subjective villains as "Wall Street profiteers" and "warmongers."

Said the report of the resolutions committee, a document regarded as the precursor of the new party's platform:

"The lords of American monopoly have gorged themselves with profit, yet they proceed at the same time to impoverish our people. . . . The genuine peace-loving and humanitarian spirit of the American people has been cynically used to further the global aims of Wall Street. . . .

"The Marshall Plan, skillfully propagandized as a great humanitarian venture, does not seek the development and self-recovery of the countries of Europe. It divides Eastern and Western Europe into hostile camps. . . . [It] seeks to strengthen American monopoly's control over the internal economies of Western Europe."

To many of the devout the "Wallace myth" is crumbling. The White Knight has ridden off the stage—in the wrong direction and with a strange wench a-pillion. Some see in it a sort of Hitlerian tragedy: a great leader trapped by the flames of his own ambition. They shake their heads sadly and ask one another, "What's happened to Henry?"

To assess "what's happened to Henry" one comes up immediately against that strangely complex personality, the mystic-humanitarian-demagogue. Efforts at analysis usually are predicated upon one or the other of those attributes.

For example, a famous economist who worked closely with Wallace throughout his Washington career and who translated many of his ideas into popular prose, thinks he has been swept up in a sort of religious frenzy.

"Henry is a deeply religious man," he said recently, "and with a tendency toward the metaphysical. It's not uncommon for people like that to get the notion that the hand of God is upon them; that they have become 'the chosen instrument' for carrying out some mandate of divine will.

"Intolerance is a part of this sort of religion. If you aren't a true believer in every point of the Decalogue you are a sinner. There aren't any degrees of faith; it is all or none; you are all good or all bad."

"Henry, I think, believes sincerely in everything he is saying today. He thinks we are going to hell at home and courting war abroad. He has arrived at the conclusion that he has a divine mission to rescue America from this plight. Some inner light tells him that he is God's instrument in this work of salvation. He brings to his side whoever professes a belief as passionate and as inflexible as his own, and casts out everyone else.

"I don't think it was just an accident of phrase-making that made him call that crowd a 'Gideon's Army.' I think it had a positive significance, for Henry Wallace at least."

Another view is that of an able Washington reporter who has observed Henry Wallace closely since 1935.

"Wallace's career up to now has been that of thinker," he said, "a man of ideas and great dreams. He has never been a lucid thinker nor a good expositor of his ideas. But his ideas were usually the right ones.

"Now he's called upon to translate his ideas into action, to be an executor as well as a thinker. For the first time in his career Henry Wallace is called upon to supply the answers to his questions. And he's giving all the wrong answers."

Among those who have known Mr. Wallace for some years in Washington and who observed his recent performance in Chicago there is little disposition to question the sincerity of his beliefs. They think he has come honestly, if not logically, by his current obsession toward reactionism and war.

But they remember that he was ever a gullible man, an easy convert to almost any scheme provided it was served up with a garnish of broad humanitarianism. And they also remember that there have been conspicuous traces of naïveté—almost of immaturity—in his make-up.

So it isn't entirely out of character that Henry Wallace, in the most dramatic decision of his career, should take his stand on a platform of "something for everybody," a statement of social and economic objectives almost utopian in its scope. Nor is it out of character that in focusing his vision on the twin sectors of reaction and war his blind spot should encompass the reasonable alternatives.

There is certainly a challenging plausibility in the Wallace thesis. All the evils he complains of are visible to the naked eye, and the international horizons are darkly obscured by suspicion and hate.

One need not go behind the apparent symptom, the unexplained bogey, to instill fear in the heart of the multitude. A great merchandising genius thought up the word "halitosis" and millions of the uncontaminated pay him homage every year.

Henry Wallace has drawn a fearsome indictment of American democratic capitalism. He has highlighted its every defect; blacked out its modest virtues and its relative achievements. As a prophet of doom he rallies the frightened—as well as the deliberately scheming—behind his crusade. He promises with one stroke of his righteous sword to strike down the dragons and the evildoers, and to deliver a bright and shining America into the hands of its rightful inheritors.

The short cut to salvation is an always fascinating theology. Its propulsion is fear and its rhetoric the plausible cliché. It puts a minimum strain upon the exhorter and doesn't confuse the faithful with doubts. But history fails to show that it has ever led to eternal glory in either religion or politics.

The Rise, Fall and Hopes of the G.O.P.

by Cabell Phillips

THE PLACE of the Republican party in national affairs today is approximately that of an uneasy and dyspeptic back seat driver who also happens to have a lien on the car. The G.O.P. doesn't like anything about the man at the wheel, accuses him of running through red lights and skidding on the turns, and is convinced, moreover, that he is reading his road maps upside down. It proclaims its alarm in strident and ill-tempered language and swears that, so help it, if the conveyance holds together until 1952 it will throw the driver out and take over the wheel itself.

Almost eighteen years have gone by since a Republican administration ran the Government of the United States. Only twice, in all that time, have the Republicans seriously threatened Democratic control, and both times were in off-year, non-Presidential elections. The first was in 1946 when, to their surprise and confusion, they gained a narrow margin of control in both the House and the Senate. The second was last year when they came within two seats of capturing the Senate and twenty seats of taking the House.

The result of this latest upsurge is that in the Eighty-second Congress the Republican party is a minority in name only. Because there are enough dissenting Democrats in both chambers to string along with them on many controversial issues, the Republicans are in a position to control many aspects of national policy. This gives them one of the rarest offensive advantages in the whole strategy of poli-

From the *New York Times Magazine*, July 8, 1951.

tics—power without responsibility. If they cannot initiate policy, at least they can shape it or block it. If the policy turns out well, they can claim the credit. If it turns out badly, they can, with that easy illogic that is countenanced in politics, blame the other fellow.

There is no better illustration of this than the recent G.O.P. victory in forcing the Truman Administration into a showdown on the dismissal of Gen. Douglas MacArthur. The Democrats, almost to a man, would much have preferred to let the controversial old soldier "fade away" after his return from Tokyo. But the Republicans set up such a clamor of protest that the Administration had no choice but to yield to an elaborate investigation of Far Eastern policy.

Just what tangible political gains will come out of this cannot be foreseen now. But that the investigation was held at all is an evidence of the Republicans' strength.

This dawning sense of power, plus the exciting statistics of last November's election, have acted like a shot of vitamins into the wearied carcass of the G.O.P. elephant. Republicans believe, and there is much independent opinion to support them, that the country is really "ready for a change" this time as against the deceptive appearance of readiness last time.

They can find omens of this wherever they look.

There is, for example, widespread uneasiness over our involvement in the Far East, an anxiety which the Republicans themselves have done as much to foster as they dared. High prices and high taxes, in spite of an unparalleled dollar prosperity, are universally unpopular. Public confidence in the Administration and in the President have been shaken by such disclosures as those of the R. F. C. and crime investigations (both headed by Democrats). Senator Joe McCarthy's vituperative attacks on the State Department have stuck firmly in the public consciousness. And finally, it is reasoned, the Democratic candidate in 1952 will not have the ineluctable benefit of the Republican-controlled "worst" Congress to belabor at all the whistle stops across the land.

But there is a more somber side of the picture that afflicts the thoughtful. The Republicans are having a very tough time of it getting together on any sort of program and solidifying their strength. They seem to be making many of the tactical mistakes and personal blunders that cost them victory last time. The party wears a positive tinge of isolationism, despite the best disclaimers of nearly everyone concerned. Pronouncements of party doctrine often are left to be uttered by the least tactful and responsible party leaders. Legitimate partisanship on many issues is frequently distorted by vindictiveness. Party unity has all but been destroyed by splits over basic political doctrine, over fundamental economic theory, and over regional and sectional prejudices.

One of the worst blows to harmony within the G.O.P. has come through the controversy over the firing of General MacArthur. Initially it seemed that the President's "affront" to the great military hero of the Pacific was just the sort of cement needed to bind the warring factions together. Senator Taft promptly took his stand at the General's side, and others of lesser stature fell obediently into line.

But the attractions of the MacArthur crusade have begun to fade. The other side of the story on Korea as supplied by Secretary Marshall, General Bradley and the Joint Chiefs of Staff brought some sober second thinking. When the National Committee met in Tulsa recently, the whole MacArthur issue was handled as gingerly as if it were a vial of U-235. It is obvious that a lot of Republicans want no part of the "MacArthur package" as a political issue, and they resent the efforts of Senator Taft and others to force it on them.

But in spite of these handicaps, there is a tinge of destiny about the Republican party today. Whether the signs are as fallible as last time no one can say. But there is a consensus among the political pundits that there may now be a more prophetic validity to the campaign song, "This Is the Hour," that vibrated *ad nauseam* through the Philadelphia convention hall late in July, 1948, than there was then.

So let's put the G.O.P. briefly on the dissecting table to see what it is, what its bloodlines are and how its pulse rate looks at the moment.

The Republican party, like its ancient foe, the Democrats, is part reality and part idea. In its temporal body it can best be likened to a pyramid.

At the broad base of this pyramid are the 18,000,000 to 22,000,-000 citizens who have affirmed their Republicanism by voting for Republican candidates with more or less regularity for the last ten or twelve years. They have come within a few percentage points each time—from minus 5 to plus 2—of comprising one-half the total voting population of the country.

The second layer is composed of the 300,000 to 400,000 who

call themselves "organization Republicans." These are the party janizaries, the volunteer precinct workers, local and state committeemen and so on, who hold the party together between elections and who man the ramparts when the call to battle sounds.

Still more important are the "angels" who supply the party's working capital. In 1948 the National Committee and its immediate affiliates spent $3,500,000 in the unsuccessful effort to get Gov. Thomas E. Dewey elected to the Presidency. Even in this nonelection year, it has set a goal of $1,200,000 for running expenses and to build up its kitty. This money comes in driblets from the faithful, and in much larger measures from 300 or 400 capitalists and their families to whom Republicanism is both a creed and a civil obligation.

Superimposed upon the financiers, and frequently in mortal conflict with them, is the party's Congressional representation. Its members are the real architects of party policy between conventions and it is their collective action that dictates what posture the party assumes in the public eye.

Finally, at the capstone of the pyramid is the 104-man (and woman) National Committee or, even more precisely, the fifteen-man (and woman) executive committee. Guy George Gabrielson presides over this menage as chairman from his $25,000 a year headquarters in a dignified Georgian mansion on Washington's Connecticut Avenue. He is the party's business head and its main catalyzer of action. He keeps the publicity pipelines full and endeavors to maintain a proper pitch of indignation against all things Democratic.

Organizationally, the Republican party is a pretty lively outfit these days. It has made a strong comeback from the shock it suffered in 1948. As it proved in the Congressional elections last fall, it has rebuilt solidly at the precinct level where strength is essential. It has wooed back into the fold many of the "angels" who deserted it after the Dewey-Warren débâcle, and its finances are on a relatively sound basis. And it has been alert to exploit every opening the Democrats have afforded.

Equally important in seeing the party whole is discovering what it has been.

Ralph Waldo Emerson once wrote, "The two parties which divide the state, the party of the conservators and the party of the innovators, are very old and have disputed the possession of the world ever since it was made. This quarrel is the subject of civil history."

Democrats and Republicans alike have defended ground on both sides of that fence at various times, but essentially the Republican party has been the party of the conservators, the steadfast exponents of "the least government is the best government" school of politics.

Paradoxically, it came to birth on a wave of liberalism, rising out of the ashes of the discredited Whig party in 1854. It was spawned by a colorful and rambunctious alliance of disillusioned progressives and malcontents who wanted a Federal government more sympathetic to their needs and less dedicated to the whims of the big bankers and merchants of the Eastern seaboard.

Abe Lincoln rallied them under the common banner of Abolition (although that was not what he set out to do). From 1860 to 1865, in spite of the heavy distractions of the Civil War, the Republican party was a dynamic, responsive instrument of the people themselves.

With Lincoln dead and Abolition no longer an issue, the coalition that had sired the Republican party fell apart. The Empire Builders moved in and took over. The pathetic Andrew Johnson, who tried to carry on the Lincoln tradition, was demolished. He was succeeded by Grant and by Hayes, Garfield and Arthur, each of whom held to the passive concept of government and the Presidency.

These were the impressionable, formative years of the Republican party. The nation was launched upon one of the most incredible periods of material prosperity and economic expansion in all history. Wealth was the sole criterion of success. Great political bosses arose —the Mark Hannas, the Matt Quays, the Tom Platts who, in the words of Mark Sullivan, "stood with one foot in the world of politics and one in the world of big business, and were the medium through which each served the other."

This was the age of the Robber Barons, the Empire Builders, the age of the last great flowering of Adam Smith's laissez-faire theories of economics. The whole concept of a free reign for capitalist adventure, and of a minimum role for government, was consistent with the national character of the time. And it colored the character of the Republican party for decades to come.

William McKinley was the first to seek to alter this passive and acquiescent concept of government. He reintroduced the idea into the Republican credo that government had an obligation to serve the people as well as the great property interests. Among other things, he was the first President to make affirmative gestures of friendship to the then-struggling labor movement, and organized labor remained predominantly Republican until the advent of the New Deal.

But if McKinley caused furrows to crease the brows of the G.O.P. stalwarts of that day, the erratic and bombastic Teddy Roosevelt, who followed him, frightened them very nearly out of their wits— and for good cause. His first message to Congress in November, 1901, was a bristling 20,000-word document setting forth a "Square Deal" that seemed just as revolutionary to the conservative statesmen of that day as the program of the New Deal was to seem thirty years later. He, like Lincoln—and unlike any Republican President since his day—captured the imagination, loyalty and faith of the people themselevs.

Taft, who succeeded him, was cast in the familiar mold of the late nineteenth century. T. R. became disenchanted with the genial but ineffectual Ohioan and formed his Bull Moose party to oppose him. But his comeback failed, of course, and two terms of Democratic rule under Wilson ensued.

Traditional Republicanism was again enthroned in the Harding-Coolidge-Hoover era. The complacent, passive role of these Presidents as contrasted with the soaring idealism and the dynamic statesmanship of Woodrow Wilson makes this period of the Nineteen Twenties seem almost like "the lost decade" of American political history. Republican power, which had ruled the White House for eighteen of the twenty-one administrations since Lincoln, was engulfed in the cataclysm of the Great Depression.

Wendell Willkie, the earnest but politically naive "Wall Street farm boy" who took the 1940 Republican convention by storm, gave the party its first transfusion of new blood and new ideas since the days of Teddy Roosevelt. The Old Guard lined up to fight this alien force with almost as much vigor as the Democrats. But the progressivism which Willkie left in his wake took hold in some of the untended crannies of the party structure. It is a flourishing but still parasitical growth today, surviving in spite of the best efforts of the parent plant to ignore its existence.

Thus, the Republican party in its mature, latter years is seized of that "subject of civil history" of which Emerson wrote. It is host to a variety of stresses and impulses that are mutually antagonistic.

Whose is the clear and certain voice of Republicanism today?

Is it Herbert Hoover's, warning ominously from the sepulchres of the past? Is it Robert Taft's, exhorting to a stern and self-righteous piety? Is it Governor Dewey's, crying "reform or perish"? Is it the sulphurous maledictions of Joe McCarthy, or the patient homilies of George Aiken?

These aren't captious or unfriendly questions. With a little rephrasing they could be asked just as well of the Democrats. But they do help to illustrate the harsh factionalism into which the Republicans, struggling to adjust their past to the present, have fallen.

Predominant among these factions is the conservative, at times isolationist, Old Guard wing of which the undisputed boss is Senator Robert A. Taft, of Ohio. He is backed by a majority of Republicans in both houses of Congress and by the most influential segment of the national committee. And to a considerable body of citizens at large who are disturbed by what they regard as a trend toward "socialism," he is a stern and enduring symbol of old-time Republicanism.

Taft is the Truman Administration's most remorseless foe. With incisive logic and a devastating irony he hacks away, on and off the Senate floor, at every aspect of its policy. He has aligned himself with Senator McCarthy's crusade against Communists in government. He challenges the competence of Defense Secretary Marshall and calls insistently for the head of Secretary of State Acheson.

Asserting his leadership now in foreign as well as domestic affairs, he made short work of the bipartisanship which the late Senator Arthur H. Vanderberg, of Michigan, had fathered. He has been a consistent critic of foreign aid programs. He led the fight to put curbs on the assignment of troops to Europe. And when the dispute over Far Eastern policy erupted a few weeks ago, he threw his weight into the controversy on the side of General MacArthur.

So it is not merely in jest that Senator Taft is called "Mr. Republican." In its dominant aspect today, the Republican party reflects *his* image, not he the party's.

The opposing faction, derisively called the "me-tooers," lacks the cohesion and discipline of the Old Guard. For one thing, it has no acknowledged leader. For another, its adherents are motivated almost as much by anti-Taftism as by any positive alternative to the Taft program.

In a large sense this group represents the fruit of Wendell Willkie's heresy. These are the Republicans who have rebelled against the rigid conservatism of the Old Guard, who acknowledge at least a limited inevitability to the New Deal revolution and who are willing to accept a fuller measure of responsibility for the United States in world affairs.

This liberal wing of Republicans claims about eight or ten members of the Senate—such men as Lodge of Massachusetts, Morse of Oregon and Aiken of Vermont, for example—and from twenty-five to thirty in the House, of whom Javits of New York, Case of New Jersey and Fulton of Pennsylvania are typical. They have no particular alliance among themselves and are given little opportunity to be heard in party councils.

Their great common denominator is a despairing and frustrated conviction that if the Republican party does not "wake up" to the realities of the times and adopt a more liberal and dynamic program, it will cease to exist as a political force.

Just whom the divided Republicans will nominate for the Presidency next year is anybody's guess, but Mr. Taft's chances at this moment seem reasonably good. He is the only important leader who has expressed a willingness to be drafted, and his agents are even now diligently probing the sentiment across the country.

The Eastern and progressive wings of the party, however, would fight hard to deny him the nomination. Governor Dewey, who is now aligned with these groups, has already removed himself from the running. But in so doing he gave his endorsement to General Eisenhower. Although the general has never intimated how he feels about this unsolicited honor, progressive Republican hopes continue to revolve about him.

Recently these hopes have been materially strengthened by Senator Taft's opposition to sending more troops to Europe and his espousal of the MacArthur strategy for Korea. Hence, it is reasoned that General Eisenhower's reluctance to get into politics might be lessened if that seemed the only way to avert the imposition of a Taft foreign policy on the United States.

This present G.O.P. dilemma, which may dim the party's prospects, illustrates a fact which is sometimes a weakness but is often a major strength of the American political system.

It is futile in a two-party system to look for unanimity and airtight cohesiveness. Our parties aren't based on dogmatism. Dogmatism leads to rigidity and rigidity leads to splintering, as one may observe in the unhappy experience of France.

Our two parties are rather—and necessarily—coalitions of many beliefs and shades of opinion held together by some elastic congeniality of aims or even by force of habit. The vitality of the parties rests upon their ability to compromise and to live with their inner conflicts; to find the broad road between dogma and free thought that offends the fewest and gratifies the most.

The trouble the Republicans are having today is finding their way back to that broad middle road. Too many big wheels are rolling in too many directions, and gathering speed as they go. The Republicans are afflicted not by too much dogmatism but by a sort of anarchy. The big question is how and when and by whose magic this situation is going to be tidied up.

Part **2**

THE EISENHOWER ADMINISTRATION

Inquiry into McCarthy's Status

by John B. Oakes

THE MOST TALKED about man in the capital today is, next to the President, a junior Senator from Wisconsin named Joseph R. McCarthy. His name arouses deeply felt emotions on the part of seasoned politicians as well as political novices; his face has become familiar to nation-wide audiences, and his methods of political warfare have given a new word to the language. He is the most bitterly attacked figure in public life and yet even his most earnest foes in the halls of government have thus far done little to stop him.

This article is an effort to describe his position in Washington, to set down objectively the arguments Democratic and Republican leaders make for and against him, and to explain why both his friends and enemies handle him with care.

Senator McCarthy first shot to national prominence with his attack on alleged Communists in the State Department just three years ago, although in the words of one of his most fervent Senate admirers, "he didn't know a damned thing about communism." Many people think that he still doesn't, but few will argue that he lacks the ability to seize on popular issues, dramatize them, use them ruthlessly for his own purposes and make political profit out of them. His critics charge that in doing so he shows a disdain for traditional American concepts of freedom and fair play, but his tactics have thus far been crowned with personal success.

From the *New York Times Magazine*, April 12, 1953.

Senators speak with something like awe of McCarthy's facility for turning even his defeats to his own advantage. When President Eisenhower submitted the name of Charles E. Bohlen to be Ambassador to Russia, the first rumblings of opposition came from Republicans who honestly resented Bohlen's connection with the Yalta conference. It wasn't McCarthy's show at all. But with his unerring flair for publicity, McCarthy intervened, seized public attention with his own special brand of allegation against Bohlen, and, as far as the public was concerned, became leader of the anti-Bohlen forces.

The result is that the eleven Republican votes eventually cast against Bohlen took on something of the color of a McCarthy bloc within the party, although it is probably true that most of these votes had nothing to do with McCarthy at all and it is even likely that there would have been a larger anti-Bohlen vote if McCarthy had not played so prominent a part in the opposition.

Even if as a result of this Bohlen incident McCarthy suffered a net loss in prestige (which is doubtful), he was able immediately to divert public attention by issuing his famous statement that his committee had managed to get Greek shipowners to agree to cut off all trade with Communist-held ports. McCarthy was in the headlines again, and the ineradicable public impression was created that he had been able to accomplish something the State Department had been incompetent to do. The fact that McCarthy was trespassing into the field of foreign relations constitutionally reserved to the Executive may have shocked a small segment of the public, and it certainly irked a good many Senators. But a frequently expressed reaction on Capitol Hill is that most people don't care how trade with Communist countries is stopped, so long as it's stopped, and that McCarthy would get the lion's share of the credit because he had got the lion's share of the headlines.

McCarthy's new position as chairman of the Senate Committee on Government Operations is a development that has significantly enhanced his status. It is one thing to make charges and speeches on one's own, as McCarthy has been doing during the past few years; it is quite another to have the prestige, the funds and the facilities afforded by the chairmanship of a committee of the United States Senate. McCarthy has exercised his prerogatives so vigorously that undercover protests have already been heard from members of his own committee. For instance, a former high official of the Truman

Administration was subpoenaed one afternoon recently to appear before the McCarthy committee on less than twenty-four hours' notice, hardly enough time to enable him to collect data that he might have been questioned about even if he had been told what the subject of his interrogation was to be—which he wasn't. Other members of McCarthy's committee didn't know the subpoena had been issued until the victim himself so informed them.

Few politicians could have survived the kind of report that was unanimously submitted to the Senate last January by a subcommittee that had been investigating charges of political, financial and ethical misconduct against Senator McCarthy. Yet after the report had been filed, nothing more was officially heard of it. One reason was that in the present narrow division of the Senate, in which the Republicans outnumber the Democrats by one vote, it was certain that an effort to unseat any Republican Senator would be defeated on partisan grounds alone. Therefore, no matter what were the merits of the report, a Senate vote would have had the effect of supporting McCarthy and rebuffing his critics; and so the critics did not press the issue.

Broadly speaking, the position of the anti-McCarthy group in Washington is that the Senator is a potential menace to the civil liberties of Americans and to the constitutional structure of our Government.

One of the most thoughtful of Southern Democrats put it this way: "What he has done is to build up an atmosphere of suspicion and mistrust throughout the country. While he may exert little direct influence on the Senate, he undoubtedly does exercise a large negative influence by creating a fear psychology on the part of Americans everywhere. Our confidence in each other is being broken down, which is a very dangerous state for the people of this country to be getting into. It is the same kind of spirit that Hitler built up in Germany. You can't really understand how McCarthy operates unless you watch him as I have done in committee. He has a talent for arousing the animal instincts of human beings. I think McCarthyism, like communism, is a completely evil thing."

Another said he felt so strongly that "this is a disgusting thing to be associated with," that he was thinking of retiring from the Senate in protest. He recalled that some years ago the highly respected Senator Baldwin of Connecticut quit Washington to accept a judicial post in his home state—a move sometimes attributed to his resentment over the attacks he had endured at McCarthy's hands.

Whether or not McCarthy is able to drive Senators out of the Senate, there are many people who think he is exerting a directly negative effect on personnel within the Government. "Why would anybody of intelligence or ambition go into the information services of the State Department after the performance McCarthy put on at the Voice hearings?" asked one legislator. "He's created an atmosphere in which existing personnel in the agencies must necessarily be extremely reluctant to submit anything but the most innocuous reports, for fear of what they may be called to answer for on political grounds sometime in the future. As a matter of fact, I think McCarthy has gone far in discrediting our own Government in the eyes of all the world."

The bulk of the Republicans, on the other hand, have quite a different view. The almost universally expressed attitude of the G.O.P. leadership at the Capitol can be summed up this way: McCarthy causes headaches but he has done some good by awakening the public to the danger of communism; he is not a serious threat to liberties; his Senate influence is vastly overrated by press and public; despite the Bohlen and Dulles incidents he has no intention of leading a revolt within the party nor does he have the following if he wished to do so.

When asked what he thought of McCarthy's influence, one of the most powerful leaders of the Republican party brought his fist down hard on his desk, pushed his chair back and stormed at the interviewer: "I'm not going to discuss McCarthy! The press has built him up, which is just what he wants. But he was the most active person in the exposure of communism in the State Department—and I don't think anybody has been injured by him who shouldn't have been injured. If it hadn't been for his methods, we would never have got the dramatic issue of communism in the State Department before the public. He may be a nuisance. But he's no danger to the country or to our liberties. I believe in many of the things he stands for and though I may not agree with everything he does, I am not going to be forced into a position publicly critical of McCarthy."

Another of the top party leadership observed: "Generally I approve of his objectives if not his methods, but some of his methods may have been the only way to obtain the results he was seeking. I don't agree that he's dangerous. Joe isn't vicious—he's more like an irresponsible boy. There's nothing sinister about him. But if you hit him, he'll hit you back and he doesn't give a damn where he hits you."

A third G.O.P. leader, who recalled with some amusement but apparently no resentment that not many months previously McCarthy had smilingly threatened to defeat him if he supported a certain measure, said: "McCarthy is an adventurer. The more you attack him the better he likes it. He's having the time of his life. But he has no real influence in the party."

Another of the topmost legislative leaders says, "McCarthy will go along with us on the basic issues. Today we can depend much more on McCarthy than on some other Republicans I could mention. When he gets really unreasonable—as he did in the Bohlen case— he loses whatever influence he might have had; the thing takes care of itself."

From these comments it is evident that the legislative leadership of the G.O.P. has no desire to "discipline" McCarthy because on the whole they claim he represents no great danger and may actually be doing less harm than good. There is another reason, too.

Although the subject is rarely mentioned, there is an implicit recognition on the part of some of these same political leaders that McCarthy has been and can be very useful at campaign time. The 1954 elections are only eighteen months away, and political students of both parties seem to be pretty much in agreement that, however small his following in the Senate, McCarthy does have considerable pulling power in the country at large. They say this even though McCarthy ran far behind the Eisenhower-Nixon-Kohler ticket in Wisconsin last November. But he won.

Apart from these special reasons that particularly affect the Republicans, no member of Congress—Democratic or Republican— cares personally to tangle with McCarthy. "You may get a lot of moral support for fighting Joe," said one of his friendlier colleagues the other day, "but if you lose your seat in the Senate—as Millard Tydings or Bill Benton did—that's no good." Senators remember that McCarthy is credited—whether rightly or not—with the electoral defeat of Tydings, an entrenched conservative from Maryland, and Benton, a wealthy liberal from Connecticut. They don't relish the thought of his coming into their own states against them.

"Every man in public life lives in a glass house," says one Democratic Senator whose private contempt for McCarthy is equaled only by his public silence on the subject. "There are few if any people who haven't done something some time in the past that could be used against them in a political fight waged by an opponent willing to bar no holds."

One of the most thoughtful men in Government pointed up the dilemma in this way:

"It is very difficult for a liberal who was active in the Thirties to survive political life in the Fifties. Take my case. As soon as I became convinced there was any evidence of Communist control in liberal organizations I belonged to, I dropped my membership—formally and completely. But do you think that explanation would do me much good in the atmosphere of today against political opponents who wouldn't scruple to cite my 'guilty record' against me? That's one reason why you won't find me leading any fight against Senator McCarthy or his friends. I'd immediately be accused of attacking him merely in self-defense—and I'd lose the battle before I had begun.

"You know, there's usually some truth in the McCarthy charges. The broad allegations, inferences and suspicions are built up on a 10 or 15 per cent basis of fact. It all reminds me of a piece of land I once owned that contained some of the most beautiful wild roses you'd ever seen. The only trouble was that mixed in with the wild roses were masses of poison ivy. I spent many hours trying to rout out the ivy without destroying the roses; but sometimes when I was hot and tired I wouldn't care too much and I'd rip out roses, ivy and all. The sad part of it is that when I got through taking out the ivy, I'm afraid there weren't any roses left." The speaker paused reflectively. "There is some Communist ivy in our country that has to be ripped out, but I hope we're not going to destroy the flower of our liberties in the effort."

"Why didn't we Democrats do anything about it?" commented one strongly anti-McCarthy Southerner. "Well, if the Democrats attacked him that would only help keep the Republicans lined up with him. Anyway, it's an Administration problem. They could cut the ground from under him if they really wanted to."

And that raises the question of just what the Administration attitude is. "I believe," said one observer very close to the top command, "that McCarthy doesn't like being on the 'outs'; I think if we meet him half way, he'll show a willingness to get along with us. We may not be able to control him, but I think we can flatten out his curves. The best way to reduce his influence to the proper proportion is to take him on as part of the team. If Dulles had refused to talk over the Greek ship problem with McCarthy, the latter would only have reacted more strongly than ever and would have gone on making more independent arrangements. And there's nothing that could have been done about it." Whether the peace treaty between Dulles and McCarthy will stick is anybody's guess, but most Washington observers feel that McCarthy has clearly emerged the winner. The crack is going around that any day now Mr. Dulles' appointment list will read somewhat as follows: "11:30—Signor Tarchiani, the Ambassador from Italy; 12:00—Mr. Bruggman, the Minister from Switzerland; 12:30—Senator Joseph R. McCarthy, the Ambassador from Congress."

Within the Administration there are some individuals who feel that McCarthy is—as one of them told the writer—"the shrewdest, toughest and most dangerous" man in Washington. But even those who think this way say they are at least temporarily reconciled to the Administration's present policy of killing McCarthy with kindness—or, in the expression universally heard, giving him enough rope to hang himself. One observer commented that the only trouble with this theory is that if you give him enough rope he'll hang you.

In any case, even his worst enemies in the Republican high command—and there are some powerful ones who are convinced McCarthy is aiming for the White House in 1956—believe that the present strategy is the wisest for the moment and the most likely to cut him off from Senate support. "If the President singled him out for denunciation, that would only make a martyr of him," says one. "He's having a field day with remnants of the last Administration," says another. "But that will end. He's still hitting pay dirt—but it will soon be running thin."

And some of his enemies are hopeful that if the hostilities in Korea are terminated, "that will make of McCarthy a dead duck." They reason that he would then no longer be able to play on the fears and suspicions of those Americans who think the Korean war is a useless war and seek an outlet for their resentment, which McCarthy supplies.

Among the Republicans who see in McCarthy a very real potential danger to their party and the country, there are some who are willing to predict in strictest privacy that "if the Senator keeps on going, there's going to be a hell of a blow-up with the White House sooner or later." And there are some who hope that the blow-up will come sooner rather than later because they believe that the whole issue of Presidential leadership is involved in the McCarthy case.

The President—
After a Year

by James Reston

PRESIDENT EISENHOWER'S first year in the White House has been a
severe test of his leadership and a period of education for his inexperienced Administration. He describes it as a time of transition
for himself and the country, and he remarks, somewhat ruefully, that
periods of transition are tough on everybody.

The President's record is mixed and subject to a wide range of
interpretations (the defense cut is a triumph to some and a potential disaster to others). He has reversed the trend of more Government intervention in the life of the nation, and cut 183,000 off the
Federal payroll, but for a good part of the year, baffled by the size
and complexity of the Government's home-front operations, he
merely sat on the fence in the middle of the road.

In the more familiar fields of military strategy and foreign affairs,
he took several fundamental decisions. He knew enough about what
was going on in the five-ringed circus of the Pentagon to cut the
military budget by nearly $5,000,000,000. He was confident enough
in his estimate of the world situation to take risks with the Russians.
Above everything else, he had the courage to be timid in Korea.

Some of the qualities for which General Eisenhower was chosen
by the people in 1952 have been confirmed in these past twelve
months, but some have not.

The popular but fantastic father-image—of the great man who
was going to wipe away our troubles—has, of course, collapsed. It

From the *New York Times Magazine*, January 17, 1954.

was never real and nobody knew it better than the President himself.

The other Eisenhower—the one known as Ike—is still around. He has demonstrated what really needed no demonstration—namely, that he is a conciliator of unusual ability, and that this city, after twenty years of noise and contention, was ready for a President who didn't insist on identifying and challenging every fool on Capitol Hill.

The Eisenhower personality, however, has not proved to be enough in political life. He came here from NATO with a soldier's concept of loyalty. Members of the Eisenhower "team" in the Army worked together in harmony despite differences of opinion. They liked "Ike" but, if they hadn't, it would have made little difference, for it was their tradition to take orders and Eisenhower could "break" them if they didn't.

The members of the Eisenhower political team are in a different position. Their loyalty goes, not only to their party chief, but to their own constituency, their own prejudices and above all, their own re-election, and it took Mr. Eisenhower some time to adjust to their notion of loyalty.

For example, his closest personal friend in the Senate during the Presidential campaign was Frank Carlson of Kansas, chairman of the Post Office and Civil Service Committees of the Senate. Yet the Senator abandoned the President on the fight over postal rates just at the moment when Mr. Eisenhower needed him most. The President was astonished.

Later the President was to find that whenever his program came into conflict with a Congressman's local interests, the chances were that the Congressman would leave him flat. And that even went for the President's party leaders on Capitol Hill.

The President reacted to this in two ways. For a time he merely complained privately about it and took refuge in the doctrine that the President could not interfere with the Congress. He tried charm and persuasion. He held more lunches and meetings with members of Congress than any President in modern times. Late in the last Congressional session, he did quite a bit of telephoning to committee chairmen and key legislators in the hope of gaining their votes, but it wasn't until late in the year that he began to realize that personality and persuasion worked a little better if backed up by patronage and a little discreet coercion.

The death of Senator Robert A. Taft of Ohio was a turning point in his attitude toward the Hill. Congress was more or less the Senator's preserve. The President hesitated to intervene against the man he defeated for the Republican nomination but when Mr. Taft died, leaving an immense vacuum, the President changed. He abandoned any notion he may have had that the Presidency should be subordinate to the supreme legislative power, and adopted the more modern theory that it can be, within generous limits, autonomous, self-directing and capable of asserting a powerful legislative initiative.

The first year is best described by a phrase Secretary of State Dulles used the other day in Paris on another subject. It has been a period of "agonizing reappraisal" for an Administration that had very little experience with the mysteries of big government.

They have had to reappraise themselves and their prejudices; their campaign promises and their new responsibilities; their finances and their commitments; their allies and their enemies.

This is always an agonizing exercise, and it was particularly so early last year for a variety of reasons. The Administration had no dependable majority in the Congress. The national economy was fluttering between inflation and deflation. The war in Korea was dragging on without hope of victory or honorable retreat. The Allies were bored with an American leadership they did not trust and could not do without. And the Russians were in the midst of another mysterious upheaval following the death of Stalin.

The "team" President Eisenhower gathered together to help him with these problems was a typical businessman's team, but it did not coincide precisely with his promise to "mobilize the best brains of the country."

He did not even mobilize the best brains of the Republican party in the selection of his Cabinet. And in the selection of the White House staff all he did was to mobilize the best brains of his campaign train and his headquarters at the Commodore Hotel in New York and move them to 1600 Pennsylvania Avenue.

What kind of an Administration, then, do we have?

It is, to begin with, a serious Administration: industrious, pragmatic, amateurish but orderly, punctual, frugal and pedestrian. One wing of the last Democratic Administration was rough, earthy, highly political, spendthrift and unpredictable. Another wing was urbane, ideological, erudite, facetious, argumentative, witty and highly articulate.

This is not an articulate Administration. There is scarcely a member of the Cabinet who can make a moving extemporaneous speech. It is humorless, obvious, unintellectual (almost anti-intellectual) and lacking in the one thing it has talked so much about—a crusading spirit.

Nevertheless, the differences of approach, manner and personality have been dominated in both cases by the hard facts of history and geography. The new Administration has talked a lot about rugged individualism and "liberating" the captive peoples of the Communist world, but its actions have avoided the extremes of both conservative economics and venturesome strategy.

It has put honor before peace, peace before solvency and prosperity before any doctrinaire concept of economics. It has reduced the spending, the taxes, the overseas garrisons, the draft, the Federal payroll and the operations of the Federal Government. It has drawn in and pulled back and cut down, but it has done what conservative Governments usually do—it has slowed the pace of its more liberal and radical predecessors, and in the process has probably gone a long way toward conserving the American economic and foreign policy revolutions of the Thirties and Forties.

The President concentrated in the past twelve months on three things: (1) getting a new estimate of the Soviet menace and the United States commitments to meet it; (2) organizing an economic planning staff in the White House to watch the national economy; and (3) pulling his new team together through diligent use of the Cabinet and development of the National Security Council.

The question of "peace" dominates Eisenhower. He is more at home in this field than in others. Like Churchill, who has also made a reputation as a warrior, his sole remaining ambition is to avoid a depression and complete the victory he did so much to win in 1945. Also he has a special personal reason: He has never forgotten the teachings of his pacifist mother who once said to him, in her disappointment at his soldiering: "Never forget that they who live by the sword shall die by the sword."

Accordingly, he has paid more attention to this problem of peace in the last twelve months than any other, and he took one decision in the process of his study that may very well influence the judgment of history on his entire period in office.

This was the decision to act on the assumption that the Communists would probably not make a major war in the foreseeable future. The assumption was not new. Europe had already accepted it. Mr. Truman and his Secretary of State, Dean G. Acheson, had talked a lot about it, but Eisenhower acted upon it. He made the truce in Korea, and consciously started the "policy of detachment" —of reducing America's overseas commitments, of bringing more of America's power into a "mobile reserve" at home, and relying more on air power and atomic power than in the past.

The principal act of the first year, whether one agrees with the act or not, was that the Eisenhower Administration did in Korea what the Truman Administration wanted to do but was afraid to do, at least partly because of Republican opposition.

After the election, President Eisenhower concentrated on this problem. He went to Korea. He asked the Joint Chiefs of Staff and the Secretaries of State and Defense for a survey of all the nation's overseas commitments, and by the beginning of April he had made a decision.

This was as follows: (1) The danger of an all-out war was remote. (2) The power of the United States was over-extended. (3) The cost of the military programs we were proposing to our Allies was jeopardizing their economies and causing trouble within the Allied coalition. (4) By maintaining smaller forces overseas and relying more on a bolder diplomacy and the deterrent effect of our air power, the enormous cost of the military establishment could be reduced and progress made toward balancing the budget.

Whether the strategy determined changes in the budget or the budget was primarily responsible for determining the new "strategy of detachment" is still a source of considerable argument here. But the decision was made, and the first major implementation of it was to make the necessary concessions to get a truce in Korea.

In the field of world strategy, the President has obviously sat at the head of the table. He has had the confidence to second-guess his former colleagues at the Pentagon. Also, he has used the National Security Council more effectively than ever before. This is the Cabinet committee that sits as the highest policy-making body in the Government.

It had never met more than thirty-four times in any other year since it was started in 1947, and that was in 1951, during the critical decisions of the Korean war. Under Eisenhower in 1953, it met fifty-one times, usually on Thursday mornings at 10 o'clock for a period of two and a half hours. The President presided over it forty-eight times, missing only twice when he was in Denver during the summer and once when he was at Augusta during the Christmas holidays.

This council has been an important factor in the Eisenhower Administration. It has done a lot to educate and develop the inexperienced Cabinet. The paper work of the council has been greatly improved by the President's principal assistant for security affairs, Robert Cutler of Boston, who worked for years with the late James Forrestal, the principal architect of the council system in Washington.

Cabinet members are constant and punctual in attendance. They come well briefed by Mr. Cutler's advance "papers." Each session opens with an intelligence briefing by Allen Dulles, the head of the Central Intelligence Agency. It has been in this body that the major strategy decisions have been talked out, and it is perhaps fair to say that, as a result of these sessions, the usual inter-departmental fights on major foreign policy questions in Washington have decreased.

The President has not paid so much attention to domestic developments during the year as to foreign. This has been apparent in his answers to questions at his news conferences. He gets the fine point of the question on foreign affairs, but misses the obvious point on the domestic question.

Early in the Administration his first major acts were to reduce the activities and authority of the Federal Government. All wage and price controls were removed. The Secretary of Agriculture, Ezra Taft Benson, began warning the farmers about the dangers of a protective agriculture policy, and on May 22 the President signed the Submerged Lands Act, leaving to the states the title to seventeen million acres of submerged land and resources along the United States coastline.

About mid-year, however, the President began to pay a great deal more attention to domestic problems. Farm prices were off, way off. Price and employment figures began to cause some concern with the Administration. An Administration that had been worrying about inflation began to be concerned about deflation.

Prof. Arthur Burns, formerly of Columbia and now head of the President's Council of Economic Advisers, and Gabriel Hauge, the White House assistant on economic matters, spent more and more time briefing the President.

Soon a kind of economic planning board was set up within the Executive. This was headed by Professor Burns and called the Interdepartmental Advisory Board on Growth and Stability. Members were Hauge, Marion Folsom, Under Secretary of the Treasury; Abbot Mills of the Federal Reserve Board; Walter Williams, Under Secretary of Commerce; Rocco C. Siciliano, an Assistant Secretary of Labor, and Paul Morrison of the Bureau of the Budget.

It is the assignment of this board to watch the economy and to draft plans to be used in the event a dip reaches the point where Federal intervention is essential. If defense spending drops, the board recommends incentives, such as the recent tax cuts, and gets emergency measures in line to deal with any real emergency.

This is one political problem the President does not want to muff: he is as well aware as anybody what would happen to his party if the so-called Hoover Depression were to be followed by even an Eisenhower Recession.

"The American economy," the President said in his State of the Union Message, "is one of the wonders of the world. It undergirds our international position, our military security, and the standard of living of every citizen.

"This Administration is determined to keep our economy strong and keep it growing. At this moment we are in transition from a wartime to a peacetime economy. I am confident that we can complete this transition without serious interruption in our economic life. But we shall not leave this vital matter to chance. Economic preparedness is fully as important to the nation as military preparedness."

The last Republican President to lay down a program before the American people was Herbert Hoover on Dec. 6, 1932. At that time, even when the bottom was already falling out of the national economy, he developed a theme which provides an interesting contrast.

The Federal Government could permit of no privilege to any person or group, he argued, but then he added:

"It should act as a regulatory agent and not as a participant in economic and social life. The moment the Government participates, it becomes a competitor with the people. As a competitor it becomes at once a tyranny in whatever direction it may touch."

Though the new Republican President's statement clearly differs from this, the conflict between the two approaches is still not over in Washington.

The first year has been marked by some odd contradictions. For example, the President made clear throughout the year that he favored a lower tariff policy, but other members of the Administration persuaded him to appoint two comparatively high-tariff advocates to the Tariff Commission. Similarly, he has permitted men with records of opposition to the Federal Trade Commission and the Public Housing Administration to be appointed to these agencies.

His dealings with Senator Joseph R. McCarthy and the Republican National Committee illustrate this same ambivalence. For months he carefully avoided any critical word about the Senator's tactics, insisting he could not comment on the activities of any legislator. Then, late in the year, when the whole country was saying that McCarthy had challenged the President's foreign program, he finally issued a statement rejecting the Senator's policies regarding Communist China and our Allies.

Time and again he talked about his responsibilities as head of the Republican party. Yet he paid little attention to the National Committee, which was often following the McCarthy line.

Nevertheless, Eisenhower's first year is not unlike the first year of many other Presidents. It has been a year of learning. It did not bring the avalanche of new legislation that marked the first Roosevelt year, or produce any startling innovations, but conservative Governments are not supposed to produce startling innovations. They are supposed to conserve.

Has Eisenhower Changed the G.O.P.?

by William S. White

TO WHAT extent has President Eisenhower remade the Republican party? How long will the reformation endure? As the campaign takes shape, questions such as these are increasingly asked. Not in many years, and perhaps never in history, has the highest figure of a party so dominated the essential image of that party that is projected to the public. The President's role has been, consciously or not, the role of the mediator, the binder-together, not simply of the factions within his own party but of the interests of thousands and perhaps millions in both parties.

It seems clear that to the public at large he has been a very unpartisan sort of partisan. It is a commonplace of political experience that three years after his inauguration he is to many people plainly not identified with all the acts of his Administration. Certainly this has been true in those matters—take the lowering of the farm subsidies—where there has been local or sectional or class resentment at *Administration* policy that, according to Congressional mail, usually involves little or no resentment of the President himself.

Again, not in many years, and perhaps never in history, have all the lesser politicians in all wings of a political party put such urgent and total trust in the power of a President to carry them all through. The Republicans have lost since 1952 a whole series of important political contests in which the President's name was not on the

From the *New York Times Magazine,* March 18, 1956.

ballot, but are nevertheless almost absolutely confident that, with his name back on the ticket this time, all will be well.

Before it is possible to attempt to answer the ultimate questions as to what the President has done to the Republican party and how long his handiwork may last it is necessary to consider history.

The shortest way, perhaps, to put the business is to say this of the Republican party: It was born and brought up in protest, passed its middle years largely in acceptance and conformity and of later years has been like an elderly man examining and re-examining the basic postulate of his life.

The Kansas-Nebraska Act of 1854, which legally laid the Western territories open to slavery, resulted in the formulation of indignant local movements that took the name "Republican"—first, officially, in Ripon, Wis.

The seedbeds were in Indiana, Ohio, Wisconsin and Vermont, although the belligerent political liberalism of the first Republicans was within six years somewhat diluted by a concept of fiscal conservatism ("sound money") that has persisted to this day.

The Republican platform on which Abraham Lincoln won election in 1860, over a divided Democratic party that was a much older political organism, was liberal in the matter of "free soil," but conservative in the matter of high tariffs.

In fact, the least changing of all the Republican party's generally changeable and fluid characteristics is to be found at one place of great power, and one alone. That place of power is the Treasury Department.

In the lifetime of men now in middle age there have been incomparable disparities between the personalities and the philosophies of Republican Presidents. Take, for example, Calvin Coolidge and then Dwight D. Eisenhower.

But, allowing for some admitted overstatement to permit the point and allowing for the fact that time to some extent must change all frames of reference, there is a considerable validity to the point that all Republican Secretaries of the Treasury are much the same. Take, for example, Andrew Mellon of Pennsylvania and the present Secretary, George M. Humphrey of Ohio.

True, they differ, but in infinitely less degree than the difference between Presidents Coolidge and Eisenhower.

The present G.O.P., a version of a series of transformations that began at about the time of the gusty Theodore Roosevelt, is an amalgam of all these forces:

(1) Old-line orthodox Republicans, of whom Mr. Humphrey is the nearest to a perfect example in the Eisenhower Administration, although he does not fit the mold in an absolutely ideal sense.

(2) "Modern" Republicans, who have been greatly influenced in many directions by the New Deal and Fair Deal—men like President Eisenhower, who are hardly partisan at all in the ordinary sense; men like Secretary of Defense Charles E. Wilson, who are partisan only in a rather mild and institutional way, and men like Thomas E. Dewey and Attorney General Herbert Brownell, Jr., who are deeply partisan but partisans of the new and not of the old form of Republicanism.

(3) Ex-Democrats, Southern as well as Northern, although mostly Northern, who have found at least a temporary home in the Republican party more or less simultaneously with a forward movement in their economic affairs that has taken them from the city flats to the ranch houses, or their equivalents, in the suburbs.

(4) What are called "Independents," a fugitive term, indeed, and one subject to much debate in the political profession. The late Senator Robert A. Taft of Ohio, perhaps because he spent the greater part of his mature political life in the common Republican frustration of the long Roosevelt-Truman years, was wryly inclined to suspect that an "Independent" was simply a crypto-Democrat whose true colors were revealed only in the voting booth on Election Day. There are, currently, some Democrats who would turn this quite about. They would suspect that the "Independent" is really a crypto-Republican—and for evidence they would point to the results of 1952.

At all events, it is this somewhat variegated, but not necessarily inchoate, mass that now makes up the Republican party of 1956.

How did it get into this condition, and, specifically, how did the Republican party of the harshly unrewarding Thirties and Forties spring forward in this present decade to a point where, for practical purposes at least, it appears a majority and no longer a minority party?

To begin with, of course, the Democrats themselves opened many opportunities for the realizing of this state of affairs—although the wit to seize and exploit these opportunities was not, of course, among their gifts to their opposition. Anyway, the Democrats at minimum had got a bit tired, a bit fat, a bit careless and, in general, perhaps a bit noncombative. This brief summary, however incomplete, is enough for present purposes.

From the conventions of 1940 onward the Republicans (and here they begin most clearly to appear like the introspective elderly man mentioned at the outset) were suffering a series of inner convulsions and mind-searchings of the kind that sometimes presage a recovery from illness or ineffectuality.

In 1940, in 1944, in 1948 and again in 1952 the traditional, orthodox and historically dominant Republicans—the "Taft Republicans" as they are now generally known—lost, one after another, contests of incalculable importance to the less orthodox, more liberal, more internationalist and predominantly Eastern wing of the party. Taft himself was rejected for the Presidential nomination in 1940, losing out to an erstwhile Democrat, Wendell Willkie. He stepped aside in 1944 "for John," and Senator John W. Bricker of Ohio wound up on the lower end of the ticket with Thomas E. Dewey of New York at the head.

In 1948 it was again Taft and Dewey—and Dewey won the nomination. In 1952 it was again, in many senses, Taft and Dewey, for Taft remained the undoubted choice of the orthodox Old Guard while Dewey acted as the New Guard's acute and hard-handed field marshal for General Eisenhower's nomination.

These victories for the New Guard—the "moderns," the relative "liberals," or whatever one may choose to call them—were fundamental. They signaled an unbroken, accumulating rise to power of a section of the Republican party that was prepared to come to some terms, to some degree, with the liberalism that Franklin D. Roosevelt had stamped upon the general political movement in this country with an almost indelible trace and that the dogged Harry S. Truman had sought to defend to the end.

One meaning of all this in historical terms was that the locus of power in the Republican party was removed from the Midwest to this side of the Appalachians and agreeably settled into what had already for generations been the center of power in finance and in all forms of national opinion-making.

The Republican party came to have Eastern domination at the top in nearly every significant sense. And it is, of course, in the

East that the Government sits, that, for the most part, the most powerful organs of the press operate, that all "mass media" have headquarters and that business itself is largely headquartered.

Another and more immediately practical meaning is that the Republican party, now in critical affairs under new control, has simply put itself into position to win national elections by accommodating itself to certain political realities rather than stolidly preparing itself to lose national elections by refusing to make any accommodation at all.

The new party has now come a long way, geographically and in certain other senses, from the prairie Republicanism of Mr. Lincoln. But in some ways it has come closer to validating his concepts than did the old Midwestern-based party, for that old party, although living in Mr. Lincoln's land, maintained the "sound money" and tariff policies of his time but had almost no trace of his liberalism in other matters.

The reformed party, the product, as it was, of the progressive rejection at four national conventions of the stand-pattism of the Old Guard, met the Roosevelt-Truman revolution not with a simple, adamant, win-or-die resistance everywhere, but with a counter-revolution of its own.

This counter-revolution, based almost wholly on the pragmatic economic hopes and desires of people and their wishes for an end to vehement political disagreement in the nation, made its appeal through the centers of both political parties, moving to the right, of course, wherever it could without compromising its basic design, and straight to the ultimate mind of the predominant post-war thought of the United States. This thought had been (and perhaps it still is) characterized by what might be called a centralism of view on almost all matters.

What has President Eisenhower done to the Republican party as it now stands? He has expanded it, up to now, at least, into something far larger than it has been. For the American Center is now much larger, in the general estimates of detached viewers, than it has been in perhaps many generations, and the Right and the Left are in consequence far smaller.

President Eisenhower has fashioned this party into an instrumentality for the "moderates," who may, for practical purposes, be largely identified with the middle class. The middle class, of course, is the storied backbone of parliamentary-capitalistic countries; here and now it is not merely the backbone but very nearly the whole torso of the country.

Although political writers are uniquely qualified not to attempt even timid economic judgments, it does seem on common sense and inexpert observation that the middle class is vastly bigger and the so-called upper and lower classes immeasurably smaller than was the case, say, even just before the onset of the Second World War. The term "class" is, of course, used here mainly in the economic sense; any other definition is thought unsuitable if not invidious in the United States.

Thus, what is at hand in the Republican party of President Eisenhower is, in its simplest terms, an enormous, a historic and, perhaps for us here, an unexampled triumph for the middle class. What the old Republicans continually feared in the Franklin D. Roosevelt days, "class warfare," has not occurred; or, if it has, the winning class has won so handily that, looking back, one can hardly see the after-marks of any conflict at all. It may be that this is so because the victorious class has been expanding at so Gargantuan a rate as more or less to blot up the other classes.

And all this has had another, and arresting, effect on the Republican party itself as now reformed and constituted. It has inaugurated a day of great importance in politics for the rich and sentient amateur of the kind who never quite could put his modern heart into the old party, mainly because its quasi-isolationist outlook went against both his deepest interests and his more sophisticated and more hospitable view of the round world.

Along with the march into active Republican politics of this rich amateur there has been a march, in the same sense, of many not-rich but up-and-coming business and professional executives (in advertising, in communications, in law and so on). These men have enjoyed the adventure, not simply for its own sake, but for the opportunity it has offered for the exercise of their special skills.

The Old Guard has, of course, mainly held its ground in Congress, much as the Democratic Southern Old Guard held its ground all through the Roosevelt time. But in the truly national Republican party, at those moments and at those places where the highest of policy is made and where Presidential candidates are chosen, the Old Guard has been largely isolated.

Will the reforms in the Republican party made by President

Eisenhower, or symbolized by him, long endure? Will this new coalition of the "moderates" survive as long as did the Roosevelt coalition of what might be called in this context the "immoderates," the alliance of the Bourbon Southern planter and the Detroit auto worker?

The question is, of course, unanswerable on a score of grounds, but some considerations that would be involved in its ultimate answer might be suggested. The coalition plainly and in the nature of things is not held together by an absolutely impervious cement any more than was the old.

The accommodations made within the core of the Republican party have not been made with the glad assent of the Old Guard, as any loss to the Republicans of the President's sort of popular leadership would make instantly apparent. The Old Guard has not conceded the game in any sense; it has conceded an inning or two as it has conceded that the President as of *now* is indispensable to the larger party success for which all Republicans hope, of course, in November.

Already there have been rumblings and grumblings from the Taft wing of the party at the limited sort of campaign, paying little heed to what the Congressional politicians see as their necessities, that Mr. Eisenhower proposes to wage. The heir of Senator Taft as the Republican Senate leader, William F. Knowland of California, has formally put these complaints in a general warning against the "overconfidence" that he sees both in the White House and in the pro-Eisenhower Republican National Committee. What Congressional Republicans fear is that an Eisenhower-Republican victory may not be otherwise a Republican victory and that the new masters of the party are not overly concerned with the fortunes of its now dispossessed masters.

There is no intention, in short, among the orthodox Republicans that the new face of the party shall endure forever—or even for any substantial number of future years. The anti-third-term constitutional amendment will in this connection be seen to be increasingly important as time goes on. If the President is re-elected for a second term he will be the first Chief Executive in history to be on prior notice that his practical influence on the party *must* begin to decline almost as soon as he takes office.

A formidable drive by the orthodox to recover power will begin within a year from next November's elections though it is probable that the old Republican will not go all out in this design until the Congressional elections of 1958.

In a curious sense, therefore, the liberal Democrats and the Old Guard Republicans have much in common: each group fears an eventual descent into something like oblivion if the Eisenhower kind of Republicanism, with its tendency ever to enlarge the center at the expense of right and left, should long prevail.

And in the current Republican discussion of the second place on the ticket—shall it be given again to Vice President Nixon or to another—lies one of a number of latently dangerous possible dilemmas.

There is no doubt whatever that the President, if he chose, could dictate the precise identity of his running mate and that the Republican convention would go along. If, however, the President should choose to leave the question open, or substantially open, an explosive contest, scattering about all kinds of cement, undoubtedly could and might develop.

Again, there are more fundamental questions. To what degree can the "moderns," the "moderates," the relative liberals, keep essential control of the party in the future? To what degree will the Democrats be able to heal the party's split personality represented by the North-South wings, and to what degree will they be able to present a more coherent party front, appealing to the centrists without losing all touch with the urban liberals who are so important to it in the long slope of time?

What will be the future state of the national economy and will it continue to promote or will it begin to reduce the thus far rapidly expanding middle class? What of foreign policies and the world outside?

No, not much can be said surely of this future, as not much can be said, for certain, of any future in any sense. It can only be said now that this is the point to which the Republican party has now come and that these are some of the reasons why it has come there.

America's "Four-Party" System

by James MacGregor Burns

ONCE MORE, as Congress quits the capital and the party chiefs make ready their convention halls, we are witnessing the glaring paradox of American politics.

The paradox involves both major parties: next week in Chicago Democratic Congressmen will, most of them, help adopt a platform and choose a candidate, both of which will be considerably more liberal than their own record on Capitol Hill. A week later Republican Congressmen, having deserted President Eisenhower on issue after issue in Washington, will enthusiastically help draft him in San Francisco to run again.

How can such odd behavior be explained? We shall find that we can make better sense of the coming conventions and campaigns —and of American politics generally—if we abandon the idea that politics in this country is simply a battle between Republicans on one side and Democrats on the other.

Actually we have four parties all fighting one another in a vast guerrilla war. Here is how they line up on the political spectrum:

A little left of center, as Franklin Roosevelt used to say, is the Roosevelt-Truman party—the party of the New Deal and Fair Deal, the party that has tended to embrace the bulk of organized labor, Negroes, Catholics and other groups centered especially in the large urban states. This is the *Presidential Democratic* party that will convene in Chicago a week from tomorrow.

From the *New York Times Magazine*, August 5, 1956.

In the exact center is the Eisenhower party—the *Presidential Republicans*. They are middle-of-the-road on domestic policy and generally internationalist on foreign; they attract especially the modern business and suburban groups; they fight the Presidential Democrats for control of the urban states. The Presidential Republicans convene in San Francisco two weeks from tomorrow.

A bit to the right of the Eisenhower Republicans is the *Congressional Democratic* party. It is led by perhaps a dozen men—by Speaker Sam Rayburn in the House, Majority Leader Lyndon Johnson in the Senate, by the chiefs of the more important committees. As a result of Congressional politics and machinery, this party responds especially to Southern and border-state attitudes and interests.

Much farther to the right are the *Congressional Republicans*—the party of Senate Minority Leader William Knowland and House Minority Leader Joseph Martin, of a dozen ranking committee members. This party claims to be the "real" Republican party; its great leader, the late Senator Robert A. Taft, was "Mr. Republican." Its geographical center is in the Midwest. It is also strong in Northeastern and Western rural districts. In foreign policy it leans toward isolationism.

The lines between these four parties are not, of course, sharp or clean-cut. Some Congressional Democrats, such as Herbert Lehman of New York and Estes Kefauver of Tennessee, belong to the Presidential Democratic party, while some Congressional Republicans, such as Senator Leverett Saltonstall of Massachusetts, are part of the Eisenhower party. Indeed, our system actually is made up of scores of state and local parties attached to leaders seeking or holding office. But to view our politics as a four-party system puts several things in clearer light.

Take the case of the two Republican parties. The Congressional Republicans will loudly back Eisenhower's renomination not because they agree with him but because they like him and above all because they need him. They need him to build up a huge Republican tide this fall that will sweep a Republican majority back into Congress and allow the Congressional Republican party to regain control of the machinery on Capitol Hill. The Congressional party, in short, will lean on the Eisenhower party for victory this fall, but it will not promise to support the Eisenhower party's policies in Congress next year.

For their part, the Congressional Democrats need a Presidential candidate who can withstand Eisenhower's appeal and who can help the Congressional party hold its majority in House and Senate.

Viewing our politics as a four-party system helps explain why President Eisenhower had such difficulty with the Republican Congress during his first two years of office, and less trouble with the Democratic Congress just ending. Note on our four-party spectrum that *both* the Congressional parties are more conservative than *both* the Presidential parties. The Eisenhower Republicans are far closer in outlook to the Congressional Democrats than to the Congressional Republicans. The result has been that the President has found unexpected support from the Democrats on Capitol Hill. The Republicans in Congress have been somewhat isolated on the right, while the Presidential Democrats complain that Lyndon Johnson & Co. have not made a record of opposition to the Administration on which their Presidential nominee can wage an all-out assault this fall.

Examination of our four-party system also shows why some of the key political battles of recent years have taken place not between Republicans and Democrats but within each broad party fold. The angry encounter between Taft and Eisenhower in 1952, climaxed by the former's rout at the Republican convention, was at least as significant as the later Presidential contest. Four years earlier Harry Truman beat Dewey and the other Presidential Republicans by accusing them, in effect, of "guilt by association" with the party farthest to the right on the political spectrum—the Congressional Republicans and their "do-nothing Congress."

If our four-party system goes according to form, how will it shape political developments in 1956 and the years immediately ahead?

The Eisenhower Republicans will so dominate the convention that the Congressional party will hardly be in evidence during the San Francisco proceedings. The Congressional Republicans will agree to a platform more liberal and internationalist than they would like, but they will go along, knowing that the planks will not be binding on them next year.

A test of power between the two Republican parties would come if the Vice Presidential nomination were thrown open, but the President's support of Nixon would probably preclude this. Harold Stassen's move against Nixon seems to have backfired, but Stassen may well have put himself in a stronger position to lead the Presidential Republicans after Eisenhower leaves the White House— whenever that may be.

The Democratic convention will afford a better glimpse of the conflict between the Presidential and Congressional parties. The strength of the Johnson-Rayburn party will be measured by the platform concessions allowed it by Presidential Democrats intent mainly on holding their Negro-liberal-labor support. The Congressional Democrats will probably grumble over the civil rights plank, but they will go along with it in Chicago because they know they need not do so in Washington.

The nomination fight will also test the strength of the Congressional party. It will mainly support Stevenson (though reluctantly) because he seems the most moderate of the Presidential Democrats. If Stevenson is stopped, the Congressional Democrats will then swing their weight around in the ensuing melee, hoping to come out with an acceptable dark horse such as Symington. But in any straight contest with the Presidential Democrats the Congressional party will be beaten.

The conventions will also serve as tune-ups for the autumn campaigns. In part, those campaigns will be a direct encounter between the two Presidential parties—Eisenhower versus Stevenson, perhaps —running on their respective platforms. In part they will be a series of separate and sometimes obscure little battles in scores of states and districts where Congressional candidates will be seeking to keep or gain office, not on the basis of their party's national platform but on the basis of far different platforms of their own.

These differences within the parties will be lost amid the open artillery duels between the Presidential candidates and the infantry charges between their respective running mates. Even more, party leaders in all camps will suavely gloss over these differences. But the differences will be there, ready to surface later on. How serious will they be? The answer depends in part on the outcome of the four-party battle.

On Nov. 6 next, two parties will win and two will lose. G.O.P. leaders are hoping that both Republican parties will win. They are busy building a war chest for Congressional candidates and extending the President's coattails as far as possible. These efforts have a touch of irony, because a sweeping Eisenhower victory might pull into office enough Congressional Republicans to regain control of House and Senate.

Would this really be a victory for the Eisenhower party? That party would confront much the same situation that it did in 1953. It would face the same type of committee chairmen—including Joseph McCarthy undoubtedly heading the Senate Committee on Government Operations. History might well repeat itself. After he first took office in 1953, Mr. Eisenhower tried a variety of methods to win support from the Congressional party. He tried a hands-off policy—plus patience. He tried friendliness and persuasion—most notably by inviting every Congressman to lunch. He tried what he called "salesmanship." Nothing worked very well; the man who had won a reputation as a conciliator of bickering allies in wars hot and cold could not bridge the deep gulf between the two Republican parties. The President was becoming increasingly bitter toward the Congressional party—until the Democratic capture of Congress in 1954 made it easier for him to work with Capitol Hill.

Indeed, if both Republican parties win this fall, Mr. Eisenhower may be even worse off than he was in 1953 and 1954. He will not be a candidate in 1960 and his power will ebb as Congressmen begin to build alliances with Mr. Nixon or other possible successors. Even more important, he may not have the necessary physical resources for the job.

For nothing is more exacting of a President's time, energy, and political talents than dealing with his Congressional party on the Hill. It is a job that cannot be effectively delegated, because potent Congressmen want to make arrangements with the President himself, not with underlings. It is a job for which there is no pat formula or rule book; every Congressional situation and personality calls for a different marshaling of Presidential influence and resources.

A case in point is Franklin Roosevelt's great success with Congress when he put through the enduring elements of the New Deal during the "Second Hundred Days" of 1935. His program was a result not of some "magic touch" but mainly of a simple capacity to work throughout the day and late into the night applying pressure. Over the phone, in little notes, in face-to-face interviews, he wheedled, pleaded, teased, cajoled, promised, and sometimes threatened—and on bill after bill he kept one or two jumps ahead of the opposition.

Would the situation be any better if both Democratic parties won —if Stevenson, say, entered the White House and the Congressional Democrats kept their majorities and their chairmanships in Congress? Probably not. A Democratic President might have the time and energy to lead his Congressional party, but his job would be far bigger than Mr. Eisenhower's. For a Democratic President would face a bloc of Congressional leaders inflamed over school segregation and civil rights and divided from the Presidential Democrats over many other matters. The Southerners brought Roosevelt's New Deal to a halt during his second term; they stymied much of Truman's domestic program. There is no reason to expect that another Democratic President would have much better luck.

A third possible election outcome is a victory for the Eisenhower Republicans and the Congressional Democrats. Such a result would continue the present relative harmony in Washington between the Administration and the present chieftains on Capitol Hill. It would be a victory for the two parties in the center—for the two parties that have shown how well they can get along together.

Many Americans would welcome such an outcome. In a time of prosperity and muted cold war they like the politics of the center. Others will argue that this is really the politics of dead center—it will work as long as the Administration need not consider moving in new directions, but it will fail if new problems call for fresh and vigorous programs.

But the main drawback to a victory for both Presidential Republicans and Congressional Democrats is one that involves Americans of all parties. This drawback is the lack of responsibility and accountability that lies at the heart of such an election result. For such an outcome means coalition government, which in turn means that neither party clearly takes up the responsibility for government nor the equally vital job of opposing.

The recent defeat of the school bill is a case in point. Who was responsible for its failure? The Congressional Republican party deserted the President to support an anti-segregation amendment that they knew would eventually defeat the bill. The Democrats split into fragments. The result is chaos: all parties but one argue for more Federal aid to education; all parties but one want segregation ended —but a bill embodying these ideas fails. The tragedy is not simply that the bill was murdered but that everyone can argue that someone else was the culprit.

On other key issues this fall—liberalizing world trade, resource development, foreign aid, spending, taxation—there will be no clear drawing and discussing of the issues in party terms, but a vast game of finger pointing as the voters struggle to discover who was responsible for what. And we would face this same situation in the 1958 and 1960 elections should Republican-Democratic coalition politics continue.

It seems, in short, that no matter how the election next November turns out, we will have to go on with our four-party system and all the deadlock and confusion that it involves. Is there any way out?

Mr. Eisenhower tried to find a way out after his first year in office. Robert J. Donovan, the Administration's unofficial historian, informs us that the President was so exasperated by the Congressional Republicans that he almost decided to abandon the Republican party. He toyed with the idea of starting a new party—one that would have been "essentially his" party, supporting "enlightened" foreign and domestic policies (in short, the Presidential Republican party today). In the end, fearing that the new party would become merely one more of the many unsuccessful third party efforts in American history, he dropped the notion. He decided to work within the Republican fold.

At this point, however, fate dealt him a hard blow. To unite the two Republican parties from within called for the time and energy that his health breakdowns of the past year made impossible. No one has more bargaining power with a Congressional party than a popular President able to accept or reject a draft for renomination. Such a President can reward and punish; under certain conditions he can draft good Congressional candidates and quietly sidetrack others. But either because of his health or because of divided counsels in the White House, Mr. Eisenhower let the opportunity slip. For example, he refused to help Senator Alexander Wiley against the Wisconsin McCarthyites, even though Wiley had long supported the Eisenhower party on foreign policy.

Nevertheless, Mr. Eisenhower's instincts were right. Our parties can be strengthened more effectively from within than from without. Even if he wins a second term, however, it is probably too late now for the President to accomplish the hard job of bringing the Congressional Republicans into closer cooperation with the Presidential party. If the job is to be done, it must be shouldered by someone whose power is on the rise, like Vice President Richard Nixon, but some will doubt that he has the necessary conviction and tenacity.

Can the Democrats unite their two parties into an agency that can govern—or oppose—in a responsible fashion? As masterly a politician as Franklin Roosevelt tried and failed. But certain things are running in the Democrats' favor, at least in the long run. One is the slow rise of a two-party system in the South—a development likely to bring the Southern Democrats more in tune with the Northern. Another is the increasing pressure on the Presidential Democrats to deliver on their platform promises or face defeat at the polls.

The Democratic convention next week may give some clue to the ultimate direction of the Presidential party. Adoption of a platform that straddles key issues such as education and segregation will suggest that the Presidential party is willing to yield to the Congressional party for expediency's sake. Another clue, assuming Stevenson or someone of his stripe is nominated for President, will be the choice of his running mate. Democratic selection of a Northern progressive, such as Senator John F. Kennedy, rather than the usual liberal-conservative hybrid ticket, would represent a significant new departure for the Presidential party.

One thing is certain: only persistent and determined leadership from the White House can enable the Presidential parties to bring the Congressional parties into alignment. The Congressional parties recognize this. That is why they wage a continuous war, except during election time, against Presidential power through such varied means as the Bricker amendment and Congressional investigations. As so often in American history, more effective government and more responsible opposition will call for a fruitful combination of Presidential power and popular support.

And until this happy condition is achieved, we can stop looking down our noses at the French. We have a multiparty system, too.

Impressions of the President —and the Man

by Arthur Krock

"NO MAN is an Iland, intire of itselfe," but a President of the United States is a far larger "peece of the Continent, a part of the maine" than the general Man to whom Dr. Donne explained that every funeral bell tolled for him. And no "peece" of any Continent that a myriad of agronomists might test with every microscope, every chemical, every sieve in their collection is as thoroughly analyzed as the chief of the American Union.

From the moment a citizen is nominated for the Presidency by a major political party this analysis begins. It grows steadily in the three usual dimensions throughout his White House incumbency, and to these the fourth is added as the President passes into history. Not a grain of his flesh, not a cell of his brain, not an impulse of his heart is out of bounds for the contemporary researcher. And the more complex the man who becomes President, the more conflicting the portrait studies from life which the objective historian must compose into a probable likeness.

This analytical process has been gaining in volume and perspective every year since the deaths of Lincoln, Wilson and the two Roosevelts—all complicated men. But, since it lacks the vital element of perspective when the subjects are living persons, the analyses of Truman and Eisenhower as yet are only working papers and footnotes.

That is the limitation of an attempt such as this to evaluate the

From the *New York Times Magazine*, June 23, 1957.

private individual and public executive who currently is the President of the United States.

The outer man fulfills the American ideal of the democratic leader who has risen to eminence by the possession and employment of the simple virtues and by the endowments of mentality and personal charm. The President's stature is a happy compromise between the short and the tall. His usual complexion is ruddy under the golfing tan. His blue eyes are kindly, but penetrating. His voice has the rough grain that is accepted as the token of virility, and his accent is the kind known as "Midwestern" that is prevalent in North America.

His manner is genial; his ways and reflexes are kindly. His bearing is soldierly, yet his well-tailored civilian clothes never seem out of character. His smile is attractively pensive, his frequent grin is infectious, his laughter ready and hearty. He fairly radiates "goodness," simple faith and the honorable, industrious background of his heritage.

Like Truman, he is an uncomplicated man. But, like any incumbent of the White House, his inner reflexes must in great measure be matters of speculation in his time. And documented explanations of baffling factors in many of his public acts must also await the opening of the archives and the publication of memoirs.

Meanwhile, his public acts raise, among others, these questions:

Does President Eisenhower's staff system make him too dependent on subordinates for the choice and synthesis of the public matters laid before him, and for the selection of those to be admitted to his presence?

Does his obvious preference for business and military men as companions imply at least a mild distaste for the company of the professional politicians with whom his two predecessors surrounded themselves in leisure hours?

If his doctors, after the President's two illnesses, had not advised frequent changes of scene and recreation, would he have absented himself from his desk and from Washington on the present scale? If so, does this imply that he is irked by his heavy and incessant duties?

Granting that the President has been responsively and informatively asked, and has answered, more questions about the large and the small of Administration activities than any predecessor, why does he at times appear to be totally unaware of an event that dominates the news of that day?

Considering the severity of his moral code, that impelled him to accept literally the need of a "crusade" as justification for his own entrance into partisan politics (which he vowed was out of bounds for a "professional military man"), why has he neither publicly rebuked nor otherwise disciplined some subordinates who have been exposed for what at least may be classified as acts designed to mislead or deceive Congress, the people, or both?

Why on occasion does the President, usually at news conferences, weaken an effect of forceful leadership he has just established, and thus revive obstructions to his programs by the very politicians against whom he had taken the initiative?

On the basis of a mass of documentary evidence—largely supplied by the transcripts of the White House news conferences—and in consequence of constant observation of the President and the testimony of qualified sources, I have formed conclusions as to the points raised by several of these questions.

These conclusions are that the President is remarkably well informed in a vast field of Government operations; that his occasional unawareness of a major event is merely the result of special concentration at the time on some difficult administrative problem; and that, while perhaps he wishes he were not President more often than some of his predecessors did, he enjoys the power and the glory and is absorbed in his task. No intelligent man so plainly concerned as Eisenhower with the judgment history will make of him could be a lazy or reluctant President.

But I suspect that the White House staff system—the President's own idea—vests too much "screening" authority, and hence too much power, in certain members. Conceding the need for their solicitude that his illnesses have created, I think these assistants have excessively sheltered the President from public persons he should see and from intra-Administration situations he should know about. Some of these situations might revise the President's belief that his Administration is more completely conducted than Truman's, and that the standards of all his policy-making personnel are what he pledged they would be—or else.

Agreed answers to these and other questions posed above will not even begin to come in the President's lifetime; they elude the facts in the unbounded field of speculation. But this is the man Dwight D. Eisenhower appears to this reporter of the times in which the President has played so great a role in war and in statecraft:

Fundamentally, he possesses and automatically practices the simple virtues of mental and moral integrity, humility, candor and compassion as those words are commonly construed by the American people. These are his strength as a popular leader and custodian of the awesome powers of his office. But they also have been a source of weakness because of a certain simplicity inherent in his make-up that the moral code of the Army has intensified.

This brought him into politics with the belief that another man's word deserved to be rated as good as his own until or unless proved otherwise; with the conviction that the orders of a superior would be scrupulously executed by his subordinates; with confidence that respect for the American system and the Presidency would produce the truth from those to whom he had given his trust; and with the attitude that impels him neither to forgive nor forget certain kinds of personal attack which politicans easily condone as "campaign oratory."

When the attack is directed against those who happen to be the kith and kin of a President, Eisenhower is implacably unforgiving. It was Senator McCarthy's slur against his favorite brother, Milton —not McCarthy's remarks about the President himself—that caused Eisenhower to bar the McCarthys from the social function to which all other Senators and their wives were invited.

These are endearing qualities that account for much of the President's success in war and in voting referendums on him as the leader of the nation. But on occasion these admirable traits have operated to his disadvantage in dealing with the many politicians whose experiences in the trade of getting and holding office persuade them to follow a very different code. And until the third month of his second term, there were evidences that this discovery had strengthened in the President a natural distaste for professional politicians and for strictly political issues that impelled him to neglect them—at the peril of his programs, as it proved.

In the apparent effort to continue to govern by copybook maxims that made his first term an unusually agreeable personal chapter in Presidential history, the re-elected Eisenhower stood aloof from the problems created by the play of professional politics. Not until he saw, largely through the anxious eyes of his advisers, impending consequences which threatened some of his basic aspirations for the Republic, did the President come to grips as a politician with politicians. Even then he had periods of hesitation.

This is illustrated by his approaches to Congress and the people on his budget for the fiscal year 1958, especially those sections dealing with national defense and mutual security ("foreign aid").

The President honestly deplores the size of the budget—$71.8 billions—but he had affirmatively resolved, though with difficulty to his political philosophy, the question whether to request the continuation and expansion of public welfare projects previously established by Congress, or to propose that some be abandoned and others indefinitely deferred. True to his nature he made these animations public—at news conferences and in conversation with legislators.

His purpose was to encourage Congress to try to find sound economies he had been unable to find, and to eliminate certain of its own projects that the President felt could not be eliminated by the Executive without disrespect to Congress as the institution he reveres. Once, for example, finding Senators Johnson of Texas and Byrd of Virginia with their heads together and asking what they were talking about, the President, informed it was "about cutting the budget," replied: "Go ahead and cut it all you can."

His fumbles at news conferences, remarkably few in a record so out-giving, are traceable, I think, to his efforts at times to speak personally and not to be President. And that, of course, is impossible.

These tactics, for all their honesty and dedication, were the worst possible for the preservation of the budget to the degree the President holds absolutely essential to national security and that of the free world. Not only did they feed the popular protest against the budget's size, but they passed to Congress the initiative to satisfy that protest. Moreover, the President's hot-and-cold discussions of the budget acted as a stimulant on his Secretary and Under Secretary of the Treasury to add to the record their own apprehensions about mounting budgets.

The President, in this period absorbed with getting Congress' approval of the Middle East resolution to help allay the crisis in that area, and then the meetings with French and British statesmen to try to repair the relations broken over Suez, finally partly saw, and partly was made to see, that his tactics with the budget had seriously imperiled the appropriations sought for national defense and mutual security.

Only then did he begin a salvage campaign with a televised address to the country. But, still clinging to his distaste for "desk-pounding," the President spoke as if he were doing a rather dull chore. And at his news conference the following day he diluted what effect the speech might have had on the budget-slashers, the Republicans in particular, by lavish concessions of the right to dissent and the constitutional duty of Congress.

The damage done by this soft approach was instantly manifest, and his advisers found him ready at last to take and maintain a hard line. This he laid down in a second and vigorous televised speech, and at his next news conference. Also there is evidence that the White House switchboard was busier than it ever had been in his time with Presidential appeals for support to members of Congress. The President concluded the hour had come to employ some of the pressures politicians understand, and that in such circumstances there are pressures available he conscientiously can use.

His behavior toward the emergence of his first "bad press" is another and very revealing item in an analysis of the manner of man that is Dwight D. Eisenhower. Until recently most commentators, like most politicians and the mass of the people, were disposed to exculpate the President from the sins of omission and commission that are charged to every Administration.

He was allowed to stand aside from or above the political battle longer than any President in recent history—the more remarkable a conformity to the popular mood because most of those whose writings have nation-wide circulation follow a political philosophy opposed to the President's. Also, these observers had implied the opinion that Eisenhower is a *roi fainéant*.

But with the development of the Mideast crisis and the issue with Congress on the budget, this prevalent group among the commentators took direct and daily aim at the President. Now and then the criticism was so severely personal that a member of his staff would lay it indignantly before him, to discover that the President was not indignant, not disturbed in the slightest, unless he thought some factual premise had been misstated. Then he would discuss means of correction, sometimes by himself at the next news conference. But as to the personal criticisms he would say, "I was criticized worse than that in the war. And they haven't yet called me what they called Lincoln" [or McKinley, or both Roosevelts or Truman].

Sometimes he explains he is a fatalist and a gospel believer: hence criticism does not disturb nor praise exalt him. What will be will be, and usually it will be right. He felt, he said, he knew the people, he believed in them; he thought they knew him and believed in him. So long as these things were so, he could do his duty as he saw it with confidence that he would be sustained. If and when that confidence was misplaced, he still would do his duty as he saw it.

A calm and judicious man, his intimates agree. "But [one exclaims] if he would pound his desk just once in a while!" The reference is to troubling Republicans, in especial, and Congress, in general, and should not be taken to imply that Eisenhower has learned at all times to subdue his quick temper. This, however, he shows only rarely, and then to aides in whom his confidence has been thoroughly established. At Cabinet meetings and other high-level conferences there is no question who is boss. But the knowledge is never conveyed by the clatter of a jumping ink-well.

The President is warm in speech and behavior, but he can spread the chill of an iceberg drifting into warmer seas. Generals are famous for this refrigerative quality, yet Eisenhower displays it on occasion with a suddenness that suggests it was born in him. Sometimes the chill appears to be the reflex of boredom or of an inner repugnance for artificial amenities: a graduate of Columbia University recalls he felt "as if President Eisenhower handed me my diploma from the deep-freeze." Sometimes a question at a news conference evokes that steely glint from the President's eyes.

It happens rarely. No President since White House news conferences began has submitted with such patient tolerance to—indeed has ever been asked—the personal questions put to Eisenhower, to which he invariably responds as if the questioner had the status of his doctor, his attorney or even his pastor.

But, though his predecessors have been supplied by public taxes with yachts and fishing camps, he froze at an implication that helicopters were being bought by public funds for his recreational use. And when a reporter asked if he had been "filled in" on a large affair of government—the phrase revealing an unconscious acceptance of the critical line that the President doesn't know what is going on in Washington unless someone chooses to tell him—he chillingly remarked that this was a "strange" locution.

This instant effect on him of the language employed was one of the many demonstrations provided by the press questioning periods that the President's mental process is penetrating and alert. This quality is often obscured by the prolixity of his replies, in which numbers and genders collide, participles hang helplessly and syntax is lost forever.

But these flaws invest the diction of most Americans who like to talk—which the President very much does. And though both the point and the purpose of a question sometimes are washed away in the surge of the reply, the news conference transcripts, in this writer's opinion, acquit the President of making it a practice deliberately to use language "to conceal thought." He shoots with a No. 12 shotgun, but he generally shoots at the target.

The President is loyal, once he has chosen an official associate or a friend, and his confidence is a substantial thing. But he is no Grant, to be steadily imposed on; no Truman, to stand stubbornly by an erring subordinate "because his enemies are also mine." In several instances, at least, known to me, the President has been disillusioned as to the quality of judgment he thought he saw in an assistant, or has become convinced an aide was "pulling against the team." Then the offender promptly has felt the chill that impelled him to seek the more comfortable air of private life.

Yet the President's axiom is that everyone is entitled to make the small mistakes; the big ones he will attend to himself. And the temporary or even protracted period in which a member of the Administration comes under heavy and effective political bombardment does not slacken his support of that subordinate to the slightest degree if the President has originally set his seal of approval on the activities under fire and believes they have been pursued in loyalty and good conscience.

This has been thoroughly established by the President's unswerving championship of his Secretaries of State and Agriculture. In the frequent storms as well as the infrequent calms that John Foster Dulles and Ezra T. Benson have passed through in their Cabinet service, they have had the unswerving backing and praise of Eisenhower, publicly and privately expressed.

He seems to abide stanchly by an administrative principle that also is a reflection of his personal code. This is, mistakes of the head are pardonable; mistakes of the heart are unforgivable. The first, he realizes, can make a public servant expendable, however devoted he may be, if they damage the standing of the Administration in public opinion, and in that higher interest the offender must depart. But what he estimates—on the evidence as it reaches him through the staff screening system—as even one mistake of the heart, though it may not be so judged in public opinion, is one too many.

Eisenhower is not unique among Presidents for the passion with which he seeks an enduring peace and a stable order in the world. No chief of this nation could have been more zealous in this pursuit than Eisenhower's immediate predecessor, and the Truman Doctrine was the most effective deterrent to war that statesmanship devised in its time.

But because Eisenhower was trained to arms, and led to victory the largest military forces ever assembled, there is a spectacular quality about his consecration to the ideal of peace, and to his conviction, not only that war is outmoded as a solvent of international disputes, but that another war will revert what is left of mankind to a cycle that by comparison will make the Dark Ages shine like the Renaissance. For he has looked into the gulf of chaos, littered with the corpses of humanity, from a point of vantage in the arsenal of nuclear weapons that is shared perhaps by only half a dozen other people in the world.

This is, this can only be, a glimpse of Eisenhower, the President and the man, in the notoriously deceitful half-light of the contemporary scene. Explorers into the true nature of the world's cloistered elect can be as mistaken about what they think they see as explorers of the planet.

Columbus thought he had found India when the land-birds flew to the mainmast of the Santa María from the Caribbean islet. And if Keats' "stout Cortez," who, boring factualists remind us, really was Balboa, had been plodding through Illinois instead of Darien, he might with eagle eyes have stared at Lake Michigan, and gone to his grave in the belief it was the Pacific Ocean.

Part  3

THE KENNEDY ADMINISTRATION

"A Total Political Animal"

by Tom Wicker

ONE OF THE "Irish Mafia" recently swung his feet up on his White House desk and declared: "Jack Kennedy is a total political animal. In this job, he has to be." Down the hall of the busy West Wing, one of the Kennedy intellectuals put the same thought more elegantly. "The President," he said, "never takes time off from politics. He can't."

Both those remarks make John F. Kennedy seem a bit like a high-level ward boss, stuffing ballot boxes and pelting the opposition with dead cats, or an old-time glad-hander, amusing the folks while raiding the till. And, since his first battle with Congress—the Pier Six brawl for control of the House Rules Committee—he has been widely viewed as a President who spends half his time twisting Congressmen's arms and extorting votes for his bills via rack, thumbscrew and rubber hose.

In fact, Mr. Kennedy is neither so partisan a leader as Harry S. Truman nor so spellbinding a performer as the old master, Franklin D. Roosevelt. The number of twisted arms on Capitol Hill does not add up to mass mayhem, and some of the President's best friends in that precinct are Republicans. Some are even Southern Democrats.

This is true despite the fact that Mr. Kennedy approaches members of the Congress as tirelessly, if not as successfully, as he stalked delegates in the good old pre-convention days of 1960. He wants as

From the *New York Times Magazine*, April 15, 1962.

many of them as possible to vote for his program regardless of party and section, and he is a relentless and persuasive pursuer.

Mr. Kennedy is also a realistic bargainer who does not expect something for nothing. It is not out of the goodness of their hearts but out of the depth of their horse sense that the Kennedy forces rely as little as possible on arm-twisting (defined as forcing a vote from an unwilling victim).

They know that, efficacious as it may be in dredging up the one or two votes needed on a close and crucial issue, arm-twisting can hardly be employed on each of the more than 500 members of the House and Senate on every important bill for four years—let alone eight. "You can twist a fellow's arm once or even twice," observed a Kennedy lieutenant, experienced in the art. "But then the next time he sees you coming, he starts to run."

The President, for one, believes his true task as a politician in the White House is broader than that of dragooning votes out of reluctant Congressmen—though he often is the one who makes the "big call" to the right man at the right time. He cites three more important functions:

First, he must influence his own party in the selection of able, attractive candidates who not only can win but can handle their offices once they've got them.

This sounds nobler than it sometimes is. When Philadelphia's Democratic boss, Representative William Green, Jr., was threatening to oppose Mayor Richardson Dilworth for the party's gubernatorial nomination, Mr. Kennedy had to take firm measures. Not only was a Democrat of Mr. Dilworth's stature needed to lead the ticket against an expected Republican drive but neither the Pennsylvania party nor Mr. Kennedy's legislative forces in Washington could afford to see the efficient Green machine splintered by a Dilworth campaign against "bossism," like that waged the year before by Mayor Wagner of New York against Carmine De Sapio.

Mr. Kennedy played it cool. He let Mr. Dilworth speculate openly about a Wagner-type campaign. He let his ally, Gov. David Lawrence, paint this danger in operatic tones to Mr. Green. When the President judged the latter ripe for the kill, he telephoned him and with a mixture of bluntness and persuasiveness made it plain that Mr. Dilworth was the choice from the top and that the alternative was a damaging intraparty battle. Mr. Green, who did not achieve his eminence through an unwillingness to listen, got the message and acquiesced in the choice of Mr. Dilworth by the state Democratic caucus.

Second, a President of the Kennedy persuasion must also willingly do the political drudgery of raising the vast sums needed to finance modern campaigns, and encourage good organization and precinct work for all the party's candidates.

At fund-raising, Mr. Kennedy is a dandy. His presence, like that of any President, is magic at a $100-a-plate dinner. On a Western tour last fall, he spoke at three of these affairs and raised almost $700,000 for the state and national parties.

At organization (for other than his own past and prospective candidacies), Mr. Kennedy has yet to prove himself. A few Congressional Democrats are grumbling that the party is running behind time in readying itself for the 1962 campaign—a matter of hundreds of state and local races rather than the single national campaign Mr. Kennedy was able to wage in 1960.

The top political figures at the White House, from the President down, confess that they have not devoted as much time to party organization as they have to legislative affairs. Theoretically, however, the able performance of these functions would secure a strong base in his own party for a President. He would then face the third task defined by Mr. Kennedy—a subtler operation, of broad implication.

This is to be the kind of President whose backing can help his party's candidates to win, but whose programs have a broad enough appeal to attract support from more than one party or one section, and whose personal performance does not deeply alienate important national forces.

Dwight D. Eisenhower generally achieved national support because he was a great hero and father-figure in whom people of both parties believed they could put their trust. (He did not always have the political skill to transform this support into national leadership.)

Mr. Kennedy started with no such built-in advantage. His has been the slow and painstaking task of sensing, using and shaping national opinion and confidence to achieve a base of support wider than the badly split Democratic party. He believes, too, that only through acute awareness of politics in its broadest sense can he convert hard-won national backing into an instrument of national leadership.

It was in this sense that he was described as a "total political animal." He seldom moves, acts or speaks without a realization that everything he does will produce its reaction, on a few or many people, and help or hurt his ultimate ability to get things done.

The most innocuous executive order and the most important legislative project must be considered in terms of how they will affect voters generally, specific groups, the attitude of the Congress, national unity in foreign policy, the fortunes of the President's chief supporters, and his own prospects for re-election. He is helped in such judgments by his great knowledge (acquired in his long quest for the Presidency) of the variety and complexity of the country, and of the various forces at work within it—down to the precinct and district level.

Many a member of Congress has been startled to have the President tell him that some relatively obscure vote "won't hurt you in your district as much as you think," and spell out the reasons. He has been known to thank others for their support this way: "I know that was a tough vote for you and we won't let you down next fall."

Mr. Kennedy has worked hard for the support of business groups like the National Association of Manufacturers; yet, on his Western tour, he reverted to a straight New Deal line on resource development and social welfare. He has angled for support among minority groups, unions and interests as sharply defined as dairy farmers and as amorphous as sports lovers.

He has leaned over so far to avoid the appearance of being influenced by his Catholicism that he has been criticized by other Catholics. And the only groups he has really attacked are "extremists" of far Right and far Left.

When Mr. Kennedy became the first Democratic President to address the N.A.M., he explained the basic reason for this approach. Many N.A.M. members had voted against him, he said, but "we are together now, and I will be the President of the United States for the next three years, and I am most anxious that while we may not agree on all matters, goodwill, at least, will prevail among us."

When he sought a means of developing and operating communications satellite systems, for instance, Mr. Kennedy moved with intuitive caution. He found merit in a proposal by Senator Robert S. Kerr of Oklahoma that would have turned the project over to private communications companies, but he knew such a bill would be regarded among his liberal supporters as a "big business" plan.

He found merit, too, in the ideas of Senator Estes Kefauver of

Tennessee, who wanted to have the Government develop the communications system. But that was sure to be regarded among business leaders as socialism.

Mr. Kennedy veered from either alternative and proposed broad-based private ownership of the system. He would have signed either the Kerr or the Kefauver bill, however, if one had been the choice of Congress. In fact, a Senate committee now has approved a compromise between the Administration proposal and the Kerr bill.

With his frontal attack on the problem of civil rights in the late Forties, Harry Truman alienated the Southerners in his own party and drove them into an opposition to him that was in some ways deeper than that of the Republicans—whom he also roundly denounced.

Mr. Kennedy, on the other hand, has moved more vigorously than Mr. Truman in the field of Executive action to assist Negroes and apparently has retained wide support among them. But by proposing only a modest civil-rights legislative program, and making little noise about it, he has sought to avoid bitter-end Southern opposition in Congress. Of the ninety-odd Southern Democrats in the House, fewer than fifty are regarded as hard-core conservatives opposed to any liberal legislation.

The President has been willing, too, to consult privately with such Southern leaders as Representative Howard W. Smith of Virginia. He has maintained good personal relations with almost all of them, and in March he seemed perfectly at home at a Florida party dinner where he endorsed Senator George A. Smathers—who had supported him on only 49 per cent of the Senate's votes in 1961. In Mr. Truman's day, a Presidential endorsement might have been the kiss of death for a Southern politician. Certainly no one would have got it with that kind of record.

The President also has sought support among Republicans. His stump oratory is filled with imprecations on nameless trolls who oppose progress, education, welfare, etc., but he seldom flails the Republicans by name. Influential Congressional Republicans like Senator Everett M. Dirksen are welcome at the White House, always present when the President signs an important bill before the television cameras, and often consulted in advance on important matters. Senator Dirksen has given valuable help in return, most recently in getting the United Nations financial support bill through the Senate.

During the 1961 minimum-wage debate, Senator Jacob K. Javits, the New York Republican, mentioned in a conversation with Mr. Kennedy his desire for a minor amendment of importance to New York City hotel and restaurant men. The next day the Democratic leadership quickly accepted Mr. Javits' amendment, earning a measure of his gratitude and costing themselves nothing. Other Republicans have found the White House equally helpful.

One of Mr. Kennedy's most resounding defeats resulted from a departure from these ingratiating methods. He sent to Congress a reorganization plan to create an Urban Affairs Department, and announced that Robert C. Weaver, a Negro, would be the first Secretary. Anyone voting against the plan, it was strongly implied, would be voting against having a Negro in the Cabinet.

This was a little too partisan and a lot too obvious; it aroused Southern Democrats and angered Republicans who might have supported the Urban Affairs Department or Mr. Weaver or both, but who did not want to be coerced into doing either. In a "we'll show you" mood, these groups combined and smashed the plan in the House, 264-150.

On the whole, however, Mr. Kennedy has been a conciliator, not a Trumanesque knight-at-arms. When the House Armed Services Committee sought to involve him in a constitutional battle over the B-70 bomber, he carefully skirted a public showdown—not only to avoid antagonizing Congress as a whole but to maintain his good relations with the committee's powerful chairman, Representative Carl Vinson of Georgia, a useful ally in many other areas.

Despite these strategies, there remains on any close issue the tactical problem of rounding up a majority, particularly of the House of Representatives. It is then that a Representative may learn, for instance, that a watershed project in his district will go into the next budget—a prospect he is not anxious to jeopardize.

Another may be given a detailed statistical analysis of why his vote for a bill on widgets will not hurt him as much as the appearance of voting against the President. Or a Democrat may be told bluntly that since he opposed Mr. Kennedy on the last two votes, he will be expected to come through for the widget bill, or at least to stay off the floor and not vote against it.

The mere admission of strong Presidential interest in widgets puts a Senator or Representative on notice to be careful, before a word is spoken to him. From V.I.P. tours of the White House to the authorization of public works, an Administration in power has numberless opportunities to help or hinder, punish or promote, the men of Congress. It can be defied, but not lightly.

The most effective approach to a recalcitrant legislator, however, is often the simple one of providing him with all the facts about the issue. Even conscientious members of Congress have difficulty in tracing every nuance of the bill drafters and following every obscure change made in committee. They are vulnerable, therefore, to rumor and misinformation.

A Congressman from a widget-making district may believe the widget bill will cut production and cost jobs. It is important to convince him that it won't. Or a non-widget Congressman may think the bill's terms also will affect some other interest in his district, when, in fact, there is no relation.

On the other hand, some features of a bill actually may cause side effects that reduce support for it. Sometimes these can be removed, even when the cost is great. The Administration ruthlessly trimmed various categories of workers out of its minimum-wage bill in 1961, picking up votes with every slash—an estimated twelve, for instance, when laundry workers were eliminated.

In this kind of vote-seeking, Mr. Kennedy himself is a big asset. Even his opponents concede his powers of persuasion in direct confrontation. An editor recently left a White House luncheon convinced that he had been wrong in his opposition to the Administration's plan to buy $100,000,000 in United Nations bonds. It was only later that he realized the President had advanced no substantive arguments that hadn't been voiced at his news conferences.

It was the President who made the phone calls last year that persuaded some of the more conservative legislators—Senator Spessard L. Holland of Florida, for one—in a conference committee to restore much of the money that had been cut out of the foreign-aid bill by the House.

However, even the Boston accent on the telephone doesn't always work; it didn't when Mr. Kennedy called Representative Harold D. Cooley of North Carolina, soliciting Southern votes in the Rules Committee fight. But vote counters in the House report that a major factor in increased support for the trade bill was the President's personal presentation of the issue, complete with charts and graphs, at a White House reception in January.

Mr. Kennedy's fourteen years in the Congress taught him that all the arm-twisting in the world won't sway some votes. Representative Wilbur D. Mills of Arkansas, the chairman of the Ways and Means Committee, is solidly committed at home, for instance, to vote against the President's medical-care bill.

That may outrage some proponents of the measure, but Mr. Kennedy is mindful that Mr. Mills also will be the floor manager of his trade bill, and has already guided his tax reform bill through the House. In addition, his committee in time will have to handle the unemployment-compensation bill and other major legislation. It would be neither sensible nor fair to treat Mr. Mills as an enemy.

The proof always, of course, is in the pudding. Mr. Kennedy is already under heavy pressure from labor and liberal elements to "fight harder"; conservatives alternately deprecate his legislative record as falling short of his promises, and criticize him for the iniquities of those promises. Even non-aligned political students find the Administration's achievements to date little more than a start.

Thus, the political animal is not yet the king of the beasts in the Washington jungle. Few would suggest, however, that he is not constantly on the prowl.

Report on the "Rampageous Right"

by Alan Barth

FRUSTRATION, WHICH PRODUCES tantrums in babies, can lead to equally irrational fits of rage in adults. Unhappily, the contemporary world is, in many respects, a frustrating one. It is rotating not only on its axis but on all its axioms as well. It is involved in profound change—in its international power relationships, in its economic organization, in its social arrangements. And so it confronts many Americans with inevitable alterations in ways of life they cherish and with insurmountable obstacles to ways in which they want their country to move.

In foreign affairs, the United States and the Soviet Union are locked in a classic stalemate which forbids either side to work its will without limit but which affords at least a precarious assurance of continued peace. Colonialism is disappearing, new economic groupings are in process of formation among nations, new developments in weaponry have rendered traditional modes of enforcing national policy altogether obsolete. These are but the most obvious of the conditions in America's relations with the world outside which serve to frustrate American aims and ambitions.

At home, the country is undergoing a tremendous transformation in the pattern of its race relations, involving a long-delayed emancipation of Negroes; for some persons the transformation seems to mean an economic threat and a serious loss of status. In addition, the urbanization and industrialization of American life have brought

From the *New York Times Magazine*, November 26, 1961.

demands that the Government assume new social-welfare responsibilities—in relation to schools, to slum clearance and housing, to relief of the indigent and the aged; and these are opposed by some members of the community as contrary to traditions of free enterprise and individual initiative.

These frustrations are experienced in an atmosphere of continuing international tension and fear. Americans have lived in a steady state of crisis ever since the Second World War. That war was hardly ended before American troops were engaged in a bloody struggle in Korea, to be followed by a prolonged period of "cold war" which produced a harrowing sense of strain and anxiety. Moreover, the terrifying possibility exists that atomic weapons may be launched against American cities at any time in a sudden, surprise attack. Concern about this possibility is exacerbated by confusing and conflicting exhortations from Washington regarding the dangers of radiation and the advantages of fallout shelters. All in all, the future seems an uncertain one. The widespread fear arising out of real and imagined perils is hardly conducive to the rule of reason.

That there is a great deal of frustration in the land today is made evident by a proliferation of societies, leagues, committees, councils and crusades which propose to stop the clock—or to turn its hands back to some easier, earlier time when men could move more readily and directly to achieve what they wanted. How to classify these groups politically raises a difficult problem in semantics.

They are commonly called "Rightist"—a term which connotes conservatism. But in sober truth there is nothing conservative about them. They are much more in a rage to destroy than a fervor to conserve. They tend, as Under Secretary of State Chester Bowles remarked of some of them just the other day, to be saying: "Stop the world, I want to get off." Clearly, these "Rightists" have nothing in common with such conservatives as, say, Dwight D. Eisenhower or Herbert Hoover. Prof. Richard Hofstadter of Columbia University, in a most insightful essay about the "Rightists" some years ago, called them "pseudo-conservatives."

Sometimes they are referred to as the "radical Right." But the fact is that there is nothing radical about them. They offer no novel solutions to the problems that plague them; indeed, they offer no solutions at all. They are immensely discontented with things as they are and furiously impatient with almost everyone in public office who can in any way be held responsible for their frustrations. But it cannot be said that they hold any clearly stated objectives or have any specific program either in common or individually. They are fundamentally and temperamentally "aginners." And perhaps the commonest characteristic among them is anger. They can fairly be called, if nothing else, the Rampageous Right.

But if they defy designation under any simple political label, it is nevertheless possible to find certain lowest common denominators of philosophic outlook which may help to describe them and to set them off from the parties and factions which engage in the traditional pulling and hauling, the compromising and accommodating that are customary in the American political process. Here are some of their identifying traits:

First, they tend to see complex problems simply and to define problems in terms of "either-or" choices. For example, Senator Thomas J. Dodd, addressing a huge rally in the Hollywood Bowl in October under the sponsorship of the Christian Anti-Communist Crusade, said: "The only alternative to total defeat in the struggle with communism is total victory."

Whatever the merits of this formulation as rhetoric, it suffers from the logical fallacy of the excluded middle. Obviously there are a number of possible alternatives. Total annihilation is one of them. So is continued stalemate. So is some sort of temporary accommodation conferring neither victory nor defeat upon either side but providing for reciprocal concessions which might relax tensions while allowing life to go on for a while longer on the planet.

The "either-or" solution is a formula for frustration. It pits what is unattainable against what is intolerable and precludes all rational and feasible middle courses. In international affairs it makes negotiation impossible and assures for any compromise, no matter what gains or advantages it may embrace, a taunt from the "Rightists" that it amounts to abject surrender. It is hard to escape a conclusion that the essential negativism of the "either-or" approach is designed to frustrate rather than forward any kind of agreement.

This "either-or" approach is adopted by the Right in regard to domestic as well as foreign affairs. It expresses itself in an insistence that there can be no middle ground between pure capitalism and complete communism. In Southern California, automobile bumpers abound with stickers reciting the slogan, "Socialism is Communism." To the people who like to see things so simplistically, blurring the vital distinctions that make free choice possible, socialism is an epithet applied indiscriminately to almost any form of collective endeavor. Thus, any governmentally operated insurance program to provide medical care for the elderly is denounced as Socialist. So are Federal aid to education, Federally financed scholarships for college students and Federal support of scientific research—although there appears to be nothing particularly Socialistic about the same activities when supported by state tax revenues. Public assistance for the indigent, public housing, the Tennessee Valley Authority, even the progressive income tax are all looked upon as satanically inspired deviations from capitalism.

Those who support any of these programs as pragmatic ways of dealing with community needs are unsparingly defamed as Communists or as Communist stooges or Communist sympathizers. Robert Welch, organizer and leader of the John Birch Society, has coined the word "Comsymps" to elide any distinction among these categories.

In one other area the Rightist disposition to prohibit any kind of moderation deserves notice. Southern segregationists have joined hands with the professional anti-Communists, ideologically as well as politically. Almost a full century after Abraham Lincoln proclaimed the emancipation of Negroes in the United States, segregationists can present only a solid wall of "massive resistance" to Negro demands for any of the fruits of emancipation.

Their standard defense for this resistance is a stubborn assertion that the Negro demands are merely a product of Communist agitation. In many parts of the Deep South today, the National Association for the Advancement of Colored People is regarded by ignorant whites as a Communist, or Communist-dominated, agency. The close alliance between the White Citizens Councils on the one hand and the John Birch Society and the Christian Anti-Communist Crusade on the other should not be ignored.

A second common denominator of the Rightist groups is that they subscribe wholeheartedly to the conspiratorial, or devil, theory of history and tend to attribute every frustration to betrayal by traitors. It is out of the question for them to acknowledge honest differences of opinion or to consider the possibility that problems may arise in foreign affairs either through some skillful action by the enemy or through innocent error by conscientious, though fallible, public officials at home.

They have no uncertainty, for example, as to why "we lost China" —as though it was ever "ours" to lose. China was lost to communism, these angry Rightists assert unhesitatingly, not by the Chinese but by traitorous Americans who gave it away out of fealty to the Communist conspiracy.

How did the United States get into so disadvantageous a situation in Berlin—an island in a Communist sea? Softness toward communism, or worse, at Yalta or Teheran or Potsdam, the Rightists answer with easy assurance. And what more proof of the proposition can be demanded than the fact that Alger Hiss committed perjury before the House Committee on Un-American Activities?

As Professor Hofstadter has put it, "Hiss is the hostage the pseudo-conservatives hold from the New Deal generation. He is a heaven-sent gift. If he did not exist, the pseudo-conservatives would not have been able to invent him." They have made him into a prototype to explain every national misfortune from Laos to outer space.

The Communist conspiracy, to these fixed-focus interpreters, is omnipresent, and very nearly omnipotent. It permeates every American institution and intrudes its poisonous influence into every aspect of American life. They see the Communists exercising power, if not actual control, in religious organizations, especially in the National Council of Churches of Christ, which appears to stand convicted of Communist inspiration, in their view, by its very tolerance and humanism.

The Rightists insist that the Communist conspiracy has infiltrated the leadership of the country's great labor unions, the faculties of its principal universities, even the editorial offices of important newspapers. In a speech just the other day one of the most vehement of the Rightists, T. Coleman Andrews, Commissioner of Internal Revenue in the Eisenhower Administration and, subsequently, an ardent advocate of abolition of the income tax, called The New York Times "the uptown Daily Worker," adding that the nation's capital also had its "Daily Worker—The Washington Post." Tolerance of diversity is not a characteristic of the Right.

The close consanguinity between the segregationist and the anti-Communist strains in the Rightist movement is illustrated by their common attack on the Supreme Court. To the segregationists, the Court's unanimous decision in 1954 that segregated public schools violate the Constitution affords, of itself, proof positive that the Justices were subverted by communism—the all-purpose explanation for every frustration.

The anti-Communists find the same proof in Court decisions upholding the constitutional rights of persons charged with Left-Wing leanings. Robert Welch found it possible, therefore, to say quite flatly that "Communist influences are now in almost complete control of our Federal Government" and that the Supreme Court of the United States "is one of the most important agencies of communism."

The third of the common denominators characterizing the Right-Wing groups is a deep distrust of democratic institutions and of the democratic process—a distrust, in short, of the people. The Rightists never regard *themselves* as gullible or susceptible to Communist subversion; but they appear to be convinced that all their countrymen are outright simpletons ripe for a shift of loyalty at any moment from the Capitol to the Kremlin.

Thus, copying the organization of the Communist party, Mr. Welch declared that "the John Birch Society is to be a monolithic body. . . . Democracy is merely a deceptive phrase, a weapon of demagoguery, and a perennial fraud. . . . The John Birch Society will operate under completely authoritative control at all levels." And, with an ominous implication that he might in the future be quite willing to seek overthrow of the Government by force and violence, he asserted that his society could not rely on "politicians, political leadership or even political action."

The anti-democratic character of the extreme Right is perhaps most plainly manifested by its pronounced preference for military over civilian leadership. A most disquieting degree of cooperation has developed between leaders of the extreme Right-Wing groups and high-ranking officers of the American armed services. It was this cooperation that elicited from Senator J. W. Fulbright last summer his celebrated memorandum to the Pentagon asserting that too many military officers were meddling in American domestic politics under the guise of anti-communism and on the pretext of indoctrinating American troops.

The military programs of indoctrination have been aimed, in point of fact, at civilians as well as at men in uniform. The public information officer at the Point Mugu, Calif., Naval Missile Center took it upon himself, for instance, to "indoctrinate" more than sixty groups of civilians over a five-month period. He "taught" them that the nation's schools and churches have been infiltrated by Communists, that American newspapers should not be believed because the press is pro-Communist and he attacked the Governor of California for having criticized the John Birch Society.

In the summer of 1960 at the Glenview, Ill., Naval Air Station and in February, 1961, under military sponsorship in Houston, courses were given with the collaboration of Dr. Fred C. Schwarz for civilians and military personnel, adroitly mingling anti-communism with extreme Right-Wing politics.

Senator Fulbright's memorandum and the subsequent removal of Maj. Gen. Edwin A. Walker from his command of the Twenty-fourth Division in Germany touched off a major national controversy regarding military programs of indoctrination which impinge on political affairs. That controversy is likely soon to be acted out dramatically in hearings before the Senate Armed Services Committee. General Walker himself has now resigned from the Army— and in a letter to the Senate Committee has flung down a gauntlet which may make him the new champion of the far Right.

General Walker's letter seemed deliberately contrived to drive a wedge between civilian and military authority in the United States. Complaining bitterly about "censorship" as though civilian officials had no business exercising control over military officers in regard to political activities—and about "the power of little men who, in the name of my country, punish loyal service to it," the General seemed to be trying to convince the country that civilians have been improperly and illegally putting a leash on the military.

He uses the term "censorship" in curious ways, speaking of "censorship of victory on the field of battle" in regard to the Korean War, "censorship of action" that led to the fall of the Chinese Nationalist Government in the Nineteen Forties and "harassment through censorship of execution" during the war in Greece.

Asserting that American boys enter on military service without adequate understanding of the enemy or knowledge of communism, General Walker says, "If it is now to be the case that commanders are restricted, or constrained by censorship, to certain limited areas of communication in their indoctrination of their soldiers, then the deficiency in training will go unremedied."

This is astonishing and alarming language for a professional soldier. A paragraph later, the General observes that "our defense is based on the concept of a civilian military establishment with regular Army support" and adds that "to presume a military coup by such an army is patently preposterous." So it has always been in the United States. But when one reflects upon the conduct of General Salan in France, can one feel wholly comfortable about military officers who denounce civilian leaders as corrupt and treasonable and who work hand in hand with Rightist groups which have rejected democracy?

What is the strength of the extreme Right today? The number of its adherents cannot be determined with any accuracy; and, as has been observed with regard to the subversives on the extreme Left, numbers do not afford a satisfactory index to influence. A score or more of Rightist groups are now vying with one another for supremacy.

Most formidable among them in terms of membership, money and notoriety are the John Birch Society and the Christian Anti-Communist Crusade. The sheer extravagance of some of Robert Welch's utterances may have somewhat dimmed the luster of the former and diminished the breadth of its appeal. It takes a fairly strong stomach to subscribe to Mr. Welch's statement that "Dwight Eisenhower is a dedicated, conscious agent of the Communist conspiracy."

Dr. Schwarz' Christian Anti-Communist Crusade, which has said nothing quite so shocking, is now busily expanding its operations from a Southern California base to national proportions. Dr. Schwarz says that 70,000 persons contribute to his organization. In point of fact, he has had some impressive endorsements, including a hearty pat on the back from C. D. Jackson, the publisher of Life, and television sponsorship by such considerable industrial firms as the Richfield Oil Co., the Schick Safety Razor Co. and the Technicolor Corp. The Crusade seems to be well-heeled and shrewdly led.

Most frenetic of the fanatics is the group calling itself the Minutemen, whom President Kennedy derided in his Southern California speech last week. They have actually organized themselves into armed bands of civilian guerrillas—waiting, no doubt, for Der Tag.

Undoubtedly the extreme Right is going to exercise a powerful negative influence in the difficult and inevitably frustrating years immediately ahead. Its weight will be thrown against Federal aid to education, against medical care for the aged, against generosity to the indigent—the municipal authorities of Newburgh, N. Y., seem to reflect its welfare philosophy—against civil liberties in general; and in foreign affairs it will strive militantly to represent any concessions to the Russians or to the Chinese as treasonable, any consideration for this country's allies as craven and any squeamishness about extermination of the human race in an atomic holocaust as subversively sentimental.

Lacking any realistic affirmative program, however, the Right is unlikely to be able to grasp the reins of political power in the United States. Genuine conservatives devoted to the nation's traditions, values and institutions will be reluctant to identify themselves with the extremists or to make common cause with them.

The Rightists will no doubt seek to capture control of the Republican party but they are unlikely to succeed. Their darling just now is Barry Goldwater. But the Senator will be obliged before very long to choose between the support of the Rightists and the support of real Republicans who will not care to forsake the traditions of their party for a forlorn kind of fascism.

This much can be said with assurance: the American people are not about to do away with the income tax or social security or the intelligent use of their Government for the accomplishment of public purposes; they are not about to substitute military for civilian authority; they are not about to forgo self-government for the sake of some evangelistic fuehrer. The Right may make itself a nuisance; but it will not make itself into a government. It is not a wave of the future; it is a voice of frustration and despair, a wail from an irrecoverable past.

Historic Change in the Supreme Court

by Anthony Lewis

A HISTORIC TERM of the Supreme Court is drawing to a close. It rates that adjective because of a single momentous decision—the decision in *Baker v. Carr,* opening the doors of the Federal courts to legal attacks on the apportionment of seats in state legislatures.

The apportionment case was decided just three months ago, on March 26. But it has already started to remake the political map of the United States. In Georgia and Alabama, Federal courts have ordered rural forces to relax their ancient hold on the legislatures. In Maryland the legislature, acting under a judicial ultimatum, has redistricted its lower house for the first time in forty years. In two dozen other states legal or political action is under way on reapportionment.

A lawyer who has been a student of the Supreme Court's work for many years remarked soon after March 26 that the decision in *Baker v. Carr* had been "inevitable." Then he added: "But twenty years ago, or even ten, it would have been inconceivable."

From "inconceivable" to "inevitable" in a decade or two—so swiftly does the course of decision run. But why the change? That is the great question posed by the apportionment case. What had happened to Court or country that made the justices see the issue differently in 1962 from the way they might have, indeed had, seen it a few years earlier?

From the *New York Times Magazine,* June 17, 1962.

In this respect the apportionment case is part of the larger question of change in the Supreme Court. For of course it is not the only example of a revolution in constitutional doctrine in recent years. Two others come quickly to mind: the standards of fairness imposed on state criminal proceedings and, best known to the public at large, the Court's attitude toward racial segregation.

Perhaps it would be useful to approach the general question of the changing role of the Supreme Court by a particular examination of each of these areas—criminal procedure, segregation, apportionment. Seeing what the Court has done there, and considering why, may suggest some general reasons for the great shift in the Supreme Court's place in the American system of government over the past twenty-five years.

Recall, first, the dominant mood of the Supreme Court a generation ago. The issues then were the right of the states to set maximum hours and minimum wages, the right of the Federal Government to use its tax and commerce power to deal with the Depression. In short, the Court's concern seemed to be with property, not what we today would call human liberty.

It was in that setting, in 1936, that the Court for the first time in history set aside a state criminal conviction because the defendants had been mistreated. The case was called *Brown v. Mississippi,* and it is worth recalling the facts set out in Chief Justice Charles Evans Hughes' opinion.

Three Mississippi Negroes were charged with murder. One was hanged from a tree and told he would hang there until he confessed; at the trial he still bore the marks of the rope on his throat. The two others "were laid over chairs and their backs were cut to pieces with a leather strap with buckles on it. . . . In this manner the defendants confessed the crime, and as the whippings progressed or were repeated, they changed or adjusted their confession in all particulars of detail so as to conform to the demands of their torturers."

The Supreme Court decided that convictions based on confessions obtained by such methods denied the "due process of law" guaranteed by the Fourteenth Amendment.

Since 1936, in a steady progression of cases, the Court has struck at the use of coerced confessions. It has outlawed psychological as well as physical coercion. And in many other aspects of criminal law, despite protests from state officials and from dissenters within the Court, new restraints have been put on the states.

In 1956, over strong dissent, the Supreme Court said that a state which allows appeals in criminal cases cannot deny the right just because a prisoner is too poor to buy a trial transcript; it must supply the transcript or an adequate substitute. The Conference of State Chief Justices charged gloomily that the decision threatened "an almost complete breakdown in the work of state appellate courts," but nothing like that has occurred.

Just a year ago the Court, again by a narrow division, overturned the well-established rule that state courts were free to admit illegally seized evidence. It has put down for argument next year the question whether it should now require the states to supply free counsel to impoverished defendants in all criminal cases, abandoning the present rule assuring counsel only in cases involving the death penalty.

The course has been clear in the area of criminal law: despite resentment at new restrictions on the freedom of the states, and despite some misgivings within the Court from time to time, the Supreme Court has moved steadily in the past twenty-five years to impose uniform national standards of fairness on state criminal proceedings. State law enforcement faces Federal judicial scrutiny today to a degree unthinkable a generation ago.

Why?

It seems evident, first, that in moving against the third degree and other forms of unfairness and inequality in the criminal law, the Court was reflecting a national moral sentiment. Perhaps this arose from the experience of totalitarian brutality in other countries. Whatever the reason, Americans were plainly less willing to tolerate police misbehavior in any state, regardless of the political niceties of Federal-state relations, than they were in earlier years. Many Americans have a national conscience that is injured by any state's misbehavior. And more and more the national ideal is prevailing over state orientation.

A second point to be made is that, if higher national standards were to be imposed on law enforcement in this country, the Supreme Court was the only agency that could do the job.

The inmates of state prisons hardly had the kind of political power likely to spur legislative reforms. State courts tended to be dominated by local feelings and dislike for criminals. One of the happy effects of intervention by the Supreme Court has in fact been growing sensitivity on the part of local courts and political groups to the needs of fairness in criminal procedure. Intervention has spurred self-reform.

In 1938, two years after *Brown v. Mississippi,* there came a significant decision in the racial area. For the first time the Supreme Court emphasized the "equal" aspect of its 1896 rule that a state could provide "separate but equal" facilities for Negroes. Over bitter dissent, the Court held that Missouri did not meet the rule by sending Negroes to an out-of-state law school; it must provide legal training within its own borders.

There followed a series of unanimous decisions on higher education tightening the "separate-but-equal" standard. Finally, in 1950, the Court all but made segregation a legal impossibility. It held that Texas had not provided equality by establishing a separate law school for Negroes. In directing the (white) University of Texas Law School to admit a Negro applicant, Chief Justice Fred M. Vinson wrote:

"[The white law school] possesses to a far greater degree those qualities which are incapable of objective measurement but which make for greatness in a law school. Such qualities, to name but a few, include reputation of the faculty, experience of the administration, position and influence of the alumni, standing in the community, traditions and prestige."

It took no great thinker to realize that, when such intangibles were placed in the scale, no segregated school for Negroes was ever likely to be found "equal." Four years later the Court cut through the legal web and held that segregated schools were inherently unequal and denied the "equal protection of the laws" guaranteed by the Fourteenth Amendment.

The school decision followed other great victories for the Negro in the Supreme Court—cases establishing the right to vote and serve on juries and buy property without discrimination. But schools were by far the most inflammatory issue in the South, and the Court was well aware of that. Nevertheless, it decided against segregation, and unanimously.

Why?

Once again no complicated motive need be sought. The Supreme Court was reflecting a national moral consensus on segregation—perhaps anticipating a feeling that had not yet fully taken shape.

In 1896, in establishing the "separate but equal" rule, the Supreme

Court had relied on the sociology of its day. It said there was nothing individuous to the Negro in segregation unless "the colored race chooses to put that construction upon it."

But after Adolf Hitler and South Africa, no court could say with a straight face that separation of human beings on account of race or color was a stamp of inferiority only if the segregated so regarded it. Most of the world knew, and the United States was at least coming to know, that segregation was intended as a demonstration of one race's superiority over another.

Moreover, there was again the fact that unless the Supreme Court acted there would be no action. Discrimination made the Negro politically powerless in his own state. Ever since Reconstruction, Congress had happily left to the Supreme Court the enforcement of constitutional guarantees against racial discrimination. The Federal legislative path to reform was blocked by the South's power in the Senate. Closing of the judicial path might produce intolerable social pressures.

The Senate Majority Leader, Mike Mansfield, made the point during the recent Senate civil-rights debate. Our recent constitutional history, he said, "makes clear that progress toward the equalization in practice of the ideals of human freedom will not be halted indefinately. When one road to this end fails, others will unfold. If the process is ignored in legislative channels, it will not necessarily be blocked in other channels—in the Executive Branch and in the courts."

Finally, the problem of legislative districts. It is an old problem; rural areas have refused for decades to relinquish the power given to them by unrepresentative districts in state legislatures.

In 1946 the Supreme Court seemed to close the doors of the Federal courts to the aggrieved city-dwellers. Justice Felix Frankfurter said the districting question would lead the courts into a "political thicket." The cure, he said, would have to be a political struggle by the disenfranchised.

A dozen times since 1946 the Court had held to the hands-off attitude on apportionment and related questions. Then, last March, it abruptly changed direction. The extraordinarily swift reaction to *Baker v. Carr* helps to suggest why the Court decided as it did.

Here, in contrast with the much less than deliberate speed with which school segregation has been abandoned, the Supreme Court's lead has been followed with exuberant enthusiasm by lower Federal and even state judges and by political figures. No recent constitutional decision has had such widespread effects so fast.

It seems evident that on the issue of legislative apportionment a moral explosion was waiting to be set off. Almost everyone, including the beneficiaries of the evil, knew that an evil existed. But Justice Frankfurter's advice to work for political change was useless; the political system provided no way of escape. The Supreme Court supplied the key, opening the way for political as well as legal forces to work for orderly change.

Perhaps in 1946 it still seemed possible that the rural oligarchies in control of state legislatures would listen to reason. But by 1962 that hope had passed. It was plain that only the Supreme Court could cure the disease of malapportionment eating away at the vitals of American democracy.

There, then, are our three examples of dramatic change in Supreme Court doctrine during the past quarter-century. Surely they do suggest some generalizations about why the Court has shifted as it has in its own view of its role.

One constant in the three examples was the ethical element. In intervening in behalf of the abused criminal suspect, the Negro, the citizen disenfranchised by malapportionment, the Supreme Court has been responding to what it deemed to be a moral demand—a demand of the national conscience. Moreover, the national conscience had found no way to express itself except through the Supreme Court. The Court moved in only when the rest of our governmental system was stymied, when there was no other practical way out of the moral dilemma.

The conclusion is that the Supreme Court has tended in recent years to act as the instrument of national moral values that have not been able to find other governmental expression. If the Court has changed, it is because we have changed.

The unhappy recent history of the world has rearranged Americans' hierarchy of values, and so it should be no great surprise that the Supreme Court emphasizes interests different from those of the past. We are more concerned, now, about abuse of official authority, mistreatment of racial minorities and sabotage of democracy than we are about the state powers in a federal system.

This is not to say that everyone agrees on moral goals, much less ones that are judicially attainable. The nine justices cannot be expected to march in happy unanimity toward a legal heaven whose definition all applaud.

Only in the field of race relations—where, ironically, public reaction has been the most divisive—have the justices been regularly in agreement. They have apparently found the moral imperative more obvious. But even here it seems doubtful that unanimity can long be preserved as the Court reaches the difficult questions of how to distinguish "private" from "public" discrimination.

Outside the racial area the Court has been deeply divided. Justice Frankfurter has been the principal spokesman for the view that the Court should be hesitant to impose its moral ideal in a complex political structure. He dissented not only from *Baker v. Carr,* but, for example, from last year's decision outlawing illegally seized evidence in state criminal trials.

This does not mean that Justice Frankfurter likes unfair apportionments or illegally seized evidence—far from it. He is simply a believer in the independent power of the states, wisely or unwisely used, and such a skeptic about the perfection of judges that he hesitates to bind government to rigid judicial formulas.

Justice Frankfurter, of course, is not alone in his doubts about an expansive role for the Supreme Court as keeper of the national conscience. Most of today's critics of the Court are disaffected only because they dislike some particular result—say, the outlawing of school segregation. But there are some who, like Justice Frankfurter, have deeper and more general philosophical objections.

One is that judges are not necessarily competent to make broad moral judgments. Law school trains a man to work his way through conflicting principles in construing a contract or a statute. But does it equip Supreme Court justices, or the lower court judges who must carry out their decisions, to pass judgment on great social questions such as race relations and legislative districting, where there are few guidelines—few easily defined principles?

Even more strongly pressed is the thesis that reliance on the courts to cure society's ills saps the strength of democracy. The late Judge Learned Hand put it most colorfully when he said that he did not care to be ruled by "a bevy of Platonic guardians."

The more citizens rely on the courts, it is argued, the less will they fight issues out where they ought to be fought out in a democracy—

in the political forum. Justice Frankfurter has often spoken admiringly of Britain as a country where misuse of official power is quickly argued out and corrected in the legislative arena, Parliament.

Those who believe in the moral role that the Supreme Court has increasingly come to play would not deny the difficulty of the job it gives to judges. But they make the point that it is a duty compelled by a written Constitution. The framers of the Constitution and its amendments deliberately chose to use phrases such as "due process" and "equal protection"—phrases that express no more than moral ideals, that must be given content by each generation. It is our judges who have been designated to supply that content, and their sources of inspiration must be national values.

Justice Frankfurter, for all his concern about judicial power, sees no escape from a judge's duty to give the Constitution concrete meaning. "It must be an impersonal judgment," he once wrote. "It must rest on fundamental presuppositions rooted in history to which widespread acceptance may fairly be attributed. . . . But in the end judgment cannot be escaped."

Another time, Justice Frankfurter spoke of the Supreme Court's right to enshrine in the Constitution "those liberties of the individual which history has attested as the indispensable conditions of an open against a closed society"—in short, deep-rooted national ideals of liberty.

And this is not Great Britain. It is not a small, homogeneous, centralized country with a tradition of parliamentary supremacy and a deep commitment to official impartiality and decency. This is a sprawling country divided by regional and other animosities, with an unhappy tradition of corrupt and partisan officials, especially on the local level. It has a national legislature too often driven by sectional interests, and in any case too busy, to spend much time bringing local action into harmony with national ideals.

It is a country, also, that has always looked to its courts for moral inspiration. It has looked especially to the Supreme Court, whose very remoteness and freedom from sectional and political pressures have made Americans value it as a forum for the defense of human liberty.

The Court has not been a Platonic dictator and could never successfully be that. When it has tried to stand against the tide of history, as in the Nineteen Thirties, it has failed. Its great success has been as a moral goad to the political process—when it has urged politicians to do what they have avoided doing but knew in their hearts they should, as in race relations and apportionment.

There is every indication that the Supreme Court more and more sees its constitutional function in those terms. Slowly but perceptibly, with occasional retreats but with the over-all direction clear, the Court is taking up the role of conscience to the country.

What Was Killed Was Not Only the President But the Promise

by James Reston

TIME SEEMS to be trying to make amends to John Fitzgerald Kennedy. Robbed of his years, he is being rewarded and honored in death as he never was in life. Deprived of the place he sought in history, he has been given in compensation a place in legend. What was a monstrous personal and historic crime a year ago is now something even more elemental and enduring: It is a symbol of the tragedy and caprice of life, and is likely to be remembered by the novelists and the dramatists long after the historians have gone on to other things.

Will he seem different to the historians from the way the dramatists will see him? What are they likely to say of his conduct of foreign affairs, domestic affairs, the Presidency itself? Are we already confusing myth with reality, as he was always telling us we should not do?

Probably we are, but this is only fair and maybe even natural. For there was always something vaguely legendary about him. He was a story-book President, younger and more handsome than mortal politicians, remote even from his friends, graceful, almost elegant, with poetry on his tongue and a radiant young woman at his side.

He was a sudden and surprising person. He never did things when

From the *New York Times Magazine,* November 15, 1964.

other men were doing them. He went to Congress and the White House earlier than most. He married much later than his contemporaries. His war record, his political record and his personal life were marked by flashes of crisis and even by a vague premonition of tragedy. He always seemed to be striding through doors into the center of some startling triumph or disaster. He never reached his meridian: we saw him only as a rising sun.

Accordingly, it is not easy to make an estimate of his 1,000 days in the White House. He didn't have a fair chance and he didn't even give himself a fair chance. He often made his decisions alone after a series of private talks with several individuals, none of whom shared the whole process of his thought.

Oddly in one who had such an acute sense of history, he was disorderly about keeping records of what led up to his decisions, and though he had a great gift for conversation, he seems to have spent little time talking to his closest associates about how he had decided things in the past.

All this complicates the task of placing him in the catalogue of the Presidents. We do not have the record. We do not have the full story of the two Cuban crises, or his meeting with Khrushchev in Vienna, or the reasoning behind his gambles in Vietnam, or the communications that led up to the atomic test-ban treaty with the Soviets. We have only our clippings, memories, and impressions, and these can be uncertain guides.

I—Foreign Policy

Historians—and here we are in the realm of opinion—will probably rate President Kennedy's handling of foreign policy higher than his contemporaries did. It is a spotty record. He dreamed occasionally of an interdependent Atlantic world and this has become part of the legend, but the reality is that the alliance was in poor shape during most of his Administration. He courted Latin America like a thoughtful lover, but, again, the Alliance for Progress was more dream than reality.

Even so, he had a feeling for the way the world was going. He understood the challenge of change. He was fascinated by the political revolution produced by the liberation of the colonial peoples: sometimes too fascinated with it, and too inclined to give it a higher priority than it deserved. He studied and understood the intricate problems of the atomic revolution and the scientific revolution, probably better than any of his predecessors.

Yet this keen, analytical intelligence was not always a help. It enabled him to see the problems, but it often depressed him about finding the answers. I always thought—perhaps wrongly—that his intelligence made him pessimistic. The evidence that science was transforming the world seemed so clear and overwhelming to him that he was irritated by the failure of men and institutions to adapt and keep up.

In his very first State of the Union message, 10 days after he had been sworn in, he told the Congress and the nation: "Before my term has ended, we shall have to test anew whether a nation organized and governed such as ours can endure. The outcome is by no means certain. The answers are by no means clear."

His bungling of his first foreign-policy gamble, when he tried to help the Cuban refugees overthrow the Castro Government, made him all the more conscious, not only of the complexities of political decision, but of the possible consequences of failure.

The events at the Bay of Pigs contributed to his natural caution, and added to his problems with the Communists for most of the rest of his days in the White House. It is impossible to be sure about this, but I was in Vienna when he met Khrushchev shortly after the fiasco of the Bay of Pigs, and saw him 10 minutes after his meeting with the Soviet leader. He came into a dim room in the American Embassy shaken and angry. He had tried, as always to be calm and rational with Khrushchev, to get him to define what the Soviet Union could and would not do, and Khrushchev had bullied him and threatened him with war over Berlin.

We will have to know much more about that confrontation between Kennedy and Khrushchev, one now deprived of life and the other of power, before we can be sure, but Kennedy said just enough in that room in the embassy to convince me of the following: Khrushchev had studied the events of the Bay of Pigs; he would have understood if Kennedy had left Castro alone or destroyed him; but when Kennedy was rash enough to strike at Cuba but not bold enough to finish the job, Khrushchev decided he was dealing with an inexperienced young leader who could be intimidated and blackmailed. The Communist decision to put offensive missiles into Cuba was the final gamble of this assumption.

The missile crisis brought out what always seemed to me to be

Kennedy's finest quality and produced the events on which Kennedy's place in history probably depends. There is a single fact that repeats itself in the Kennedy story like the major theme in a symphony: He was at his best in the highest moment of crisis.

He could be ambiguous and even indecisive on secondary questions. He obviously trifled with the first Cuban crisis. He also temporized with the Vietnamese crisis, partly supporting those who wanted to intervene "to win," partly going along with those who reminded him that the French had suffered 175,000 casualties against the same Communist army, but never really defining his aims or reconciling his power with his objectives.

Yet always in his political life he acted decisively when faced with total defeat. He was supremely confident, almost presumptuous, in going for the Presidency in the first place against the opposition of the most powerful elements in his party. He was bold and effective when first Hubert Humphrey, then Harry Truman and finally Lyndon Johnson challenged him publicly during the campaign for the nomination. He probably won the Presidency in the critical debates with Richard Nixon. And this same quality came out in the missile crisis in Cuba.

Then he was, as Robert Frost had urged him to be, "more Irish than Harvard" but with a dash of Harvard intelligence, too. If the first Cuban crisis was the worst example of the uses of American power and diplomacy in this generation, the second Cuban crisis was the best. And the significance of this fact can be understood only in relation to the longer perspective of war in this century.

Twice in this century, the leaders of the free world have been confronted by the menacing power of a totalitarian state. From 1912 until 1914, and again from 1935 until 1939, Germany made a series of moves that clearly threatened the peace and order of the world, and during those critical testing periods, Britain, France and the United States failed either to raise enough military power or to show enough will power to avoid the holocaust. The resulting tragedies of the two great wars transformed the history of the world.

The Soviet decision to place long-range missiles in Cuba, capable of firing atomic rockets into almost any part of the United States, was a similar and in some ways even more ominous test. This lunge into the Western Hemisphere was clearly an effort to change the world balance of power in Moscow's favor, and Kennedy faced it at the risk of war and turned it back.

It is ironic that he went to his grave with many of his fellow countrymen condemning him for failing to get rid of all the Communists and all the defensive missiles in Cuba as well as all the offensive missiles. Yet this view has not been shared by most of the political leaders and historians of the world.

I saw Prime Minister Macmillan of Britain just before he resigned and before President Kennedy was murdered. "If Kennedy never did another thing," Macmillan remarked, "he assured his place in history by that single act. He did what we failed to do in the critical years before the two German wars."

Within a year of Kennedy's death, Khrushchev was removed from power, partly as a result of his humiliating defeat in the Cuban missile crisis, but something important and maybe even historic remained: The Communist world was relieved of the illusion that the United States would not risk atomic war to defend its vital interests. This new awareness greatly reduced the danger of miscalculating American intentions and led almost at once to the first really serious steps to bring atomic weapons under control.

II—The Home Front

Mr. Kennedy was more at ease in the larger world of diplomacy and the struggle between nations than he was in the world of Congressional politics and the struggle between contending national forces. He had more freedom of action in foreign than in domestic policy. He did not seem to mind the small talk of ceremonial meetings with heads of state or foreign students at the White House, and he had a rare combination of informality and dignity that made him very effective in this role. But blarneying with pompous Congressmen bored him and he simply would not take time to do it, as his successor, President Johnson, has with such marked success.

This was odd, in a way. He was a superb politician in planning and running a Presidential campaign, but he didn't really know the deck on Capitol Hill and he did not really like to play the political game there. Even though he spent most of his political life in the House and the Senate, he was always sort of a nonresident member of those peculiar clubs, always a back-bencher with a high truancy record and an excessive respect for the chairmen of the committees and the other elders of the Congress.

The very qualities of appearance, style and cast of mind that won him the admiration of the intellectual and diplomatic worlds somehow marked him as an outsider in his dealings with the Congress. He had little patience for the tiresome loquacity and endless details of legislation, and he never cared much for the boisterous bantering and backslapping of the cloakrooms.

He had a kind of gay magic as a political speaker, most of it as carefully contrived as it seemed spontaneous. He was good at the arts of Hollywood and Madison Avenue, and this delighted his fellow politicians, but he was a little too polished, ambitious and out of the ordinary to escape the envy and criticism of The Hill.

Congress likes typical Americans and Kennedy was not one. In his mature life, he probably crossed the Atlantic more often than he crossed the Allegheny range. He never seemed at home in the West. The America he understood best was bounded by Harvard Yard, the State Department, Park Avenue and Palm Beach. His political style and humor were not based on the exaggerated language and gymnastics of the American hustings but on the gentler models of the House of Commons.

Maybe these things had nothing to do with his troubles in getting a legislative program through the Congress; maybe it was just the old stubborn resistance of the Congress to change—"the government of the living by the dead"—but the fact remains that his domestic program was in deep trouble when he was killed, and some of us despaired that Capitol Hill would ever be his field of triumph.

Part of the Kennedy legend is connected with his introduction of the most radical legislation in behalf of Negro equality in this century. But again the reality is less romantic. He did not normally like to take on anything more than he had to tackle, no matter how worthy. Oddly for a man who wrote a book celebrating the heroes of lost causes ("Profiles in Courage"), he was always saying: "Why fight if you are not sure to win?" The Negro demonstrations in the summer of 1963, however, forced his hand, and he went along when some Republican leaders and his brother Robert urged that action was necessary.

Yet, on the home front, as in the foreign field, he did start one major innovation of transcending importance. At the urging of Walter Heller, the chairman of the Council of Economic Advisers, he broke with the traditional economic concepts of Capitol Hill and plunged for a large tax cut and a planned budget deficit. Liberal economists in Europe and in the American universities had been arguing for years that it was no longer necessary to redistribute the wealth of the rich in order to elevate the poor, but that the total production of wealth could be increased to the benefit of everybody if modern technology and fiscal measures were applied.

Kennedy was not by temper a fiscal reformer. He came to the White House as a rather timid liberal, but the longer he was in office the more he cried out against the restraining economic and fiscal traditions of the past and the more he appealed to the country to deal with the world as it is. He never saw his tax bill go through; he died before it was passed. But he was largely responsible for heading the country into the most prolonged period of peacetime prosperity since the last World War. There was a recession when he took over in 1961. Unemployment was up to almost 7 per cent of the work force. There was a balance-of-payments deficit of nearly $4 billion. The outflow of gold to other countries in 1960 totaled $1.7 billion. But by the time he died, this trend had been reversed, at least in part as a result of his initiatives.

III—The Imponderables

Yet even if he turned the tide of the cold war toward the control of nuclear arms, and started the trend toward acceptance of the new economics of increased production and general prosperity, this is not the Kennedy story that is likely to be remembered.

These things were only dramatic symbols of his critical mind. He was a critic of his age. He did not think we could deal with the menace of nuclear weapons unless we searched constantly for means of accommodation with the Communists. He did not think we could employ our people in the midst of a revolution in labor-saving machinery unless we changed our attitude toward Federal budgets and Federal deficits.

He did not think we could deal with the pressures of communism, rising population, or galloping automation, or that we could contain the rising expectations of the non-white races and the new nations unless we moved faster to integrate the races at home and the nations of the free world abroad. In short, he did not believe we could deal effectively with a transformed world unless we transformed ourselves—our attitudes of mind and our institutions.

This was a youthful mind asking the big questions. He was not one for big plans and grand designs, though contemporary writers often professed to see such things in some of the speeches of Ted Sorensen. Incidentally, it was always difficult to tell where the soaring rhetoric of Sorensen's bolder and more liberal mind left off and the more cautious Kennedy mind picked up, but Kennedy was not a great planner.

I once asked him in a long private talk at Hyannis Port what he wanted to have achieved by the time he rode down Pennsylvania Avenue with his successor. He looked at me as if I were a dreaming child. I tried again: Did he not feel the need of some goal to help guide his day-to-day decisions and priorities? Again a ghastly pause. It was only when I turned the question to immediate, tangible problems that he seized the point and rolled off a torrent of statistics about the difficulty of organizing nations at different levels of economic development.

Yet there is a puzzle in all this. For while he wanted to transform the thought and institutions of the nation, and regarded the machinery of the Congress as almost an anachronism, he concentrated on working—not, on the whole, very successfully—with the Congress, and he never really exploited his considerable gifts as a public educator.

"Give me the right word and the right accent," said Joseph Conrad, "and I will move the world." This was Churchill's way, and nobody admired it more than Kennedy. But while he made a few glorious trial flights, something held him back, some fear of appealing to the people over the heads of the Congress, some fear of too much talk (he hated verbosity), some modesty, maybe—always so apparent in his embarrassment before applauding crowds.

The essence of the tragedy, however, is perfectly clear. What was killed in Dallas was not only the President but the promise. The death of youth and the hope of youth, of the beauty and grace and the touch of magic.

The heart of the Kennedy legend is what might have been. His intelligence made people think that the coming generation might make the world more rational. It even made it hard for the intellectuals of Europe to be anti-American. His good looks and eloquence put a brighter shine on politics, and made his world relevant and attractive to young people all over the world.

All this is apparent in the faces of the people who come to his grave daily on the Arlington hill. In the world of their dreams,

Presidents would be young and heroic, with beautiful wives, and the ugly world would be transformed by their examples.

John Finley, the master of Eliot House at Harvard, sent me a letter which sums up this sense of loss better than anything else:

"No doubt like innumerable people, I feel suddenly old without Mr. and Mrs. Kennedy in the White House. On reflection, ours seems a society of older people; it takes a while to reach the top in science, law, business and most other things. Yet, paradoxically, only the young have the freshness to enjoy and not be wearied by the profusion and vitality of present American life.

"Not only by ability, but by sheer verve and joy, the Kennedys imparted their youth to everyone and put a sheen on our life that made it more youthful than it is. Mr. Johnson now seems Gary Cooper as President—'High Noon,' the poker game, the easy walk and masculine smile. But even Gary Cooper was growing older, and the companions and adversaries around the poker table reflect a less fresh, if no doubt practical and effective, mood. All will be well, I feel sure . . . but it is August, not June. . . ."

Always we come back to the same point. The tragedy of John Fitzgerald Kennedy was greater than the accomplishment, but in the end the tragedy enhances the accomplishment and revives the hope.

Thus the law of compensation operates. "The dice of God are always loaded," wrote Emerson. "For everything you have missed you have gained something else. . . . The world looks like a multiplication table, or a mathematical equation, which, turn it how you will, balances itself. . . . Every secret is told, every crime is punished, every virtue rewarded, every wrong redressed, in silence and certainty."

Part

THE JOHNSON ADMINISTRATION

The Candidates Spell Out the Issues

by Lyndon B. Johnson

THE CENTRAL ISSUE in this election is the oldest continuing issue of our American system—the issue of responsibility.

From 1789 to the present, responsibility has meant seeking, achieving and maintaining a consensus—a center of unity—on our nation's purposes and policies.

Amid the perils of these mid-century years, this will for unifying our strength has become a central thrust of American life—from the people and their Presidents alike. Members and leaders of both parties, Democratic and Republican, have concentrated upon broadening the vital center of American unity—and closing the dangerous door of American divisions.

The wisdom of this course is confirmed.

The world is responding to our defense of freedom and pursuit of peace through preparedness and patience. Of the many new nations born in these years, none has chosen Communism. In the steadfastness of our alliances, the growing unity of our hemisphere, the nearly universal support of the test-ban treaty, and many other measures, we see evidence of the world's trust of America's purposes.

Here at home, likewise, our American economy is responding to the growing center of unity among all its segments—the broadening consensus between business, labor, agriculture and government. This Administration is the first in a century not to have faced a recession

From the *New York Times Magazine*, November 1, 1964.

or depression. Instead, the nation has experienced the longest and strongest peacetime expansion in history—with the most stable prices in the Western world.

It is significant—and symptomatic of the new climate—that the second session of the 88th Congress this year was the most constructive and most productive of our history, with an outstanding record written by votes from both parties.

In this election, it is this center of unity which is under attack. For as the center of American agreement has grown broader, factions on the fringe have grown more determined in their opposition to—and criticism of—those in both parties who have sought, achieved or abided by the responsible consensus of our purposes and policies.

These factions wear many names. They espouse many causes. In their statements—and their actions—they demonstrate contempt toward the will of majorities, callousness toward the plight of minorities, arrogance toward allies, belligerence toward adversaries and carelessness toward peace.

On Nov. 3, the choice before American voters is not a choice between right and left, conservative and liberal, or even a true choice between Democratic and Republican views. It is a choice between the center and the fringe.

I stated earlier, in the course of this campaign, my belief that this election represents a turning-point in the history—and the destiny—of our nation. The events of recent days fortify that conviction.

Changes of profound potential have occurred within the Communist world. Communist Russia has acquired new leadership. Communist China has acquired a new nuclear capability. Clearly, it is imperative that in this period there must be continuity and stability in the purposes and policies of the United States.

Our position today is not the product of bluff and bluster. It is the product of courage, intelligence and reason—and these qualities we must demonstrate in full measure now.

Our peace, prosperity and progress rest upon the basic beliefs which a generation of responsible leadership has woven carefully into the fabric of America.

Our peace rests upon the basic belief that only men can bring peace—and a long succession of American Presidents have used our great power with great restraint, working always to lessen the dangers to freedom.

Our prosperity rests upon the basic belief that the work of free individuals makes a nation—and it is the job of government to help them do the best they can.

Our progress rests upon the basic belief that the object of leadership is to anticipate and help prepare for the future, rather than to preoccupy the people with repealing the past.

In this campaign, the attempt has been made to raise as "issues" the settled and successful policies supporting these basic beliefs. There is convincing evidence this effort has not succeeded.

The American majority has not accepted as relevant or responsible proposals such as our withdrawal from the United Nations, breaking relations with the Soviet Union, repudiating the test-ban treaty or using atomic weapons in Vietnam. The response has been the same toward proposals such as ending Social Security as we know it, withdrawing from education, selling T.V.A., stripping labor unions of their many gains, abandoning our agricultural policies or halting the program to improve life in our urban centers.

Out of this campaign, instead, there has come a strong and heartening rallying of public support to the consensus of our mid-century years. Areas of partisan differences have been laid aside. There has been a coming together of the people—a willingness to stand up and be counted in the pursuit of peace, the maintenance of prosperity and the devotion to prudent progress for all our people.

Americans realize, I believe, that the valid issues of this decade are those of the future—not the past. When the next President of the United States takes the oath of office next year, we shall be nearer the year 2000 than the year 1929. By that year 2000, there will be more than 300 million Americans—requiring more new jobs, new homes, new schools and new opportunities than we have ever provided in any comparable period of the past.

If America is to mean for those Americans what it has meant for us until now, America's political leadership must offer the highest standards of responsible performance.

There can be no stalemate within our system, no deadlock in our democracy. The talents, wisdom and strength of our people must be brought together to seek, achieve and maintain a new consensus on the quality of American life in the years ahead.

We have man's first chance to build the Great Society, where the meaning of man's life will match the marvels of man's labor. If we have leadership appealing to the best—not to the worst—within us, we can together build a good and decent society where no man or woman is the helpless victim of poverty or hatred or injustice.

Whether we honor this opportunity—or default it—is the real choice and the real issue of this election. I have confidence in the decision the people will reach on Nov. 3.

As this generation of Americans understands the price of recklessness and the cost of division, we have learned the rewards of responsibility and the bounty of unity. I believe this election will be a victory for the broad center of American life and experience. From that victory, we shall move ahead to bind up our wounds, heal our history and commit this nation to victory in the contests of this century as a nation whole—one nation, one people, indivisible, under God.

by Barry Goldwater

THE BASIC ISSUE of this campaign is clear. Either we continue the suicidal drift of the last generation away from constitutional government, away from moral order, away from freedom, and away from peace and order in the world community. Or we chart a new course of peace, freedom, morality and constitutional order based on the wisdom of our history.

That course will bring peace through strength, progress through freedom, and purpose through moral and constitutional order. It will stop the spread of socialism at home and Communism abroad.

Our Constitution gave us a government separated, balanced and dispersed. Yet we see our constitutional system changing before our eyes. We see the executive, aided by the judiciary, taking on more and more power over our lives. We see the judiciary openly seize the power to amend the Constitution—even to dictate whether children shall pray in local schools, how states shall form their legislatures, and how they shall apportion their districts. We see the 50 states being turned into just so many bureaus, their orders handed down from Washington.

And we are told that this is all good, because it brings about good results—good, that is, in the eyes of a self-appointed élite. Personal desires and social objectives take precedence over constitutional decisions.

What about the principle of legitimacy? Doesn't it matter any more whether somebody or some agency of government has the *right* to decide? What about the decision that is wrong? Once we accept the principle that the end justifies the means, there is no end but tyranny.

Equally dangerous is the alarming breakdown in law and order across the country. Crime is growing five times as fast as population. Our nation's capital itself ranks first among large cities in its rate of major crimes against persons. It has a rate four times the national average.

We are not plagued with this crisis in lawlessness because we are poor. We are the richest nation on earth. Our riches multiply each year, and our inequalities diminish.

The cause is deeper and more dangerous. Our traditional values of individual responsibility and moral obligation have been slipping away at a quickened pace. Corruption, immorality and cynicism reach to our highest offices and touch our most cherished institutions. Scandal itself casts a shadow across the darkened White House. Bad example radiates downward, while the apologists of collectivism preach that society is to blame for crime, not the criminal.

As if this were not enough, our highest court has been steadily taking away from local law enforcement agencies the powers needed to control law and order. The freedom and rights of law-abiding citizens have been jeopardized by obsessive concern for the criminal defendant.

The drift of a generation has also inverted the whole meaning of freedom. We are being told that freedom is something the Government can *give* us. We forget the cherished words of the Declaration of Independence: "We hold these truths to be self-evident, that all men are created equal, that they are endowed by their Creator with certain unalienable Rights." First, we were told government can make us free from want and fear. Now we are told government can make us free from poverty—free from worry and responsibility.

Does anybody really believe that *government* can make us rich and happy and confident and secure? Does anybody believe that there is somebody so wise and prudent and powerful that he can —or will—give us those things if we just put him in the White House?

The great wisdom of the founders and builders of this nation was to recognize that "power corrupts—absolute power corrupts absolutely." To them, freedom meant one thing: *freedom from oppressive government*. Let us recapture the true meaning of freedom and make it truly live.

Let us reaffirm our faith in the self-reliance, enterprise and initiative of the individual and family. Let us strengthen our economy of private enterprise, the mightiest engine of progress in the history of the world. Let us learn again that progress comes from work, initiative and investment—and means nothing more than fulfillment of the whole man in a society of freedom and opportunity.

Thirty-five years ago, government at all levels took command, through taxation, over only 12 per cent of personal income in this country. Today it commands 40 per cent. Thirty-five years ago, the Federal Government commanded only 4 per cent. Today it commands 25 per cent.

Government must be cut down to size or we will surely lose our free society. We will go the age-old way of tyranny and oppression.

And government must live within its means. The Federal Government has operated in the red in 29 of the last 35 years. Deficits have become normal in good as well as bad times. The present Administration has spent $27 billion more than its revenues over the last four years alone, running a deficit every single year. This fiscal irresponsibility spells the disaster of the cheapened dollar if it is allowed to continue.

When the Federal Government is cut down to size, it can then attend to its critical job of looking after foreign relations, national security and the general welfare.

And that brings us straight to the Presidency. The President, and nobody else, is responsible for the direction of our foreign policy and the leadership of this nation among all nations of the world. He is the man responsible for the state of our affairs throughout the world.

And our affairs are in *shambles* from one end of the world to the other. Our nation has lost dignity, respect and prestige everywhere—

among small powers as well as large. It has drifted into war through a policy of weakness, softness and irresolution.

There is a single cause: the "accommodation" of Communism. This Administration has completely and fatally misjudged the nature and intentions of the one real threat to the peace—international Communism. Nowhere is the bankruptcy of our policy of drift, deception, and defeat more evident than in the recent change of regime in the Soviet Union. This change clearly demonstrates that Khrushchev's "reasonable" stance was no more than a temporary and illusory diversion from the grand design. The strategy of world conquest remains the same. Only the tactics change. And we have been taken for a ride, a ride that has dangerously set back the cause of peace.

We must move as quickly as possible to rebuild a policy of strength and resolution, with the overriding goal of promoting our national interests. This is the only policy Communist leaders understand and respect.

We shall keep the peace if we rebuild our once grand alliances, now in tatters, and take a firm stand against Communist aggression. We must abandon the insane policy of trusting the word of Communist leaders and insist on concrete concessions and safeguards every step along the way toward a lasting peace.

When we take this course, peace and freedom will prevail—Communism will never bury us.

These, then, are the issues in this campaign. Which candidate will restore the Constitution, moral order and obedience to the law through personal example, popular appeal, proper appointments to the courts and support of local authorities? Which candidate will restore faith in the individual, faith in freedom, faith in fiscal integrity? Which candidate will cut government down to size and return it to the people along with their freedoms? Which candidate will restore peace in our domestic and foreign affairs?

You have the issues and you know the candidates. It is your responsibility to decide and vote.

The Great Society Is a Sick Society

by J. W. Fulbright

STANDING IN the smoke and rubble of Detroit, a Negro veteran said: "I just got back from Vietnam a few months ago, but you know, I think the war is here."

There are in fact two wars going on. One is the war of power politics which our soldiers are fighting in the jungles of Southeast Asia. The other is a war for America's soul which is being fought in the streets of Newark and Detroit and in the halls of Congress, in churches and protest meetings and on college campuses, and in the hearts and minds of silent Americans from Maine to Hawaii. I believe that the two wars have something to do with each other, not in the direct, tangibly causal way that bureaucrats require as proof of a connection between two things, but in a subtler moral and qualitative way that is no less real for being intangible. Each of these wars might well be going on in the absence of the other, but neither, I suspect, standing alone, would seem so hopeless and demoralizing.

The connection between Vietnam and Detroit is in their conflicting and incompatible demands upon traditional American values. The one demands that they be set aside, the other that they be fulfilled. The one demands the acceptance by America of an imperial role in the world, or of what our policymakers like to call the "responsibilities of power," or of what I have called the "arrogance of power." The other demands freedom and social justice at home, an end to poverty, the fulfillment of our flawed democracy and an

From the *New York Times Magazine,* August 20, 1967.

effort to create a role for ourselves in the world which is compatible with our traditional values. The question, it should be emphasized, is not whether it is *possible* to engage in traditional power politics abroad and at the same time to perfect democracy at home, but whether it is possible for *us Americans,* with our particular history and national character, to combine morally incompatible roles.

Administration officials tell us that we can indeed afford both Vietnam and the Great Society, and they produce impressive statistics of the gross national product to prove it. The statistics show financial capacity, but they do not show moral and psychological capacity. They do not show how a President preoccupied with bombing missions over North and South Vietnam can provide strong and consistent leadership for the renewal of our cities. They do not show how a Congress burdened with war costs and war measures, with emergency briefings and an endless series of dramatic appeals, with anxious constituents and a mounting anxiety of their own, can tend to the workaday business of studying social problems and legislating programs to meet them. Nor do the statistics tell how an anxious and puzzled people, bombarded by press and television with the bad news of American deaths in Vietnam, the "good news" of enemy deaths—and with vividly horrifying pictures to illustrate them —can be expected to support neighborhood antipoverty projects and national programs for urban renewal, employment and education. Anxiety about war does not breed compassion for one's neighbors nor do constant reminders of the cheapness of life abroad strengthen our faith in its sanctity at home. In these ways the war in Vietnam is poisoning and brutalizing our domestic life. Psychological incompatibility has proven to be more controlling than financial feasibility; and the Great Society has become a sick society.

When he visited America 100 years ago, Thomas Huxley wrote: "I cannot say that I am in the slightest degree impressed by your bigness, or your material resources, as such. Size is not grandeur, and territory does not make a nation. The great issue, about which hangs the terror of overhanging fate, is what are you going to do with all these things?"

The question is still with us, and we seem to have come to a time of historical crisis when its answer can no longer be deferred. Before the Second World War our world role was a potential role; we were important in the world for what we *could* do with our power, for the leadership we *might* provide, for the example we *might* set. Now the choices are almost gone: we are, almost, the world's self-appointed policeman; we are, almost, the world defender of the status quo. We are well on our way to becoming a traditional great power—an imperial nation if you will—engaged in the exercise of power for its own sake, exercising it to the limit of our capacity and beyond, filling every vacuum and extending the American "presence" to the farthest reaches of the earth. And, as with the great empires of the past, as the power grows, it is becoming an end in itself, separated except by ritual incantation from its initial motives, governed, it would seem, by its own mystique, power without philosophy or purpose.

That describes what we have *almost* become, but we have not become a traditional empire yet. The old values remain—the populism and the optimism, the individualism and the roughhewn equality, the friendliness and the good humor, the inventiveness and the zest for life, the caring about people and the sympathy for the underdog, and the idea, which goes back to the American Revolution, that maybe—just maybe—we can set an example of democracy and human dignity for the world.

That is something which none of the great empires of the past has ever done, or tried to do, or wanted to do, but we were bold enough —or presumptuous enough—to think that we might be able to do it. And there are a great many Americans who still think we can do it, or at least they want to try.

That, I believe, is what all the hue and cry is about—the dissent in the Senate and the protest marches in the cities, the letters to the President from student leaders and former Peace Corps volunteers, the lonely searching of conscience by a student facing the draft and the letter to a Senator from a soldier in the field who can no longer accept the official explanations of why he has been sent to fight in the jungles of Vietnam. All believe that their country was cut out for something more ennobling than imperial destiny. Our youth are showing that they still believe in the American dream, and their protests attest to its continuing vitality.

There appeared in a recent issue of the journal "Foreign Affairs" a curious little article complaining about the failure of many American intellectuals to support what the author regards as America's unavoidable "imperial role" in the world. The article took my attention because it seems a faithful statement of the governing philosophy of American foreign policy while also suggesting how little the makers of that policy appreciate the significance of the issue between themselves and their critics. It is taken for granted—not set forth as a hypothesis to be proven—that any great power, in the author's words, "is entangled in a web of responsibilities from which there is no hope of escape," and that "there is no way the United States, as the world's mightiest power, can avoid such an imperial role. . . ." The author's displeasure with the "intellectuals" (he uses the word more or less to describe people who disagree with the Administration's policy) is that, in the face of this alleged historical inevitability, they are putting up a disruptive, irritating and futile resistance. They are doing this, he believes, because they are believers in "ideology"—the better word would be "values" or "ideals"—and this causes their thinking to be "irrelevant" to foreign policy.

Here, inadvertently, the writer puts his finger on the nub of the current crisis. The students and churchmen and professors who are protesting the Vietnam war do not accept the notion that foreign policy is a matter of expedients to which values are irrelevant. They reject this notion because they understand, as some of our policymakers do not understand, that it is ultimately self-defeating to "fight fire with fire," that you cannot defend your values in a manner that does violence to those values without destroying the very thing you are trying to defend. They understand, as our policymakers do not, that when American soldiers are sent, in the name of freedom, to sustain corrupt dictators in a civil war, that when the Central Intelligence Agency subverts student organizations to engage in propaganda activities abroad, or when the Export-Import Bank is used by the Pentagon to finance secret arms sales abroad, damage—perhaps irreparable damage—is being done to the very values that are meant to be defended. The critics understand, as our policymakers do not, that, through the undemocratic expedients we have adopted for the defense of American democracy, we are weakening it to a degree that is beyond the resources of our bitterest enemies.

Nor do the dissenters accept the romantic view that a nation is powerless to choose the role it will play in the world, that some mystic force of history or destiny requires a powerful nation to be an imperial nation, dedicated to what Paul Goodman calls the "empty system of power," to the pursuit of power without purpose, philosophy or compassion. They do not accept the Hegelian concept of history as something out of control, as something that happens to us rather than something that we make. They do not accept the view that, because other great nations have pursued power for its own sake—a pursuit which invariably has ended in decline or disaster—America must do the same. They think we have some choice about our own future and that the best basis for exercising that choice is the values on which this republic was founded.

The critics of our current course also challenge the contention that the traditional methods of foreign policy are safe and prudent and realistic. They are understandably skeptical of their wise and experienced elders who, in the name of prudence, caution against any departure from the tried and true methods that have led in this century to Sarajevo, Munich and Dienbienphu. They think that the methods of the past have been tried and found wanting, and two world wars attest powerfully to their belief. Most of all, they think that, in this first era of human history in which man has acquired weapons which threaten his entire species with destruction, safety and prudence and realism require us to change the rules of a dangerous and discredited game, to try as we have never tried before to civilize and humanize international relations, not only for the sake of civilization and humanity but for the sake of survival.

Even the most ardent advocates of an imperial role for the United States would probably agree that the proper objective of our foreign policy is the fostering of a world environment in which we can, with reasonable security, devote our main energies to the realization of the values of our own society. This does not require the adoption or imposition of these values on anybody, but it does require us so to conduct ourselves that our society does not seem hateful and repugnant to others.

At the present, much of the world is repelled by America and what America seems to stand for. Both in our foreign affairs and in our domestic life we convey an image of violence; I do not care very much about images as distinguished from the things they reflect, but this image is rooted in reality. Abroad we are engaged in a savage and unsuccessful war against poor people in a small and backward nation. At home—largely because of the neglect resulting from 25 years of preoccupation with foreign involvements—our cities are exploding in violent protest against generations of social injustice. America, which only a few years ago seemed to the world to be a model of democracy and social justice, has become a symbol of violence and undisciplined power.

"It is excellent," wrote Shakespeare, "to have a giant's strength;

but it is tyrannous to use it like a giant." By using our power like a giant we are fostering a world environment which is, to put it mildly, uncongenial to our society. By our undisciplined use of physical power we have divested ourselves of a greater power: the power of example. How can we commend peaceful compromise to the Arabs and the Israelis when we are unwilling to suspend our relentless bombing of North Vietnam? How can we commend democratic social reform to Latin America when Newark, Detroit and Milwaukee are providing explosive evidence of our own inadequate efforts at democratic social reform? How can we commend the free enterprise system to Asians and Africans when in our own country it has produced vast, chaotic, noisy, dangerous and dirty urban complexes while poisoning the very air and land and water? There may come a time when Americans will again be able to commend their country as an example to the world and, more in hope than confidence, I retain my faith that there will; but to do so right at this moment would take more gall than I have.

Far from building a safe world environment for American values, our war in Vietnam and the domestic deterioration which it has aggravated are creating a most uncongenial world atmosphere for American ideas and values. The world has no need, in this age of nationalism and nuclear weapons, for a new imperial power, but there is a great need of moral leadership—by which I mean the leadership of decent example. That role could be ours but we have vacated the field, and all that has kept the Russians from filling it is their own lack of imagination.

At the same time, as we have noted, and of even greater fundamental importance, our purposeless and undisciplined use of power is causing a profound controversy in our own society. This in a way is something to be proud of. We have sickened but not succumbed, and just as a healthy body fights disease, we are fighting the alien concept which is being thrust upon us, not by history but by our policymakers in the Department of State and the Pentagon. We are proving the strength of the American dream by resisting the dream of an imperial destiny. We are demonstrating the validity of our traditional values by the difficulty we are having in betraying them.

The principal defenders of these values are our remarkable younger generation, something of whose spirit is expressed in a letter from an American soldier in Vietnam. Speaking of the phony propaganda on both sides, and then of the savagery of the war, of the people he describes as the "real casualties"—"the farmers and their families in the Delta mangled by air strikes, and the villagers here killed and burned out by our friendly Korean mercenaries"—this young soldier then asks, ". . . whatever has become of our dream? Where is that America that opposed tyrannies at every turn, without inquiring first whether some particular forms of tyranny might be of use to us? Of the three rights which men have, the first, as I recall, was the right to life. How, then, have we come to be killing so many in such a dubious cause?"

While the death toll mounts in Vietnam, it is mounting too in the war at home. During a single week of July 1967, 164 Americans were killed and 2,100 were wounded in city riots in the United States. We are truly fighting two wars and are doing badly in both. Each war feeds on the other and, although the President assures us that we have the resources to win both wars, in fact we are not winning either.

Together, the two wars have set in motion a process of deterioration in American society, and there is no question that each of the two crises is heightened by the impact of the other. Not only does the Vietnam war divert human and material resources from our festering cities; not only does it foster the conviction on the part of slum Negroes that their country is indifferent to their plight—in addition, the war feeds the idea of violence as a way of solving problems. If, as Mr. Rusk tells us, only the rain of bombs can bring Ho Chi Minh to reason, why should not the same principle apply at home? Why should not riots and snipers' bullets bring the white man to an awareness of the Negro's plight when peaceful programs for housing and jobs and training have been more rhetoric than reality? Ugly and shocking thoughts are in the American air, and they were forged in the Vietnam crucible. Black Power extremists talk of "wars of liberation" in the urban ghettos of America. A cartoon in a London newspaper showed the Negro soldiers in battle in Vietnam with one saying to the other: "This is going to be great training for civilian life."

The effect of domestic violence on the chances for peace in Vietnam may turn out to be no less damaging than the impact of the war on events at home. With their limited knowledge of the United States, the Vietcong and the North Vietnamese may regard the urban riots as a harbinger of impending breakdown and eventual American withdrawal from Vietnam, warranting stepped-up warfare and an uncompromising position on negotiations. It is possible that the several opportunities to negotiate, which our Government has let pass, most recently last winter, could not now be retrieved. Some 18 months ago Gen. Maxwell Taylor said in testimony before the Senate Foreign Relations Committee that the war was being prolonged by domestic dissent. That dissent was based in part on apprehension as to the effects of the war on our domestic life. Now the war is being prolonged by the domestic deterioration which has in fact occurred, and it is doubtful that all of the war dissenters in America, even if they wanted to, as they certainly do not, could give the enemy a fraction of the aid and comfort that have been given him by Newark, Detroit and Milwaukee.

An unnecessary and immoral war deserves in its own right to be liquidated; when its effect in addition is the aggravation of grave problems and the corrosion of values in our own society, its liquidation under terms of reasonable and honorable compromise is doubly imperative. Our country is being weakened by a grotesque inversion of priorities, the effects of which are becoming clear to more and more Americans—in the Congress, in the press and in the country at large. Even The Washington Post, a newspaper which has obsequiously supported the Administration's policy in Vietnam, took note in a recent editorial of the "ugly image of a world policeman incapable of policing itself" as against the "absolute necessity of a sound domestic base for an effective foreign policy," and then commented: "We are confronted simultaneously with an urgent domestic crisis and an urgent foreign crisis and our commitments to both are clear. We should deal with both with all the energy and time and resources that may be required. But if the moment ever arises when we cannot deal adequately and effectively with both, there is no shame—and some considerable logic—in making it plain beyond a doubt that our first consideration and our first priority rests with the security of the stockade."

Commenting on the same problem of priorities, Mayor Cavanaugh of Detroit said:

"What will it profit this country if we, say, put our man on the moon by 1970 and at the same time you can't walk down Woodward Avenue in this city without some fear of violence?

"And we may be able to pacify every village in Vietnam, over a period of years, but what good does it do if we can't pacify the American cities?

"What I am saying . . . is that our priorities in this country are all out of balance. . . . Maybe Detroit was a watershed this week in American history and it might well be that out of the ashes of this city comes the national resolve to do far more than anything we have done in the past."

Priorities are reflected in the things we spend money on. Far from being a dry accounting of bookkeepers, a nation's budget is full of moral implications; it tells what a society cares about and what it does not care about; it tells what its values are.

Here are a few statistics on American values: Since 1946 we have spent over $1.578-billion through our regular national budget. Of this amount over $904-billion, or 57.29 per cent of the total, has gone for military power. By contrast, less than $96-billion, or 6.08 per cent, was spent on "social functions" including education, health, labor and welfare programs, housing and community development. The Administration's budget for fiscal year 1968 calls for almost $76-billion to be spent on the military and only $15-billion for "social functions."

I would not say that we have shown ourselves to value weapons five or ten times as much as we value domestic social needs, as the figures suggest; certainly much of our military spending has been necessitated by genuine requirements of national security. I think, however, that we have embraced the necessity with excessive enthusiasm, that the Congress has been all too willing to provide unlimited sums for the military and not really very reluctant at all to offset these costs to a very small degree by cutting away funds for the poverty program and urban renewal, for rent supplements for the poor and even for a program to help protect slum children from being bitten by rats. Twenty million dollars a year to eliminate rats —about 1-100th of the monthly cost of the war in Vietnam—would not eliminate slum riots; but, as correspondent Tom Wicker has written, "It would only suggest that somebody cared." The discrepancy of attitudes tells at least as much about our national values as the discrepancy of dollars.

While the country sickens for lack of moral leadership, a most remarkable younger generation has taken up the standard of American idealism. Unlike so many of their elders, they have perceived the fraud and sham in American life and are unequivocally rejecting it. Some, the hippies, have simply withdrawn; and while we may regret the loss of their energies and their sense of decency, we can hardly gainsay their evaluation of the state of society. Others of our youth are sardonic and skeptical, not, I think, because they do not want ideals but because they want the genuine article and will not tolerate fraud. Others—students who wrestle with their consciences about the draft, soldiers who wrestle with their consciences about the war, Peace Corps volunteers who strive to light the spark of human dignity among the poor of India or Brazil and V.I.S.T.A. volunteers who try to do the same for our own poor in Harlem or Appalachia—are striving to keep alive the traditional values of American democracy.

They are not really radical, these young idealists, no more radical, that is, than Jefferson's idea of freedom, Lincoln's idea of equality or Wilson's idea of a peaceful community of nations. Some of them, it is true, are taking what many regard as radical action, but they are doing it in defense of traditional values and in protest against the radical departure from those values embodied in the idea of an imperial destiny for America.

The focus of their protest is the war in Vietnam, and the measure of their integrity is the fortitude with which they refuse to be deceived about it. By striking contrast with the young Germans, who accepted the Nazi evil because the values of their society had disintegrated and they had no moral frame of reference, these young Americans are demonstrating the vitality of American values. They are demonstrating that, while their country is capable of acting falsely to itself, it cannot do so without internal disruption, without calling forth the regenerative counterforce of protest from Americans who are willing to act in defense of the principles they were brought up to believe in.

The spirit of this regenerative generation has been richly demonstrated to me in letters from student leaders, from former Peace Corps volunteers and from soldiers fighting in Vietnam. I quoted from one earlier. Another letter that is both striking and representative was written by an officer still in Vietnam. He wrote:

"For 11 years I was, before this war, a regular commissioned officer—a professional military man in name and spirit; now—in name only. To fight well (as do the VC), a soldier must believe in his leadership. I, and many I have met, have lost faith in ours. Since I hold that duty to conscience is higher than duty to the Administration (not 'country' as cry the nationalists), I declined a promotion and have resigned my commission. I am to be discharged on my return, at which time I hope to contribute in some way to the search for peace in Vietnam."

Some years ago Archibald MacLeish characterized the American people as follows:

"Races didn't bother the Americans. They were something a lot better than any race. They were a People. They were the first self-constituted, self-declared, self-created People in the history of the world. And their manners were their own business. And so were their politics. And so, but 10 times so, were their souls."

Now the possession of their souls is being challenged by the false and dangerous dream of an imperial destiny. It may be that the challenge will succeed, that America will succumb to becoming a traditional empire and will reign for a time over what must surely be a moral if not a physical wasteland, and then, like the great empires of the past, will decline or fall. Or it may be that the effort to create so grotesque an anachronism will go up in flames of nuclear holocaust. But if I had to bet my money on what is going to happen, I would bet on this younger generation—this generation of young men and women who reject the inhumanity of war in a poor and distant land, who reject the poverty and sham in their own country, who are telling their elders what their elders ought to have known—that the price of empire is America's soul and that the price is too high.

George Wallace Figures to Win Even If He Loses

by Ray Jenkins

MONTGOMERY, ALA.

A LADY in Bell Gardens, Calif., was astonished to discover, as dusk approached one Sunday afternoon recently, a string band plunking out a country tune for a crowd gathered in the parking lot of the drab cinderblock town Legion hall. Sitting on the makeshift platform, of all people, was Chill Wills, the squeaky voiced character actor whom she had seen in half a dozen mediocre movies.

"What's this all about?" she asked.

"Ain'tcha heard, lady?" bubbled the response in warm Southern tones. "Governor Wallace is here, and he's runnin' for President. Come on over and get acquainted with George and sign up with us. It won't take but a minute."

The lady would not have given a second thought to this fanfare if she had lived in, say, Garden City, Alabama. Down here, the fiddle and the guitar and the gospel quartet are as much a part of politics as florid bombast. But this year, George Corley Wallace aims to give the nation a taste of that kind of politicking. In both form and substance, his campaign is altogether Southern, with a few disguises. Indeed, the basic assumption of this third-party movement is: if it worked in the South, it could work in the nation.

Many will look upon the Wallace venture as mere comic relief, fitting dark humor for an unusually somber election year. But the savants, both in politics and out, are genuinely alarmed that Wallace

From the *New York Times Magazine,* April 7, 1968.

just might be the monkey wrench which could jam the election machinery and profoundly affect the outcome of this year's Presidential race.

What makes Wallace run? "We intend to give the people a choice," goes the official line. "The two national parties are just Tweedledee and Tweedledum. There's not a dime's worth of difference between them."

But of course the real answer is much more complicated. It is to be found only in the man himself, and never is he more himself than he is before an outdoor rally in a suburb of Los Angeles, before a veterans' convention in Escanaba, Mich., or before a crowd of 3,000 who have turned out on a bitter cold night in Pittsburgh to cheer their champion on to victory. . . .

The luxurious grand ballroom of the hotel is overflowing long before the appointed hour. As the organ plays "The Battle Hymn of the Republic," the audience waits patiently—an audience composed of a few brave Negroes, a few more youthful non-conformists, still more teen-agers with simply nothing better to do with their evening, but mostly just average folks cutting across the age spectrum.

The organist suddenly shifts to "Dixie," and a few restrained whoops go up. But the church-like tone of the occasion is restored moments later by the strains of "God Bless America."

A hush falls over the ballroom as a white-haired minister approaches the podium. In a quavering voice, he addresses "our Lord and Savior Jesus Christ, thanking thee and praising thee for this great turnout. . . ." He calls the occasion "a revival" and thanks God for "this man who has been raised up in this emergency."

The lights are lowered, a spotlight focuses on the American flag onstage, and the audience rises for the pledge. The organist plays the National Anthem. No one sings; they simply listen reverently.

Now the mood changes. There is an anticipatory flourish as the magic moment approaches. The chairman for the evening, a well-groomed young man with a name that suggests Eastern European ancestry, introduces local dignitaries onstage. "You'll notice they're all sitting on the extreme right."

Now "The Wallace Girls," pretty local belles dressed in Confederate Gray, pass the hats—replicas of Uncle Sam's. "Put in your twenties and fifties and hundred dollar bills," the chairman admonishes good-naturedly. "Just small change." While the collection is being taken, he tells a joke about a leading portrait artist who wanted to paint the Supreme Court, but upon further reflection decided "a whitewash would do better."

To introduce the speaker, the chairman calls upon John Noble, who is presented as a man who endured "nine and a half years as a slave under brutal Communist oppression." Mr. Noble says a few words about his own endeavor, something called "The Trial Against International Communism," and introduces the man of the hour.

Somewhere in the audience a diminutive figure pops up. A thunderous roar drowns out the few boos and catcalls, and George Wallace strides briskly down the aisle and up the stage steps. For a few moments he holds his arms aloft acknowledging the adulation. Then he begins.

"I bring you greetings from my wife, the Governor of Alabama, who, as you know, has been under the weather in recent weeks. But she has given me a job to do—appointed me head of the highway beautification program. And you have no idea how boring it can be to go planting magnolia trees up and down the road."

A heckler shouts something from the back of the room. "Hey, fella," the speaker shoots back, "you got a boll weevil in your beard?" A roar of approval goes up. Confederate flags wave here and there. "That's right, George. You tell 'em, George."

After a few more jokes, he turns serious. "Now, what are the real issues that exist today in these United States? It is the trend of pseudo-intellectual government, where a select, élite group have written guidelines in bureaus and court decisions, have spoken from some pulpits, some college campuses, some newspaper offices, looking down their noses at the average man on the street, the glassworker, the steelworker, the autoworker, and the textile worker, the farmer, the policeman, the beautician and the barber, and the little businessman, saying to him that you do not know how to get up in the morning, or go to bed at night, unless we write you a guideline. . . ."

The "pseudo-intellectual" begins to take form as a kind of catch-all phantom who is monkeying with our liberties. "Joan Baaaaz—that's a pseudo-intellectual." So is "a bearded professor who thinks he knows how to settle the Vietnam war when he hasn't got sense enough to park a bicycle straight." Washington is full of pseudo-intellectuals writing guidelines which Federal judges use to destroy local institutions throughout the country. "When I get to be President, I'm gonna call in a bunch of bureaucrats and take away their briefcases and throw them in the Potomac River."

Congress itself is suspect. "You've got 535 big-talking members of Congress, and only six of them have got their children in the public schools of Washington. And yet they tell us how to run our schools. . . .

"I don't care what you people up here decide to do with your children. You can put your li'l children on a bus every morning and send them all the way across the state—if that's what you want to do.

"But when is it that the people of Pittsburgh don't know what they want to do without some pseudo-intellectual bureaucrat—usually with a beard—to write them a guideline?"

Now the delivery becomes rapid-fire and combative, fists thrusting into the air for emphasis. Both parties, Wallace says, supported the "so-called open-occupancy bill that would put you in jail without a trial by jury if you don't lease or sell your property to who they say."

But there'll be some changes made come January of 1969. "We're going to put through a legislative act that will do away with that Court decision that says a Communist can work in a defense plant without a security clearance." The strongest applause yet responds. When it dies down, he continues: "Frankly, I wouldn't trust a Communist *with* a security clearance."

He recalls that "some scum" tried to lie down in front of the President's car in California. "The President is entitled to personal respect, no matter how much you may disagree with him politically. But we can tell you this. When we get to be President and some anarchist lies down in front of our car, it'll be the *last* car he'll ever lie down in front of." This brings many to their feet in laughter and applause.

The number-one issue in this election is Vietnam, coupled with the breakdown of law and order. "And they are coupled. Those people who advocate a breakdown of law and order eventually wind up in Havana and Hanoi and Moscow."

The policeman won't be any "second-class citizen" in the next Administration. "If we were President today, you wouldn't get stabbed or raped in the shadow of the White House, even if we had to call out 30,000 troops and equip them with two-foot-long bayonets and station them every few feet apart." No one is safe any more since the courts have had their say about the right of criminals. "If you walk out of this hotel tonight and someone knocks you on the head, he'll be out of jail before you're out of the hospital, and on Monday morning, they'll try the policeman instead of the criminal."

Now shifting to infinite sarcastic mockery, he continues: "But some psychologist says, 'Well, he's not to blame—society's to blame. His father didn't take him to see the Pittsburgh Pirates when he was a little boy.' Well, I was raised in a house that didn't even have an indoor toilet. My mamma couldn't even buy me a dollar and fifteen cent cowboy suit that I saw in the Sears, Roebuck window. But I didn't go and bust the window out to get it."

Now he goes into a complicated yarn which he builds with considerable skill. The President and Governor Romney got into an argument over sending troops to Detroit. Romney didn't ask for them in the right way, it seems. "He was supposed to fill out a form in duplicate, triplicate, and quadruplicate . . . and in quintuplet, in sextuplet and septuplet . . . and even in *octopooplet*. My little wife said to me, 'You know, George, this is amusin' and confusin'. We got troops down here in Mississippi and Alabama and we didn't even ask for them."

A young man in the back of the room shouts, "Heil Hitler!" He is ignored.

Now the target becomes an old favorite. "There's a professor out in California that advocated revolution. Said, 'We ought to burn the town down.' Well, I can tell you this, if any professor in Alabama advocates burning the town down, my little wife's gonna see to it that he's a *fired* professor."

Professors are running around all over the place advocating a Vietcong victory. "I know there's good people here tonight who sincerely believe we should not be involved in Vietnam. I respect their opinion, I believe in the right of dissent. But when somebody advocates a Communist victory, he's advocating the killing of American boys, and that's treason. He ought to be drug before a grand jury and put *under* a Federal jail."

Suddenly there is a flourish on the floor. A dozen young men and women, acting on some unseen cue, stage a walkout. For a moment there is an edgy crisis, which Wallace senses. "Let's let 'em leave in peace. Please. Please do. Let's all be in a good humor tonight. You made me lose my place, anyhow."

Once the offenders have gone, he tells a funny story to restore the good mood. It goes back to 1964 in Maryland when he got 43 per cent of the vote in the Presidential primary. "In fact, we were leading early in the night. But then they announced they were going to have a recapitulation. And when they recapitulated, we wound up behind. I don't know what recapitulation means, but if anybody ever tells you 'I'm gonna recapitulate on you,' you better watch out, because they're gonna do something dirty to you."

Now he ends on a buoyant note, confidently predicting victory in November "for this people's movement." It has been a good rally. The response was so good that he went on much longer than usual—an hour and 11 minutes, to be precise. Now the throng surges down around him, and his short frame is soon swallowed up. Shouts of "President Wallace" are heard. Others gather around tables where pretty girls sell such campaign oddments as buttons, bumper stickers, tie-clasps, recorded speeches and the like for prices ranging from ten cents to $2.

Outside the ballroom, by odd coincidence, a convention of bio-physicists has brought a large number of professors to Pittsburgh from all over the nation. Many had lingered to watch the evening's affair. Some wore buttons which read "McCarthy" or "Peace." Some even wore beards. A young professor from California stood between two exhibits with the exotic titles of "zonal pump and gradient former" and "sw²dt" and watched the enraptured people stream out of the ballroom. "It's fantastic," he murmured. "They look just like ordinary people. It's what they respond to that's so startling."

Now, the nationalization of George Wallace's politics requires a degree of shifting here and there. It was easy enough to convert his slogan from "Stand Up for Alabama" to "Stand Up for America"—although the latter signs do appear a little incongruous emblazoned across the wall of the Jefferson Davis Hotel in Montgomery.

The New York Times and The Washington Post are convenient substitute targets for The Montgomery Advertiser and The Birmingham News. "The New York Times calls me a racist. Well, it's a sad come-off when you can't favor law and order without somebody asking if you're a racist. Anyway, who writes their editorials? It's just one man, and his opinion is no better than mine—not as good, in fact. Why, they even said Mao Tse-tung was a good man, and they called Castro the Robin *Hood* of the Caribbean."

Somewhat more difficult is the development of policy on such matters as the balance of payments, our attitude toward de Gaulle, or a policy for the Middle East—all matters of scant interest in Alabama.

But in the main this conversion requires no more than a few artful redefinitions. For instance, when reminded that a few years ago he shouted "segregation forever," he now says that all he really meant was "local government forever." On his up-North trips, he can now get away with statements that would have been political suicide in Alabama only 10 years ago. He once spoke admiringly of Roy Wilkins, and even said, "I have no objection to white and colored children going to school together"—hastening to add, "but I do object to courts and bureaucrats telling them they've *got* to go to school together." His celebrated "stand in the schoolhouse door," he now says, would have been made even if it had been a white student instead of a Negro who was ordered admitted to the University of Alabama by a Federal judge.

Being away from home also allows him to take the usual political liberties with history. In his out-of-state speeches, he speaks of the freedom-of-choice device to facilitate desegregation as if it were his own idea rather than a decree of a Federal court. And he never misses a chance to point out that his wife, in her race for Governor, "carried 87½ per cent of the Negro vote in Selma"—without bothering to recall that those same Negroes voted overwhelmingly against Mrs. Wallace in the only crucial race, the Democratic primary, and that in the general election, she was merely the beneficiary of straight-ticket voting encouraged by Negro leaders who were desperate to beat the repressive Sheriff Jim Clark, who was waging a fervent write-in campaign against the Democratic nominee, Wilson Baker.

He can even boast that Negroes live "within 75 feet of the Governor's mansion in Montgomery"—not adding that they occupy barely visible side-street shacks put up decades ago as servants' quarters for resplendent antebellum mansions like the Governor's official residence.

To get maximum exposure, Wallace schedules as many press conferences and television interviews as possible between rallies. These exchanges rarely develop any new information, but Wallace relishes the battle of wits and usually comes out on top.

If someone questions him about Ku Klux Klan support, he responds that "the Communist Daily Worker supported President Johnson, but that doesn't make the President a Communist." Does he accept the support of the John Birch Society? "The Birch society is anti-Communist, and I have no objection to anyone who is anti-Communist."

Is he cultivating the backlash vote? "The only backlash in this country is the backlash against government for allowing a breakdown of law and order."

Such conferences are usually attended by Wallace partisans who, to the dismay of reporters, burst into vigorous applause when their man scores a telling point.

Wallace travels by plane, even though he is genuinely horrified by flying. "It's the worst thing about running for President." He is always the first to detect any unusual noises in the engine, and a mere bump in the air will cut him off in midsentence to rush to the window and peer out. He was the first to detect an oil leakage which forced a quick return shortly after take-off from Montgomery in late February.

He usually travels in a four-engine DC6 provided by Henry L. Seale, a wealthy Dallas aviation executive and a political sympathizer. Seale once told a reporter the plane was being provided free of charge, but later he revised his statement—apparently at the urging of Montgomery—to say that a fee was being charged.

The traveling entourage usually includes a few politicians and staff aides, a couple of personal friends (such as Dave Silverman, bass-voiced cigar-smoking Montgomery jeweler), two pretty girls out of Wallace headquarters to serve as hostesses, some newspapermen, and a varying number of Alabama State Troopers, both in and out of uniform, some equipped with walkie-talkies and all equipped with firearms.

On one California trip, Wallace brought along no fewer than 16 state police officers, and before some audiences he delivered his speech from a bulletproof podium which covered him from three sides, his head barely visible above the massive walls.

These elaborate precautions raise a good deal of anxiety at home and puzzlement elsewhere. When questioned Wallace will pass off the matter lightly, saying there are "just too many anarchists running around the country" to take any chance. Or he might respond with a wisecrack: "We brought 'em along to keep me from biting myself," he said in Pittsburgh—his answer to Senator Hugh Scott's remark the day before that if Wallace bit himself, he might die of blood poisoning.

But police departments and local campaign headquarters in some places where he speaks do not look upon the security matter as a joke. His appearance is frequently preceded by convincing anonymous telephone threats of assassination or indiscriminate bomb-planting. Even at so sedate a place as Dartmouth College, there was a risky moment when hostile students surrounded his car after the speech—an episode which brought an official apology from the college.

The threat of violence also bedevils the campaign in another way; local officials are often afraid to have Wallace in their community. Two nights of tense disorder followed his appearance in Omaha early this month, and on at least three other occasions local police officials have asked him to cancel speeches because the climate appeared dangerous. He always feels compelled to honor such requests.

Is Wallace serious about winning?

He sounds increasingly so in public and private. As early as last fall, he was heard to murmur as he peered out of the plane's window over some remote plain of the Far West, "Just think! Some day I'll be President of all that!"

Winning, however, involves a certain amount of mathematical legerdemain. This is discussed at great length in a "position paper" emanating from the florid pen of a press functionary in the Wallace campaign. It begins: "Can a former truck driver who is married to a former dime store clerk and whose father was a plain dirt farmer be elected President of the United States?"

The answer is an unequivocal "yes," since the hero described is George Wallace. "With three candidates in the race," this paper proclaims, "Wallace would need only 34 per cent of the vote if the other two candidates split the remaining 66 per cent. With four candidates running, Wallace could conceivably win with only 26 per cent of the vote. It is even possible for a candidate to win by carrying 12 of the larger states with only 25 per cent of the vote."

A little history is cited to underscore the point. In 1824, Andrew Jackson led John Quincy Adams in electoral votes, but since neither had a majority the election went into the House of Representatives and Adams won. In 1876, Rutherford B. Hayes trailed Samuel J. Tilden by a quarter of a million popular votes, yet won the Presidency by one electoral vote.

Such examples as these provide a clue to Wallace's secondary strategy: He sees the possibility of bringing about some kind of 20th-century version of the Hayes-Tilden compromise which signaled the end of military reconstruction in the South 92 years ago. In a really close election, Wallace might nail down only a handful of Southern electoral votes and still prevent a major candidate from getting a majority. Matters would then be open for negotiation. He might release his electoral votes to either candidate who was willing to make "a solemn covenant with the American people." This covenant would bring about "a kind of coalition Government like they have in some other countries."

To get the Wallace electoral votes, a Presidential contender would be expected to promise faithfully and publicly that the Federal Government would abandon such obnoxious schemes as open-housing proposals. Apportionment of the State Legislatures and control of schools and hospitals would be turned back to the states, exclusively. Foreign aid would be terminated to such countries as Yugoslavia and to any nation doing business with the North Vietnamese. "Different oriented" men would have to be appointed to the Supreme Court. "That's the kind of covenant they'd have to make," Wallace says exultantly.

Even beyond the Electoral College, of course, might be the ultimate deal-making opportunity that would come if the election were thrown into the House of Representatives—an eventuality which would be brought about by the failure of any candidate to get the necessary votes. In the House showdown, each state would have one vote for President and a stalemate would be entirely within the realm of possibility.

What is missing from this wishful speculation, of course, is the possibility suggested by most reliable polls that Wallace would take more votes away from the Republican nominee of moderate or conservative persuasion—Nixon or Reagan—than from a Democrat, thereby making it possible for the Democrat to win crucial states with pluralities rather than outright majorities. When confronted with this thesis, Wallace argues that we would wind up "no worse off" since all the major candidates are equally unacceptable—even Reagan. Besides, his own polls—conducted by television studios which solicit telephone calls expressing preference—show him winning over all challengers by margins of 60 per cent or better.

There is still a final Wallace strategy. If all plans this year go haywire and the President is re-elected, the 1968 campaign can be regarded as a "warm-up race"—a standard practice in Alabama gubernatorial contests. (Like most Alabama Governors, Wallace ran an unsuccessful race in 1958 before being elected in 1962.) Wallace has long contended that the nation is ripe for a cataclysmic realignment of politics which will mean the death of one of the national parties. He envisions himself as a prime influence in this realignment of liberals and conservatives.

It does not seem to trouble him that he is selling a novel brand of conservatism, and so far he has been successful to a degree. The president of the local John Birch Society and the president of the local trade union can sit down side by side at a Wallace rally and each find something to cheer.

Wallace speaks of Senator Barry Goldwater as "a good man, but a poor candidate. He didn't have the massive support that we have among the working people."

In a rambling discourse on conservatism, Wallace gave a definition boiled down to this: Federal activity is "liberal" but states' rights progressivism is "conservative" because it "conserves our resources."

Some traditional conservatives are concerned enough over Wallace's candidacy to attempt to expose the Governor's tax-borrow-and-spend policies which have prevailed in Alabama for the last five years. Since he was inaugurated in 1963, Wallace has tripled the state debt to finance education, road-building, hospitals, and other services. His tax programs differ from his Populist predecessors' only in that he tends to hit the consumer rather than "soak the rich." In five years of two Wallace administrations, the sales tax has gone from 3 to 4 per cent, an extra three cents has been levied on cigarettes and beer, and $10 has been added to the price of automobile tags. This money has been used to provide free textbooks to school children, locate junior colleges and trade schools within easy school-bus reach of every community, and build new hospitals for the retarded and mentally ill.

The conservative weekly newsletter, Human Events, has given wide distribution to a detailed exposé of Wallace's liberal state policies. But when Human Events polled 220 leading conservative writers, politicians and organization heads, 30 per cent responded that they believed Wallace to be a fiscal conservative and 25 per cent said they did not believe he was appealing to race prejudice—figures which suggest an unawareness of Wallace's state programs on the part of conventional conservatives.

Wallace is also under conservative attack from a former Alabamian, Gov. Claude Kirk of Florida. Kirk has appointed himself as a "one-man truth squad" to go about the country exposing what he calls "the Johnson-Wallace plot" to get the President re-elected. Adapting an enemy ploy, he calls Wallace a "pseudo-conservative."

(By one of those curious ironies that permeate Southern politics, Governor Kirk's father was appointed by Wallace to a high state position—the state's adviser on how to get money out of Washington. Governor Kirk once observed that he hoped his attacks wouldn't get his father fired. Wallace snapped back that of course they would not, because the senior Kirk was more attuned to Wallace politics than his son's.)

Gearing up a national organization to run for President has proved to be no simple endeavor. In some states—notably Ohio and Idaho—it is so difficult to get on the ballot that the Wallace forces are challenging the qualifying laws in court. But campaign aides are confident Wallace will be on the ballot in at least 36 states.

As things now stand, the vehicle for running—the American Independent party—is largely a formless, memberless, *ad hoc* organization. California is the only state where it has any appreciable membership (100,000).

Wallace has picked up the support of a political bigwig here and there, such as the Arkansas segregationist Jim Johnson, and Plaquemines Parish's redoubtable Leander Perez. Former Gov. Marvin Griffin of Georgia, whose scandal-ridden administration prevented him from making a political comeback, agreed to serve as an interim Vice Presidential candidate, necessary to meet certain legal requirements in some states until someone better can be found. Other assorted celebrities, besides the movie star Chill Wills, include a retired Marine general and a 1964 Goldwater elector from California.

But in the main Wallace is obliged to rely upon political amateurs to carry the ball in local organizations. The John Birch Society has been a particularly fruitful source of local talent; in Washington, for instance, more than half of his 40-member state campaign committee are said to be society members.

Also, spontaneous, unauthorized organizations of dubious pedigree keep horning in on the act. At one time or another, freelance Wallace organizations have been put together by a Ku Klux Klansman, a Minuteman, an American Nazi. In South Carolina, two well-organized groups of Wallace backers are feuding for leadership, one claiming to represent "the little man" and accusing the other (the officially recognized one) of representing "big business."

The California party was hardly in business before its leadership fell to bickering. An insurgent group held a rump session of the party's board of directors and wrested the leadership from the state chairman, William K. Shearer, a Los Angeles publicist who has been involved in a number of successful right-wing endeavors. Shearer responded by filing a million-dollar suit against the challengers and obtaining a court order recognizing him as the official party leader. Thereupon, Wallace fired Shearer, who refused to accept his discharge and still proclaims himself loyal to Wallace.

Similar intrafactional difficulties have developed in Virginia, where Wallace's genteel conservative backers have been appalled at the unwillingness to disown unequivocally the Klan, the Patriotic party, and other such elements. When questioned about support from such elements, Wallace usually minimizes their importance and will only disavow in general terms the backing of any organization that advocates violence.

Thus, what professional tone there is in the Wallace campaign is supplied almost exclusively by Alabama. Seven top state officials—including such old political hands as State Finance Director Seymore Trammell and gubernatorial aide Cecil Jackson—have left the state payroll to put their talents into the Presidential venture. The campaign headquarters now takes up most of the space in a new spic-and-span five-story building which affords visitors an excellent panoramic view of the few crumbling mansions which have thus far escaped the wrecking ball on the edges of downtown Montgomery.

The operation is manned by a staff of 25, and one rates low in protocol if his office floor is not carpeted or his wall is not adorned with a map of the country peppered with colored pins. One lady even has four large clocks behind her desk—one for each time zone. The office bulletin board is plastered with campaign schedules, cartoons casting L.B.J. in a ludicrous light, and a campaign button which reads "Lyndon for Emperor."

The Wallace campaign has been bedeviled by embarrassing ineptitude. For instance, elaborate plans were made to hold the Wallace "national convention" at Miami Beach immediately following the Republican convention in order to take advantage of the television equipment already on the scene. But the whole deal was blown when somebody neglected his reservation duties and allowed a convention of car dealers to grab off the hall.

A half-hour TV program boosting the Wallace cause was scheduled to be shown over WMET-TV in Baltimore, but was urgently canceled when word got back to Alabama that the station beams mostly to the Negro community. Even Wallace's reliable supporters have contributed their share of gaucheries. Former Governor Griffin, asked if he would remain loyal to the cause even if he had to step aside as the Vice Presidential candidate, responded with an innocent, but profoundly inappropriate metaphor: "I'll be there when we tree the coon."

Campaign financing is one of the murkiest areas of the Wallace Presidential venture. Ask where the money's coming from, and the answer is, "from the little people all over the country who support the movement."

These mail contributions do add up to an appreciable sum. Campaign headquarters reports that an average of 2,000 letters a day arrive with donations ranging from two dimes Scotch-taped to a laboriously scrawled message of support on tablet paper, on up to three-figure checks from businessmen in such unlikely places as Wichita. The average contribution, Wallace aides say, is $5. This source, therefore, can be expected to produce less than $2-million between now and November.

There is a so-called "dollar-a-month" club, and the campaign has leased a computer which can disgorge more than 21,000 names of pledged donors on a moment's notice. But obviously this kind of financing cannot raise the kind of money which the campaign's financial managers feel will be necessary—estimated variously from $9-million to $15-million.

Many suspect that a source of campaign funds is H. L. Hunt, the Texas multimillionaire who has talked privately with Wallace on occasion. But Hunt insists he isn't bank-rolling the campaign, and Wallace once observed ruefully that the only thing Hunt ever gave him was a "bunch of pamphlets."

More likely lucrative sources are the standard suppliers of political funds within the state of Alabama—contractors doing business with the state, upper-level state employees who owe their jobs to the administration, and the like. Wallace, in what may have been a slip of the tongue, recently blurted out at one press conference that "the good people of Alabama raised $350,000" for the do-or-die effort to gain a ballot position in California. Candidates for various statewide offices have grumbled that "there just isn't any political money in Alabama this year. The well has been pumped dry."

The precarious health of Gov. Lurleen Wallace continues to becloud the whole campaign. The decision has already been made that the race will go on even if Mrs. Wallace is unable to continue as Governor. She has already sanctioned as much by saying the decision to run was "a joint decision, made by the two of us. . . . It is exactly what we told the people of Alabama we would do . . . of course, it has my blessings." Once she even interrupted her radiation treatments for cancer and flew to California to spend Thanksgiving with her husband and to make a few encouraging remarks at one of his rallies.

Nonetheless, her illness has a severely limiting effect on the movements of the candidate, who remains near his wife's bedside during the most critical moments. Already she has undergone surgery for cancer three times in the short span of two years, and has received radiation treatment for more than 10 weeks as well. Her last surgery was an emergency case, performed only two days after her husband returned from a campaign trip in Pennsylvania in late February and on the very day that he was supposed to make an important appearance in Florida. The crucial Florida trip, billed as "a major address" before 2,000 well-heeled supporters, had to be canceled while Wallace stood by in the Montgomery hospital.

Under Alabama law, only the Governor herself can determine whether she is physically incapable of carrying on the duties of office, thereby turning the office over to the Lieutenant Governor. When asked if such a step was contemplated, even temporarily, a top Wallace aide snapped without hesitation, "No, sir!"

The Lieutenant Governor is Albert Brewer, 39, who has been aligned with Wallace in the State Legislature. He is, nevertheless, an independent progressive who has long yearned to be Governor and it is regarded as inconceivable that he would function in the manner of a housewife who happened to be elected Governor. "Albert figures that if he will have to bear the responsibility," one of his close friends said, "he will make the decisions."

Should Wallace lose his status as the *de facto* Governor (although he holds no official position, he routinely occupies the Governor's office and functions as the state's chief executive), needless to say he would suffer not only a loss in prestige but in his ability to command support of the home folks in the Presidential effort. His current power is illustrated by the six out of the state's seven top elected officials who answered the call to serve as Wallace Presidential electors in Alabama. Also on the ticket are the wives of the two leading candidates for the U.S. Senate.

Meantime, Wallace sets a killing pace for his associates both at home and on the hustings. He can drive himself for 18 hours a day, stopping only to wolf down a sandwich here and there. His energy stems partly from the fact that he is a nondrinker (although he chews and puffs incessantly on cheap cigars) and that his political interests are totally consuming.

It is difficult for him to cut off the campaign spiel in his private conversations, even when he is talking to sophisticated people. His words usually just get tougher. "The way to control a riot is to shoot the first person that throws a brick. Bop 'em on the head." He likes to describe, complete with shadow-boxing gestures, how his fans gave the bum's rush to a noisy critic at one of his rallies.

He seems to yearn to win over even his most intractable critics. "Bigots, you call our people," he once sneered at a newspaper critic. Then he went on in a curious and uncharacteristic outburst of compassion: "Well, no matter what they are, they're *people,* and they don't deserve to be kicked around for their beliefs."

The Haunting of
Robert Kennedy

by Victor S. Navasky

Kennedy white but alright
The one before, he opened the door
—Crayoned sign in the window
of Kennedy headquarters in the
Negro section of Omaha.

THE FOUR HORSEMEN of Robert Kennedy's race for the Presidency of the United States are a ghost, a shadow, an image and a specter. The ghost is the idealized memory of his brother, President John F. Kennedy. The shadow, cast by the ghost, is what gets in the way of the voter trying to see Robert as a man rather than as a Kennedy. The image of Robert's ruthlessness is at least partly a legacy of his service to his brother. And the specter is of a Kennedy dynasty.

Despite the candidate's belated decision—roughly coterminous with President Johnson's withdrawal—to campaign without reference to his brother, these four restless spirits continue to haunt and at times dominate his search for delegates, for voters, for a program and, yes, for himself. It is ironic that one of the best-known of Americans is, for a significant slice of the electorate, an invisible man. They look at Robert, and they see John, or they see a stereotype, or they see the whole damn family. The candidate himself is not immune. His younger brother Teddy is reported to have remarked, after Robert

From the *New York Times Magazine*, June 2, 1968.

disregarded his advice not to run, "Bobby's therapy is going to cost the family $8-million."

For Robert Kennedy to run without reference to the Kennedy issue, as he now seems determined to do, is like an American Negro running without reference to his color. He may prefer for reasons of politics, character and/or personality not to discuss it, but for many voters it will make the difference.

No longer does he open and close speeches, as he did at Kansas State University, with references to and quotes from John F. Kennedy. Not once in nine days of following him through Indiana and Nebraska, with side trips to South Dakota, Iowa, Ohio and Michigan, did I hear him mention the New Frontier by name. He went out of his way *not* to visit the John F. Kennedy College in Wahoo, Neb., and when asked why, he mentioned only that his brother Teddy had already been there. In fact, a recurring theme of his campaign is that "the policies of the thirties were not adequate for the sixties, and the policies of the early sixties are not adequate to meet the problems of the seventies and eighties."

Nevertheless, it is not irrelevant that I boarded the plane for Indiana at John F. Kennedy Airport in New York, and the last speech I heard him make before returning home was at John F. Kennedy Square in Detroit. And when Papert, Koenig, Lois, Inc., Kennedy's advertising agency, asked the Nebraska Kennedy operation which of three or four half-hour TV films they preferred, they selected the only one in which the late President has a featured role, an updated biography originally prepared for Robert Kennedy's 1964 Senate race in New York.

The impact of John F. Kennedy on the 1968 electorate is the great subliminal issue of the campaign, so familiar that it has been assumed rather than analyzed. New York is really the only state which has been through a Robert Kennedy campaign, and it is useful to recall the words of New York Post columnist Murray Kempton, who now runs as a McCarthy delegate. At the time he said:

"I am for Robert Kennedy because he is a decent and talented young man terribly wounded whom I do not want to look upon wounded further. This is like being for Bonnie Prince Charlie; it has to do with commitment to a divine right and there are no reasonable arguments for a divine right."

The Ghost

"I'm not asking favors," Robert Kennedy told a gathering of Ohio delegates at Neil House Hotel in Columbus. "I'm not asking your support on the basis that you were friendly to a relative of mine eight years ago. . . ." But he was three hours late for the meeting because his motorcade from the airport was mobbed by thousands of black citizens. According to recent polls, 94 per cent of the black community believes that Robert Kennedy "has many of the same outstanding qualities as his brother" (as compared to only 39 per cent of the general population). "I have two pictures on my wall," said a Negro waiting during his lunch hour for Robert Kennedy to emerge from the Sheraton Cadillac Hotel in Detroit, "Jesus Christ and John F. Kennedy."

You can't hear Robert Kennedy tell the people of Nebraska City that 14 million people "go to bed hungry every night" without recalling that in his brother's day it was 17 million. You can't hear him tell a Purdue student, "I don't concede that once we get to the negotiating table we're going to fail," without recalling John Kennedy's "Let us never negotiate from fear, but let us never fear to negotiate." You can't hear him talk to a real estate group about "making a determination and a judgment" without recalling John F. Kennedy uttering the same words as he fidgeted with the middle button of his jacket at one of the live televised Presidential press conferences he originated. You can't watch Robert Kennedy's nervous and sometimes trembling hands without recalling the famous John Kennedy one-handed chopping motion. You can't hear Robert Kennedy promise to "turn the country around" without going back to the days when John Kennedy wanted "to get the country moving again." John also, according to 1960 polls, wore his hair too long.

The candidate arrives for a twilight street rally in Mishawaka, Ind., and over the loudspeaker we are told, "We loved John Kennedy when he was President, and we will love Bobby." The candidate attends a Jefferson-Jackson Day dinner at the Omaha civic auditorium, and the chairman calls him "a man who brings with him a memory of a happy time." The candidate speaks from the steps of City Hall in Nebraska City, and on the lawn a mother pushes a stroller bearing the sign: "Nebraska City's little J.F.K. welcomes you." The candidate arrives at Davenport Municipal Airport in

Iowa, and in the crowd is 85-year-old Durward Boyles, retired Rock Island Line railroad man. "I thought a lot of John," says Boyles. "My wife and I got a picture of John in a frame. He was so good to everybody we don't understand why they killed him. We think a lot of them Kennedy boys. John was so good I know Robert will be the same." The front-page, four-column lead in Davenport's Times-Democrat begins, "It was on a Tuesday in October, 1960, that Kennedy's brother, John F., drew an estimated 10,000 persons into the streets jutting off the corner of East Second and Main Streets. . . . R.F.K. will also address an outdoor rally at the same intersection." The candidate enters the lobby of the Savory Hotel, Des Moines, and a middle-aged lady asks one of the red, white and blue Kennedy girls if she can get one of those straw hats with the R.F.K. ribbon on it. Informed that they are all out, she says regretfully, "I have one at home with J.F.K. on the crown, but I didn't think to bring it."

At the beginning, I am told, Robert Kennedy was regularly requesting, in his brother's words, that the voters give him their help, their hands and their hearts. Undoubtedly his pollsters set him straight. Too many people were checking off the entry which reads, "He is trying to get elected on his brother's memory, and that is wrong." I heard him make at least 75 speeches without once providing genuine cause for the charge of demagoguery on the Kennedy issue. Of course, the point is that he doesn't have to be a demagogue. (To do so might even be ineffective demagoguery.) It's there, and there's not much he can do about it.

Early in the campaign a reporter from The Boston Herald-Traveler, who had known John Kennedy, was arguing with a colleague. "See, see!" said his friend. "Listen to him. He's trying to sound like his brother." The Bostonian replied, "You dumb sonofabitch. He *is* his brother's brother. Who the hell *do* you expect him to sound like?"

The Shadow

Robert Kennedy can't just come to town. He comes to town in comparison with his brother John. What other Presidential candidate has ever been plagued by bumper stickers reading "Bobby Ain't Jack"? When a lady standing on the lawn in Beatrice, Neb., turns to her neighbor and says, "He's shorter than I thought," isn't she really saying that he is not as tall as John Kennedy? The candidate himself senses the special shadow in which he acts. When asked why, given his sense of urgency about the war in Vietnam, he waited until after McCarthy's New Hampshire victory to declare, he says, "I probably made a mistake. But at the time I thought people would think if I won the primaries it was because of me personally, because of my relationship to John Kennedy."

Upon hearing that President Johnson had taken himself out of the race, Senator McCarthy is reported to have commented, "Until now, Bobby has been running as Jack against Lyndon. Now he's going to have to run as himself against Jack."

By that I take it he meant that Robert would have to emerge from John's shadow, from the Kennedy Administration's penumbra, and among other things explicitly repudiate some New Frontier policies, programs and assumptions. The observation has proved only partly prophetic. Where John Kennedy was preoccupied with the missile gap and the space race ("America must be first . . . not first when, not first if, not first but . . . first period"), Robert now says things like, "It is more important to be able to walk through the ghetto than to walk on the moon," and he would cut back the appropriations for development of the supersonic transport. Also, he has repeatedly acknowledged that when history assesses America's involvement in Vietnam, both he and the Kennedy Administration will bear their "share of the blame, the responsibility."

But readers of his book "To Seek a Newer World" and followers of his Senate career know that long before the campaign he was on record in favor of a post-cold-war, post-New-Frontier liberalism—one which had abandoned anti-Communism as the organizing principle of our foreign policy and had embraced community participation (à la Bedford-Stuyvesant) as the key to domestic tranquillity and progress. The difference is that until March 31, 1968, he was involved in a complicated dialectic, moving from what the New Frontier might have been and what the Great Society never was, toward a vision of his own. Johnson was the usurper, and Robert, in William Shannon's useful phrase, was "the heir apparent."

His initial campaign oratory, in which he accused the President of "calling upon the darker impulses of the American spirit," reflected the intensity of his own inner struggle. "He had to get it out of his system," says an aide. But when Johnson withdrew, he took the Vietnam issue with him and shipped it over to Paris in Averell

Harriman's attaché case. Now Robert Kennedy had a new problem: in addition to the preservation and definition of his newly emerging identity, he had to build a bridge between the issues which brought him into the campaign and the actions which might win him a majority of the delegates at the Chicago convention.

"The over-all strategy is remarkably like 1960," says Ted Sorensen, who handles day-to-day operations in the informal campaign directorate. "We have to use the primaries to impress the industrial states like Michigan, Illinois, Ohio, Pennsylvania and New Jersey that the people are on our side."

But Kennedy's rhetorical solution has been a kind of intellectual DMZ, where the Old Right meets the New Left. At least in places like Sioux Falls, S. D., Hastings, Neb., Davenport, Iowa, and Crawfordsville, Ind., the noisy code words are conservative, the quiet elaborations are progressive and consistent with positions set forth in "To Seek a Newer World." VIOLENCE, LOOTING, RIOTING and CRIME IN THE STREETS are UNACCEPTABLE and LAW AND ORDER MUST BE RESTORED (with social justice); THE WELFARE SYSTEM MUST BE REPLACED (by a job system); RUNNING THINGS FROM WASHINGTON IS UNACCEPTABLE and MUST BE REPLACED BY LOCAL CONTROL (under Federal standards); THE FEDERAL GOVERNMENT CAN'T SOLVE THE PROBLEMS OF THE CORE CITY; it needs the help of PRIVATE ENTERPRISE which will come in if given TAX CREDITS and OTHER INCENTIVES. Even on Vietnam the candidate is OPPOSED TO UNILATERAL WITHDRAWAL, but doesn't like to see AMERICAN CASUALTIES CLIMBING WHILE SOUTH VIETNAMESE CASUALTIES GO DOWN (regardless of what happens at the negotiating table). IT IS UNACCEPTABLE THAT AMERICAN BOYS ARE DYING WHILE SOUTH VIETNAMESE BOYS CAN BUY THEIR WAY OUT OF THE DRAFT.

Sorensen's memoirs quote Henry Stimson's observation: "Campaign speeches are not a proper subject for a friendly biographer." That may be true, and a close reading of Robert's off-the-cuff remarks reveals a consistent commitment to decentralization, community participation and equal justice at home, and de-escalation abroad. Nevertheless, a content analysis of his language on the stump might help explain why Robert Kennedy has yet to cast a more clearly defined shadow of his own.

The Image

Lou Harris, who was the official Kennedy pollster in 1960 but who has since parted ways with the family, found as late as May that 57 per cent of those polled nationally feel that Robert is "trying to get elected on his brother's memory." But in Indiana, in the wake of the hard-fought primary, the figure went down to 35 per cent. At the same time 52 per cent of the Hoosiers polled thought he had "many of the same qualities as his brother." He had managed to retain a fidelity to John's image while emerging from John's shadow. "He's got one national profile and different state profiles where he has campaigned in the primaries," says Harris. "The question is whether he can bring them into line." "Put bluntly," says a critic, "the question is whether he can spend enough to wrench public attitudes around on a national basis."

Robert Kennedy entered the race trying to convince the voters that he was right about Vietnam. He has ended up trying to convince them that they are wrong about him, that he is not "ruthless," "calculating," "opportunistic." His best arguments are the genuine compassion he displays when in the presence of the very old, the very sick or the very young, and his natural, bantering, non-ruthless question-answering style—considerably looser than the more controlled campaign performance of John, whose sense of humor didn't really surface until after he was President:

At Purdue:
Q.: Can you think of any reason other than your name, money and opportunism that qualifies you to run for President?
R.F.K.: Yes. (*Laughter.*)

*

At Creighton University:
Q.: What's the difference between you and Senator Eugene McCarthy?
R.F.K.: Charm . . . a sense of humor . . . and he's ruthless. I'm only kidding. I don't want to see headlines tomorrow saying, "Kennedy Charges McCarthy Ruthless!"

*

At Wahoo, Neb., where a reporter from the high school newspaper showed him the results of a student poll and asked if he had any comment:

R.F.K.: Yes. Tell those who voted for me, thank you.

Q.: What about those who voted against you?

R.F.K.: Tell them I'll get them. *(Laughter from the press corps.)*

*

Across the street from a movie marquee advertising "The Happiest Millionaire":

R.F.K. (pointing at the sign): Make that come true on election day!

Such spontaneity invariably earns him more support than he had when he arrived. Still, the relevance of his brother to his image should not be underestimated. That, presumably, is why Arthur Schlesinger, Jr., commenced his brief on behalf of R.F.K.'s candidacy (printed first in The New Republic and then as an ad in this newspaper): "I must confess a certain sense of *déjà vu* in sitting down to do this piece. Eight years ago this month many Americans were persuaded that John F. Kennedy was a ruthless political opportunist, shouldering aside more deserving and principled men in his driving ambition for the Presidency. . . . I do not think that we who argued for John Kennedy in 1960 misled anyone who bothered to listen to us. I argue with the same conviction for Robert Kennedy today."

This in turn gave McCarthy supporter Ed Costikyan, former New York County Democratic chairman, the opportunity to complain in a letter to the editor of The Times that Schlesinger was seeking "to erase the image of ruthless opportunism which Mr. Kennedy has justly earned by blackening the memory of John F. Kennedy.

"Of late it has been said again and again by Robert Kennedy apologists that John Kennedy was regarded as a ruthless opportunist when he ran for President. This was not true. John F. Kennedy's image in 1960 was one of youth, and perhaps of brashness in seeking the Presidency at his age, but not of ruthlessness or opportunism at all. Those words then, as now, were reserved for his younger brother."

The fact is that whether or not Schlesinger's description is accurate seems slightly beside the point. What is relevant is that, while John was alive, it seems to have been family policy to displace anti-Kennedy sentiment onto Robert ("I don't have to be charming. I'm not the candidate," he is reported to have said in 1960), just as it is now family-retainer policy to capture on Robert's behalf the halo of sentiment which crowns John's memory.

One thing is indisputable. If Robert functioned as a lightning rod for Jack, he was a predisposed lightning rod. Teddy can't fulfill the same role for Robert—too many people like him. "The trouble with this campaign," says a pro-Kennedy national committeewoman from a major Midwestern state, "is that the candidate doesn't have a Robert Kennedy working for him."

The Specter

The specter of a Kennedy dynasty continues to haunt the electorate. I guess it's because the prospect of a superfamily threatens the American dream that anybody can grow up to be President of the United States. In any event, one Kennedy-watcher has already informed us, "In 1992 Joseph P. Kennedy, 3rd, Bobby's eldest son, will be 40, the age at which Uncle Jack started his drive for the Presidency. John John will be 30, the same age Uncle Teddy was when he entered the Senate."

Not that everybody is distressed at the prospect. Democratic Senator George McGovern of South Dakota pointed out when he introduced Robert Kennedy at an Omaha rally, "I've had the privilege of knowing all three of these brothers. As my colleague Senator Russell has said, this is one of the most remarkable families on the face of the earth. They have overcome the handicap of wealth."

People have been conditioned to accept the omnipresence of the Kennedy family to such an extent that when I asked a taxi driver in Lincoln, Neb., who he thought would win the primary, he said, "The Kennedys have a lot going for them." It would never have occurred to him, or me, to think of any other candidate in the plural. ("The Nixons have a lot going for them"?)

Those politicians who don't view the Kennedys with alarm see the family as a convenience. Robert Kennedy himself admits, "Some political leaders refuse to do business with anybody but a member of the family. They know that Steve (Stephen Smith, R.F.K.'s brother-in-law who is directing the campaign) and Ted don't want anything for themselves, and they don't feel they can trust anyone else."

Nonetheless, unease about the Kennedys persists. For every man like the fellow on the Omaha courthouse steps who said he thought he'd go along with Kennedy because "it seems to me that maybe we can get two peas out of the same pod," there is another man who has already convicted him of guilty chromosomes. As one nationally prominent psychologist put it when I asked him if he thought the nation had any unconscious guilt about the assassination of President Kennedy, "There's not only unconscious guilt. There's also such a thing as conscious guilt. One of us killed President Kennedy so now we're saddled with the whole family. They'll capitalize on it whether they want to or not."

In November, 1963, most Americans spent four or five days at their television sets immersed in the ritual of John Kennedy's funeral. It was a powerful, profound and intense experience. They shared Robert Kennedy's sorrow and vicariously felt the grief he felt. They became, in an intimate sense, members of the family. Too much has happened since to attempt an electoral extrapolation based on such data. But one man who has given considerable thought to the Kennedy phenomenon deserves a hearing. He is Chuck Morgan, a liberal Atlanta, Ga., attorney, author and Kennedy supporter, who distinguished himself during the fight for integration in Birmingham, Ala., in the early sixties. Here is his theory:

"In 1952, Congressman John F. Kennedy let it be known that he wanted to run for the Senate against Henry Cabot Lodge. Everybody said, 'You can't do that. He's from the oldest and most respected political family in the state.' John Kennedy was elected. In 1960, when word got around that he wanted to run for President, people told him, 'You can't do that—you're too young, and you're a Catholic. Besides, if you get the nomination, you'll never be elected President.' After he was elected, and the rumor got out that he was thinking of appointing his brother Attorney General, people were outraged. They said, 'You can't do that—he's your brother. Besides, he's never practiced law.' So he appointed his brother Attorney General, and he went on to be one of the best. Then comes 1962, and Teddy Kennedy announced that he was going to run for the Senate. 'You can't do that—you got in trouble at Harvard, and you're barely old enough to vote, much less run for the Senate.' Today everybody says he's the best politician in the family. Anyway, in 1964, Robert Kennedy, who is from Massachusetts, who was working in Washington and living in Virginia, announced that he was going to run for Senator from New York. My best friends told me he couldn't do that. Well, now you mean to sit here and seriously tell me you don't think Robert Kennedy is going to be the next President of the United States? To some people, at least, this record would appear to suggest a doctrine of historical inevitability."

Report on the Phenomenon Named McCarthy

by Tom Wicker

IT MIGHT WELL be said of Gene McCarthy's Presidential campaign that nothing in it became him like the beginning of it. No matter how it turns out at the Democratic convention this week—or in November, if the improbable happens here, as it often has to Mc-Carthy—who will ever forget that romantic David-and-Goliath battle with President Johnson in New Hampshire, that astonishing outpouring of young people willing to be "clean for Gene" in order to overthrow Johnson, and the great "moral victory" that resulted on March 12?

After that, of course, Robert Kennedy jumped into the race, Johnson got out, and the year took on a different, darker quality. But I remember roaming around with McCarthy in Claremont, N. H., one cold, clear February day before anybody thought much of his chances and while most of the press was looking elsewhere. He was greeted with such overwhelming indifference in a downtown street tour that a normal candidate would have had his advance man's head; but McCarthy wasn't sure he had had an advance man.

Then he escaped to the Hotel Moody, where the Rotary Club was meeting. Somebody had persuaded President Rodney Brock to let McCarthy speak, provided he talked about public affairs instead of politics (one of the great underlying facts of American politics is that voters everywhere consider this distinction valid and politicians know it). Television cameramen came in and began routinely setting

From the *New York Times Magazine*, August 25, 1968.

_vilish tools, whereupon Brock ordered them out and made
... He was not going to have Rotary exploited either for politics
_ television, he said, and I thought this simple defiance of contemporary society and values probably would be the most admirable
event of the entire 10-month Presidential campaign that then stretched
ominously before us.

But I reckoned without Gene McCarthy. "Apparently untroubled
by the absence of television, before which most politicians bow and
scrape like valets," I reported in The Times, "the Senator spoke
in his relaxed manner and with his corrosive wit ('We don't declare
war any more, we declare national defense') and gave the Rotarians
—if not much of a show, by Ronald Reagan standards—a clear
picture of himself.

"It was a picture of a man who had set out to discuss what he
called 'two or three questions of vital importance' and who was
deeply in earnest about the need for the nation 'to turn aside from
the war in order to attend to the most pressing problem at home'—
which he defined as the rebellion of Negroes against any longer being
'a kind of colonial people in our own country.'

"He was unemotional, undramatic and nothing about his speech
or his manner was hoked up for cheap applause or enthusiasm. He
even treated his audience as though it would understand his points
and allusions and respond sensibly to his ideas. He said what he
had to say, with some eloquence but no particular flourish, and then
he sat down."

Neither Rodney Brock nor McCarthy, I wrote, could be accused
"of showing an image rather than a self," and no doubt that was
bad politics, but "in an age when the image is the idol, the old
values are inspected by avid tourists, and the flagrant falsities and
pretensions of American life deride verity, two men stubbornly being
themselves must be worth something."

That night (after taking vigorous part in a local ice hockey game)
McCarthy was relaxing in his room at a Concord motel, dropping
his sizzling sentences like pats of butter on a red-hot griddle ("The
function of liberal Republicans," he said at one point, "is to shoot
the wounded after the battle"). Somebody asked him whether the
Communists' Tet offensive, which had opened on Jan. 31, would
make votes for him in New Hampshire.

"Give it three weeks," McCarthy said. "Time to sink in. By then
it could make the difference."

Just about three weeks later everybody began to write that McCarthy was drawing crowds and coming up fast. The kids were arriving by the busload to help out in house-to-house canvassing. What had started off almost as a joke—McCarthy himself sometimes seemed not to take his candidacy seriously; asked if he would withdraw if Kennedy entered, he said it "might be less voluntary than that"—became the major shaping force of the 1968 Presidential campaign.

Viewed as no more than that, McCarthy's importance is easy to evaluate. His New Hampshire exploit exposed the political weakness of Lyndon Johnson and the political potential of an antiwar campaign. Together with Kennedy's entry and the Tet offensive, McCarthy's candidacy forced Johnson's withdrawal, which paved the way to the Paris negotiations. If none of this had happened, Richard Nixon, Hubert Humphrey and Nelson Rockefeller might well have remained overtly hawkish. Kennedy's murder came before the Democratic nomination was decided, but in the primary battles McCarthy defeated Kennedy in Oregon and ran close to him in California, and thus prevented any possibility of a delegate stampede.

Perhaps more important, McCarthy's willingness to challenge Johnson and what had seemed his unchangeable policy electrified American youth, evoked their idealism and energy, and largely justified his hopes of moving their protest against the war into normal political channels.

Standing amid the encrusted coffee cups, empty beer bottles, scattered papers and overflowing ashtrays of McCarthy's campaign headquarters on the morning after New Hampshire, Richard N. Goodwin told the young volunteers of what had been derided as "The Children's Crusade":

"The least you did was to prove Johnson is vulnerable. And by that you made a major contribution to national politics that will change the policies of the Republican party as well as the Democratic."

Even McCarthy's severest critics concede all this, but the tendency still is to regard him as a potential "footnote in history," to see his story being lost in the grief and drama of Kennedy's death, the onrush of world events and—by general assumption—the forthcoming Nixon-Humphrey campaign. But this is to weigh him only on the traditional scales of political value, and this hardly seems adequate to the McCarthy case.

McCarthy started out last Nov. 30 in the Senate caucus room—he said—to take the issue of Vietnam to the American people, at a time when it seemed that no one else would, and to "restore to many people a belief in the processes of American politics."

This frightened no one—particularly at a time when General Westmoreland and Ambassador Ellsworth Bunker had just been in Washington, assuring Americans that the end was beginning to be in sight in Vietnam. Nor was the challenger regarded as a heavyweight.

In Congress for 20 years, McCarthy had once been looked upon as one of the brighter members of the House; in the Senate, he had voted the prevailing liberal line but he was not regarded as a leader. He was celebrated in Washington as a wit and dinner companion, he had somehow managed to debate both Joe McCarthy and Barry Goldwater on national television, and Lyndon Johnson had almost—but not quite—made him Vice President in 1964. There was a school of thought that believed his challenge to Johnson in 1968 was petty revenge.

McCarthy was simply hard to credit in Presidential politics. He had not been among the earliest or loudest critics of the war; he had no visible following or base of strength; on Capitol Hill, he was regarded by insiders as too eager for speaking-date honoraria. A member of Johnson's Cabinet told me seriously and angrily that McCarthy only wanted to drive up his speaker's fees and book sales.

Worse were the charges that he was not a zealous defender of the public weal within the Senate Finance Committee, and that he had helped open some tax loopholes and refused to help close a few others. One Senator who endorsed another Democrat for the Presidency privately said his reason was that "he is a graduate of the House Ways and Means Committee, and that's a bad school."

Nine months after McCarthy's announcement of his candidacy (it was not a sudden decision he said, "nothing like St. Paul being knocked off his horse"), it is necessary to recall how hopeless and even foolish it then seemed to realize what McCarthy has accomplished and how far he has gone beyond his first stated objectives.

He has rejected virtually the whole of postwar American foreign policy. He has questioned the post-Rooseveltian theory of a strong Presidency. He has contradicted and challenged the post-World War II political fixations on anti-Communism, military strength and an activist foreign policy. In technique he has turned abruptly from both the hortatory personal style Americans had become accustomed to and the interest-group base-touching that had been regarded as elementary in a democratic system; Negroes and the poor get no special attention, either. He has rather casually promised to fire J. Edgar Hoover, and in the Oregon primary gracelessly pointed out that the well-educated were voting for him and the poorly educated were for Kennedy; it was true but, by political tradition, impolitic.

Moreover, McCarthy personally is caustic, not particularly generous to opponents, often lackadaisical and boring in his public appearances, and usually uninterested in "turning on" a crowd with the kind of oratorical passion that marked Kennedy's campaign. Once he showed up early for a speech in Los Angeles, found virtually no one on hand, delivered the speech anyway and was on his way before the audience began to gather. The District of Columbia delegation found him so uninterested in their questions that when he told them to go look up his record a Negro delegate burst out: "Record, hell! Tell us what you feel."

He alienated the Kennedy family and its associates with his sharp attacks on them, and he never developed strong political ties with the poor and the blacks, and for those reasons he has not been able to unite anti-Administration Democrats sufficiently to overcome the Humphrey-Johnson control of the party organization. The Indiana primary campaign was botched, and there was no reason to be as unresponding as he was to some delegates who might have been honorably persuaded to back him. It was inexcusable to address the California delegation in August and never mention the name of the man to whom it was originally pledged—Robert Kennedy.

Since McCarthy began his improbable journey as an insurgent candidate running against an incumbent President of his own party, something not done seriously in American politics since 1912, and since he made an issue of moral opposition to a war in which a half-million "American boys" were engaged with what the Pentagon invariably calls "the enemy," it is clear that Eugene McCarthy has broken virtually every taboo, and challenged almost every assumption of pre-1968 political life.

This reckless course, at one level, demonstrated sharp concern about the growth of state power as a force in the lives of American individuals. He did not so much oppose Hoover and Gen. Lewis Hershey personally; he said that they had become virtually unchecked centers of power, and therefore dangerous. It was after Nicholas

Katzenbach said that Congressional declarations of war could have their "functional equivalent" in Presidential interpretations of other Congressional acts that McCarthy told reporters:

"This is the wildest testimony I ever heard. There is only one thing to do—take it to the country."

Other McCarthy targets—the C.I.A., the Pentagon, L.B.J., even the Presidency—appear to derive from this fundamental reserve about state power.

At a somewhat different level, McCarthy obviously has concluded that the conditioning of national social and political development by the New Deal and cold war experiences was of increasing irrelevance to the contemporary situation at home and abroad. So have most other intelligent political leaders, notably Robert Kennedy, and to a lesser extent Humphrey, and in a more partisan sense Nixon. But McCarthy, more than any of them, turned sharply away from these experiences, apparently in confidence that such an abrupt departure from the "mainstream" would find its constituency.

It did—and a further political fact began to be evident. In an age of overwhelming and impersonal institutions—the Government, the corporation, the union, Selective Service, the city, the eight-lane highway, the beehive apartment building, Lyndon Johnson's Presidency—Gene McCarthy began to look like one man against the juggernaut, like the inner-directed and indomitable free spirit that all men wish themselves to be, at least in their romantic dreams.

Though of different political substance, this was not unlike the profound appeal Barry Goldwater once made to millions of Americans; and the Gridiron Club of Washington was more perceptive than it knew when, just before the New Hampshire primary, it roasted McCarthy unmercifully as a political Don Quixote with a dove in one hand and a white flag in the other.

So McCarthy has moved through the campaign in his relaxed, almost indifferent style, shattering assumptions, surviving Johnson and the primary battles, drawing crowds that are astonishing in size and enthusiasm, consistently leading Nixon in the polls, often leading Humphrey and Kennedy; surveys taken for Rockefeller showed that McCarthy would carry both New York and California against any Republican opponent while Humphrey would lose to either Nixon or Rockefeller.

This suggests that he just might be the "most electable" Democrat, and some Humphrey men want him for Vice President. Even some party "pros" are finally coming into his camp, and a march of maybe 100,000 people who support him is planned for this city this week.

If it is still unlikely that he will be nominated or elected President, it is nevertheless true, therefore, that by challenging and questioning and even ignoring so many things that had seemed ordained, he turned loose a political force that had been waiting for liberation and in doing so became its unlikely champion.

There is at least one institutional reason why McCarthy probably will not be nominated; it is that convention delegates in neither party are entirely responsive to public opinion. Often boss-controlled, usually party functionaries, attuned to the orthodox and the bland, placing higher value on party unity than on issues of principle, delegates do not normally reward people like Estes Kefauver and Gene McCarthy—people who do not "wait their turn" or "play on the team" or keep quiet "for the good of the party," and particularly not if a man of this type is also, in McCarthy's phrase, "the messenger who brought the bad news."

Modern delegates, like the ancient kings, McCarthy frequently remarks, usually kill such messengers, out of sheer annoyance with them. And he well knows that his 42 per cent of the New Hampshire vote "brought the bad news" to President Johnson and the Democratic delegates now gathering in Chicago.

Even against this kind of problem, McCarthy has made a contribution. Vice President Humphrey, worried about appearing to shut out a legitimate challenger, has urged that all delegates committed to him under a state unit rule be allowed to vote as individuals, and it is likely that, after 1968, the unit rule will be outlawed in the Democratic, as it has been in the Republican, party. Moreover, McCarthy's vocal and energetic supporters, free of the usual bonds of party loyalty, have raised so much fuss about unfair apportionment of delegates that New York, for instance, was forced to make adjustments, and the whole delegate and convention system has been brought under greater public scrutiny.

There also is at least one technological reason for his "electability" —television. Marshall McLuhan's "cool" medium seems just right for Eugene McCarthy, who can be cool enough to freeze a live audience. Understated, handsome, controlled, McCarthy usually comes across with considerable impact on the home screen—not least because there is very little that is contrived about his appearances.

He has almost no television drawbacks—no distracting gestures or dark jowls, no off-key or irritating voice sounds—and a way of looking frankly and directly into the camera. In Portland, Ore., on Saturday night before the primary, he first delivered to an uproarious rally crowd a sharply phrased speech, then went to a television studio and—without a note or a prompter, and in complete sentences—tossed off a half-hour *live* speech that timed out precisely.

McLuhan believes McCarthy on television conveys the "yokel quality" of "a small-town philosopher" and that this gives him a "nice, modest rapport with the young." More generally, McLuhan may have put his finger on a major part of McCarthy's appeal:

"If Canada's Pierre Trudeau is a great TV image in politics," McLuhan wrote, "it is because he is indifferent to political power. Anyone who looks as if he *wants* to be elected had best stay off TV." There is plenty of evidence to suggest that a lot of Americans go for McCarthy—and Ronald Reagan, for instance—precisely because neither looks or sounds traditionally political.

But though television helps McCarthy, it by no means explains him. He first set forth in detail his assault on postwar foreign policy, for instance, in a late-night speech on a Saturday at the Cow Palace in San Francisco—a typical McCarthy gesture of indifference to the usual tactics of communication, in which one would never schedule a major speech out of prime time and at an hour virtually guaranteed to get it ignored in the big East Coast Sunday papers.

"America in the period of the fifties and sixties," McCarthy said that night, "built up for itself a mission in which we were to take upon ourselves the duty to judge the political systems of other nations —nearly all the nations of the world—accepting that we had the right to interfere with all of those systems—if we found them to be wanting. We spoke with great flourish of making the world safe for diversity while, in fact, we were denying and even destroying diversity when it failed to meet our specifications and our standards.

"We put little confidence in diversity in Latin America unless that diversity acknowledged the authority of the United States of America or our position. Diversity in Southeastern Asia became a positive obstacle to American purposes."

This resulted in a diplomacy, McCarthy said, "assuming for itself the role of the world's judge and the world's policeman," and which rested upon such assumptions as "America's moral mission in the world; the great threat from China; the theory of monolithic Communist conspiracy; the susceptibility of political problems to military solutions; the duty to impose American idealism upon foreign cultures, especially in Asia." And the crucial point was that "gradually these assumptions, built into institutions, became more or less articles of faith and tended to escape any kind of examination or any kind of accountability to national politics or to the people of this country."

Again and again there appears in McCarthy's speeches this theme of accountability, or responsibility, of judgment and decision rather than acquiescence.

"If there is one central theme to my campaign," he said at Milwaukee the day before Johnson withdrew, "it is the President's duty to liberate individuals so they may determine their own lives, to restore that mastery and power over individual life and social enterprise which has been so seriously eroded by the growing impersonality of our society and by the misuse of central power."

This insistence, together with his reservations and fears about state institutions that could develop unchecked power over individuals, underlies McCarthy's controversial views about the Presidency itself.

A President, he has said, must first "be able to read with reasonable judgment the needs and the aspirations of the people," and then "he must also know the limitations of power." This, he said, would make it an office "which belongs not to the man who holds it but to the people of this nation; an office which must be exercised by the will of the majority . . . not in the sole interest of that majority but by their determination for the good of the entire nation."

Thus, he said, what was needed was not so much Presidential leadership in the Johnsonian sense of consensus to enact a particular program but a President who could "be a kind of channel for those desires and those aspirations, perhaps give some direction to the movement of the country, largely by setting people free." Only in that way, he suggested, could the Presidency play what he called its true role of "uniting this nation, not of adding it up some way, not of putting it together as a kind of odd-sized jigsaw puzzle, and not even to organize this nation, for to unify this nation means to inspire it."

All of this recognizes not only the limitations of the so-called "strong Presidency" (like Kennedy's troubles with Congress) but also its dangers—for instance, the extent to which Johnson waged war in Vietnam without sanction of the electorate or formal authorization from Congress. But more than that, it is an attempt to bring the Presidency, too, into the central theme of accountability, responsibility, individual judgment. The President must unify by inspiration, inspire by setting free. Institutionalized assumptions automatically accepted, carefully constructed political coalitions for acting upon those assumptions—both must yield to the interaction of responsible citizens and responsive government.

The distinction between traditional Presidential leadership and the "inspiration" McCarthy calls for is by no means clear, and how one proceeds without some supporting political coalition is even less defined. These remarks, taken with his respectable but unimpressive Senate record and his relaxed attitude, have caused serious charges to be raised that McCarthy would be a weak or passive President if elected.

He is the only candidate running "against the powers of the Presidency," Arthur M. Schlesinger, Jr., has said, and in a television interview McCarthy himself would go no further than to predict that he would be "adequate" in the White House.

By the standards of those convinced that only a President "in the forefront of the battle," in John Kennedy's phrase, can meet the demands of the age, McCarthy probably would not be even "adequate." It is incongruous to think of him driving bills through a reluctant House, for instance, or knocking labor leaders' heads together in the White House Fish Room in order to get a big strike settled.

But it is equally incongruous to think of him sending the Marines to the Dominican Republic. His Senate record and his campaign pledges show a commitment to bring all Americans, including Negroes, into "an order of justice," and his position papers on this are detailed and sensible, even if he has not shown any more passion on this than on any other issue.

Whether the low-pressure White House he seems to envision, the rather collective government of responsible Cabinet officials he has talked about, could get such a job done better and faster than a hard-driving Johnsonian Presidency is highly debatable. But where it clearly fits his campaign, and fits McCarthy, is that it envisions citizens who take part, who judge, who hold a President accountable, who therefore accept as much responsibility for the Presidency as does the President.

The very idea of a less personal, less expansive Presidency, coming from a liberal intellectual rather than a conservative traditionalist, is the essence of the thing; it is another effort, however flawed, to bring people into the act, to reduce the awesome loom of institutions over individuals, to revive their sense of participation in and control of affairs affecting their destinies.

Not all the manifestations of "participation" that McCarthy's campaign has let loose have been welcome. Zealots drowning out speakers who disagree with them, demonstrations that wreck rather than enforce fair procedures, "moral" rejection of majority decisions— none of these are ultimately conducive to either more democracy or an "order of justice." Nor, in a pragmatic sense, have they helped McCarthy in his already difficult battle with the politically orthodox men who control his party. Among other things, the fierce demeanor of some of his supporters convinces not a few Democratic leaders that, whatever he may want to do, he will be forced into leading a fourth party.

McCarthy—having set out to prove the viability of the two-party system—might diminish all he has achieved up to now in doing so. On the other hand, he might disappoint, perhaps shatter, the idealism of his youthful supporters if he accepted second place on the despised —as they see it—Humphrey ticket. No one knows how his youthful army would react to an abrupt end to his participation in the politics of 1968.

What happens to him, and them, will go far to shape the drama that will unfold on the convention floor and in the surrounding streets this week. But whatever happens, it will not be easy for McCarthy to improve upon what he already has done.

So far from putting himself forward as one who could right the nation's ills, McCarthy has seemed to see his role as that of giving the people opportunity for true political expression. He sensed that millions of Americans wanted to vote against the war, and gave them the chance when there seemed to be none; he believed people preferred orderly and democratic change to assault on the Pentagon, and he gave them hope for that, too. He gave a powerful but smothered sentiment an opportunity to find expression and make a difference, and that alone is no small contribution.

But beyond that, McCarthy has given Americans opportunity to free themselves of all sorts of intellectual bondage—to jettison assumptions, prejudices and taboos that have been shaping political life for decades. He showed, as few others have, that an intelligent politician can talk intelligently about serious affairs, and still find a constituency. And he demonstrated that a certain faith in the good instincts of the American voter is not altogether misplaced; he had no more reason than any other politician to believe that enough voters were profoundly disturbed by the war in Vietnam to sustain his candidacy, but he made the test anyway.

So the old strident know-nothingism, the safe insistence on the obvious, the appeals to the cheapest emotions and most sensitive interests of the voters—Eugene McCarthy put these ancient tools of the trade aside, and neither the Democratic party nor American politics is likely to be quite the same, ever again.

The Wrong Man from the Wrong Place at the Wrong Time

by Eric F. Goldman

LYNDON JOHNSON is about to leave the White House with every appearance of a thoroughly repudiated President. Since Herbert Hoover rode down Pennsylvania Avenue on a cold day in 1933, no President has ended his tenure with so few hosannas and so widespread a sense of good riddance.

The story, it seems, is simple: the accident of Dallas made Lyndon Johnson President, and he failed to measure up. So it appears—but in the field of evaluating Presidents, appearances can be sharply deceiving. The cardinal rule for any historian venturing into it is to remember that he is a historian, not History, and that no powers of divination have been bestowed upon him by his profession or even by his abounding faith in his own judgment. Yet I think it should be suggested, and with emphasis, that after the furies of the sixties are laid to rest, Lyndon Johnson may well rank a good deal above where the national mood would now place him.

Certainly in past instances the public esteem of a President during his period in office has borne no particular relationship to future judgment. In 1962, the late historian Arthur M. Schlesinger, Sr., asked 75 well-known scholars of American history to rate the Chief

From the *New York Times Magazine*, January 5, 1969. Copyright © 1969 by Eric F. Goldman, adapted from the book *The Tragedy of Lyndon Johnson* published by Alfred A. Knopf.

Executives up to John Kennedy. The preponderant opinion called five Presidents "great" in this order: Abraham Lincoln, George Washington, Franklin Roosevelt, Woodrow Wilson and Thomas Jefferson. Again in order, it placed in the "near-great" category Andrew Jackson, Theodore Roosevelt, James Polk, Harry Truman, John Adams and Grover Cleveland. The historians categorized as failures Ulysses Grant and Warren Harding. Popular sentiment in 1962 probably would have gone along with most of these judgments. But of the 11 men called "great" or "near-great," five—Jefferson, Lincoln, T.R., F.D.R. and Truman—were subject to widespread and sustained abuse during their incumbencies. Woodrow Wilson was also roundly repudiated, first by the Senate and then by the voters, on the issue of his most cherished program, the League of Nations. Harry Truman, a man reviled during much of his Presidency, went through an almost identical withdrawal ceremony just 16 years before Lyndon Johnson. Then, while still living, he emerged a favorite of the historians and something of a folk hero. The two Chief Executives deemed failures by a later generation, Ulysses Grant and Warren Harding, were enormously popular during their Presidencies. It is rarely remembered that when the Harding funeral train crossed the United States, it called forth a grief, respect and affection fully equal to, if not exceeding, the public reaction to the death of Abraham Lincoln.

The question of a President's just place in history is complicated not only by shifts in opinion as time passes but by the inherent difficulties of the assessment process. Schlesinger included among the men to whom he sent his 1962 questionnaire a sometime historian, President John Kennedy. J.F.K. was interested, started to fill out the ballot, then stopped. "How the hell can you tell?" he remarked. "Only the President himself can know what his real pressures and his real alternatives are. If you don't know that, how can you judge performance?" Historian-President John Kennedy's ultimate test seemed to be concrete achievements. This was an intriguing commentary on the problem of judging Presidents from a Chief Executive who, at least in domestic affairs during his short tenure, was far more notable as an opinion builder than as an achiever of specific legislation.

Of course, central to any long-range judgment of the Johnson Administration is the President's decision to commit American combat forces in the Vietnam war. I happen to be among those who became convinced that the action was a grave mistake; and if this assessment—which seems to be that of so many Americans in 1969—holds, the Vietnam war will certainly prove a heavy drag on the L.B.J. reputation. Just how heavy is quite a different matter. Other Presidents who are today called great or near-great made moves in foreign policy which are now considered serious errors. But with the passage of the years, the specific was submerged in the general memory of the man. If President Johnson or his successor can bring the Vietnam war to an end without much further damage, in time a kindly haze may obscure the pointless clomp of American soldiers across a defenseless civilization, what amounts to an American defeat, even napalm.

This is the more possible because the future might emphasize that, in a sense, L.B.J. inherited the Vietnam commitment. Three previous Chief Executives had ordered American noncombat involvement in the area. At least two of these Presidents, Eisenhower and Kennedy, believed that preventing South Vietnam from coming under Communist rule was important to American national security. None faced a situation in which the region appeared about to fall, and consequently none had to decide whether preventing a Communist takeover was important enough to justify United States entrance into the fighting war. Lyndon Johnson was forced to make that judgment, and another generation may decide that he committed an error prepared for by his predecessors and one which either President Eisenhower or President Kennedy might have made.

And always there is the possibility which many anti-L.B.J. commentators of the nineteen-sixties simply refuse to entertain: the Vietnam intervention might not have been a mistake at all. President Johnson could be right when he says, let the future decide. A Communist victory in South Vietnam, he was convinced, would be followed by a gradual fall of much of Asia to Communism, the domination of the huge region by a hostile and potentially powerful China and—because China had not been warned by a strong American stand—by ultimate war between China and the United States. If a successor to President Johnson should accept a compromise peace that was followed by such a chain of developments, Lyndon Johnson would be more than forgiven; he would emerge a figure of Churchillian stature, a wise, courageous voice crying out in a crowd of myopic and timid men.

L.B.J.'s place in the long sweep of American domestic affairs can be assessed with much more assurance. The three times in the 20th century the United States has faced up to the harsh facts of an industrializing, urbanizing civilization—at the beginning of the century, under Theodore Roosevelt and Woodrow Wilson; after the crash of 1929, under Franklin Roosevelt; and then, slowly, in the period following World War II.

The thirties were *sui generis*. The urgency was unique; so too was the public mood. The situations in the early nineteen-hundreds and after World War II were much more alike. In both instances, there was little sense that the country was falling apart. National opinion, jabbed by a zealous left and troubled by the arguments of a dogged right, was gradually forming around the proposition that the general population was being given too little access to economic and social opportunity. More laws were needed; the President ought to lead Congress in getting them.

At the start of the century Theodore Roosevelt bounded into the White House, caught up the strands of dissidence, wove them into an attractive pattern. "Teddy," the journalist William Allen White observed, "was reform in a derby, the gayest, cockiest, most fashionable derby you ever saw." T.R. moved few bills through Congress, but he prepared the way for Woodrow Wilson, who, without derby or gaiety, had the roused public sentiment, the votes in Congress and the Covenanter certitudes to grind the bills through the House and the Senate.

After World War II, the process began all over again. The opinion kept building, the opposition kept fighting and another generation of leaders prepared the way for another wave of action. Harry Truman, his expletives and vetos poised, fought off a Congress that yearned to turn back. Dwight Eisenhower, before he drifted into his second somnolent term, led the Republican party into some accommodation with the day. John Kennedy appeared, a second Theodore Roosevelt, associating social change with vigor and glamour and the mischievous cocked eye, legislating little but educating many. Then Lyndon Johnson, the cloakroom operator, reenacted the presbyter-professor Woodrow Wilson. He, too, seized the moment to execute the decade's needs—seized it so firmly and wrung it so hard that he built a monument to himself as big as all Texas in that 1965 Congress, which wrote into law just about everything that the public had decided was long past due.

And all the while, breaking out now and again, however explained or explained away, came the voice which spoke of something far removed from cloakroom chicanery, which caught the age-old American insistence that somehow, by some effort of hardheadedness and decency, ordinary men and women can be enabled to live in greater comfort and joy and to walk in the tonic air of self-respect. The voice was there. . . .

. . . when L.B.J., told by a visitor that he was rushing Congress, replied, "An old man on the Hill said to me a long time ago that there are some Administrations that do and some that don't. This one is gonna do";

. . . when he signed an education bill, a mist across his cratered face, and muttered: "Not enough, not nearly enough. But I'm proud, damned proud, to have got this much. Education—that's what's needed, and that's what every kid ought to get, as much of it as he can take, right up to his neck";

. . . when he told a group of corporation executives: "I have thought a great deal the last few days—I missed being an elevator boy by just about that much, when my mother reached up and made me go back to school after laying out for two years. When you're dealing with these [Negro] people, in your company, or in your firm, or in your business, just remember it's some daughter's father, or some boy's mother, or someone's sister, or somebody's brother that you are dealing with. And except for the grace of God, it might be you. And think how you would like it if you lived in a land where you could not go to school with your fellow Americans, where you could not work alongside of them, where you could travel from Texas to Washington, across many states, and not be able to go to the bathroom without hiding in a thicket or dodging behind a culvert. Ask yourself how you would feel";

. . . and when, addressing a White House Conference on Natural Beauty, he shoved aside his prepared text and spoke his memories of boyhood walks: ". . . those hills, and those fields, and the river were the only world that I really had in those years. . . . We were not a wealthy family, but this was my rich inheritance. All my life I have drawn strength, and something more, from those Texas hills. Sometimes, in the highest councils of the nation, in this house, I sit back and I can almost feel that rough, unyielding, sticky clay soil between my toes, and it stirs memories that often give me comfort and sometimes give me a pretty firm purpose.

"But not all the boys in America had the privilege to grow up in a wide and open country. We can give them something, and we are going to. We can let each of them feel a little of what the first settlers must have felt, as they stood there before the majesty of our great land."

History has been generous, and should be, to Presidents who have talked like that and taken action to turn the talk into laws. Probably history will be generous—and it should be—to Lyndon Johnson.

Probably—but all this is in the murky realm of speculation. There remains a hard, clear fact. Lyndon Johnson has served his whole five years in the White House with little genuine hold on the thinking or on the emotions of the American people.

What went so wrong? Obviously, he has been an able, hardworking Chief Executive, eager to serve the interests of the mass of the population, more than eager to win their camaraderie. He tried desperately hard, and he delivered in important respects. Lyndon Johnson not only put through a powerhouse program of legislation. He had taken over the Presidency at a moment of national emotional disarray and conducted a transition that is considered by many experts the most skillful the United States has ever known. He went on to preside over a country marked by that condition which so often has been the prime test of the public's attitude toward an Administration—an America that was generally prosperous, in fact more prosperous than any society in all of man's 5,000 years of recorded history.

White House aides kept telling President Johnson that the whole source of the public's disaffection was what the aides called his "courageous" stand on Vietnam. Well before I resigned from the White House staff, I became accustomed to the litany. Any war creates frustration and resentment, he was told, and discontent is always directed at the leader. Abraham Lincoln himself was assailed with unbridled vehemence. Modern limited wars, with their especially frustrating quality, exacerbate these public feelings.

Yet L.B.J.'s unpopularity cannot be so totally attributed to the Vietnam war. Actually, American wars have generally made of the Commander in Chief a rallying point for support and enthusiasm. Moreover, as early as 1965—before his foreign policy became a major divisive issue and when L.B.J. was at the height of his successes—a widespread distaste for him was plain. Many Americans have been snappish about Lyndon Johnson not so much because they were positive he was wrong on Vietnam but because they believed he was the kind of man who was quite capable of making a bad mistake and, having made it, of not admitting it or moving to correct it.

During the campaign of 1964, when the evidence indicated both that President Johnson would win easily and that the trend was as much anti-Goldwater as pro-Johnson, Lyndon Johnson would remark querulously to visitors, "Why don't people like me?" One guest, too old to be concerned about preferment by the White House and enough of a Washington character to get away with irreverence, answered the question. He said, "Because, Mr. President, you are not a very likable man." Bald as it was, this statement expressed a major part of L.B.J.'s problem with the American people. The fact that he was not a very likable man could not be concealed from the public despite all the arduous efforts of his friends and aides, myself included, who wanted so much to believe otherwise and who did their damnedest to present him in a way that would convince themselves and the country.

Lyndon Johnson may have risen from Johnson City to being the head of a family he cherished, a multimillionaire and the leader of the free world, but he had not risen above something nagging inside him. All the way to the top, and especially at the top, he was cumulatively, combatively insecure. Having started out as the apple of his mother's eye, overloved, overprotected and overpraised, he was thoroughly unprepared for a world that did not view him in such a glow. In his youth he was keenly sensitive to the fact that the Johnsons were not among the leading families of the area. He himself was gawky and no great charmer.

Maturing in an action-worshiping environment, it took him a long time to realize the high value of one resource he had in abundance: brains. By then, the asset was denigrated even in his own eyes by the low status of his schooling (a social abyss existed between his alma mater, Southwest Texas State Teachers College, and the University of Texas). And almost as soon as his career was really started, he had to function in large measure not amid the congenial ways of Texas but in the sharply different atmosphere of Washington.

Of course, the L.B.J. genes dictated that he would have had many of his personal characteristics if he had been born a graceful son of a Brahmin family. But a sense of insecurity was so thoroughly woven into the man by external circumstances that it brought to a high state of development his innate tendencies. Facing a world that he thought looked down on him, he sought constantly to prove, to himself and to it, that he could beat it. Dubious whether people liked him, he pleaded, clawed and maneuvered to have them love him. Desperately seeking proof of loyalty—from friends, aides and the public—he pushed his demand for loyalty close to the point where it meant obeisance. He was ready to give anything—his own driving efforts, sentiment, preferment for their wishes—to hold this loyalty, anything except what people wanted and what his lurking suspicion of them held back, the gift of his genuine self.

Toward the longtime members of his entourage, L.B.J. could be considerate and more than considerate. One aide who found himself overwhelmed by family medical expenses received a substantial financial gift from "a friend"; a person working with the President before a meal—be he a high official or a secretary who had been taking dictation—might be invited to eat with the family. But all the while Lyndon Johnson not only felt it necessary to keep testing the devotion of his most veteran assistants but to assert his mastery in scenes of demeaning tongue-lashing and by manipulating them with extremes of the carrot-and-stick technique. An aide would go along for some time, receiving extravagant praise. Then, for no particular reason, he was excommunicated, his work rejected almost *in toto* and the man himself scarcely spoken to. Just as suddenly, he would be reinstated, and someone else given the treatment.

The insecurity mounted in proportion as President Johnson was removed from familiar situations and types of people. In the spring of 1964, he approved a suggestion that he lunch with a group of writers who had distinguished themselves by their books on Presidents or the Presidency. L.B.J. was at a high point in his administration; his polls were soaring, his bills were rolling through Congress, he had just settled a labor-management deadlock in the railroad industry which two Presidents, Congress, three Secretaries of Labor and endless committees and boards had failed to resolve. Yet this group, markedly different from his usual associates, roused all kinds of defenses. He treated the guests warily, almost like a hostile force, and he ended up smothering their efforts at conversation by a near-compulsive monologue. In between, he got onto a protective, complaining theme that he was not given a "fair shake as President because I am a Southerner." It was an intimation of a later Lyndon Johnson who would growl about criticism of the Vietnam war: "I'll never be given credit for anything I do in foreign policy because I didn't go to Harvard."

Always fighting off the devils of insecurity, Lyndon Johnson was vain, not proud; boomerish, not confident; to a considerable extent he was grandiose, not grand, in conceiving his programs and grandiloquent, not eloquent, in expressing them. Gnawed by his inner needs, he turned a Congressional career shot through with instincts for the national good into a feral pursuit of personal domination, and a Presidency marked by a broad streak of idealism into what so often appeared an exercise in self-interest.

Self-interest—here is the only-too-well-recognized part of the L.B.J. story. As a student of history, I have read a great deal about men who are said to have been motivated merely by self-aggrandizement. I have never really believed the analyses. I think over the array of people I have known well, many of whom are not particularly noble, and they have never seemed totally dominated by self-interest. Neither was Lyndon Johnson—and perhaps Lyndon Johnson especially was not.

But President Johnson, lashed by his insecurity, fought his better angels harder than any man I have ever known. It was a hostile world out there, far removed from mother and Texas and his trusted buddies; you had to keep handling it. Most of the time he appeared afraid to rely on anything except the doctrine that life and politics and government are simply a conflict and confluence between the self-interest of various people and groups. He seemed driven to function as Machiavelli in a Stetson, part of which posture was to keep assuring everyone that rugged he-men in Stetsons would never be Machiavellis.

So lacking in confidence, so defensive and wary, those hard eyes always searching the room or across the country for enemies, he was determined that nobody and no circumstance would get the better of him by playing to his strong personal ideals and emotions. This attitude led to increasing justification for, and ever more extended practice of, his natural bent toward exorbitant secretiveness, labyrinthine maneuverings, a sanctimonious glossing over of reality, the plain withholding of truth which had no need of being withheld and the plain distortion of truth which, at least in part, was much better stated and done with.

The American public delights in ferreting out the shortcomings of its Chief Executives. A nation of President-watchers knew that Franklin Roosevelt was an incorrigible political gamesman, that Harry Truman could sound like the village calliope, that Dwight Eisenhower often tried to grin away massive problems, that John Kennedy had some of the frailties as well as the assets of the charmer. But endlessly critical, it has also shown itself remarkably indulgent, provided that the virtues of the President appear to outweigh his defects. In this balance, the critical weight is the judgment that at bottom the President is a "good man," fundamentally decent, putting the welfare of the nation first in all his really important considerations. Most Americans have believed this to be true of every President from the thirties through 1963. It was a fundamental difficulty of Lyndon Johnson that he did not leave such an impression.

His background of the Texas wheeler-dealers, his long years as a Congressional manipulator and the association with Bobby Baker, his family's accumulation of considerable wealth based on a Government-regulated television station, his very appearance and mannerisms which easily suggested the riverboat gambler—all had prepared the public for skepticism of his basic motives as soon as he entered the White House. Nothing happened to change that attitude. Even the two achievements that President Johnson considered irreproachable brought him no surcease from suspicion.

He felt that he had incontestably established his right to the national leadership by his landslide victory in the election of 1964. But millions came to feel that he had incontestably established that he was ready to double-talk about anything, including taking the country into a grisly war, in order to win votes. He believed that the great success of his legislative program after the election earned him the confidence and admiration of the nation. The great success of that drive was, among other things, his great undoing; it made more people more sure that he did everything only by political legerdemain and only for political advantage.

It was within this context that the charge of credibility gap cut so deeply. Other modern Chief Executives—widely popular ones like Theodore and Franklin Roosevelt, Dwight Eisenhower and John Kennedy—had been known to play fast and loose with facts. President Johnson not only played faster and looser; he did it amid a widespread conviction that self-serving deceit was part of his essential make-up.

This distrust militated powerfully against his whole Presidential leadership. It went beyond stripping him of much of the credit for his domestic legislative achievements; with the credit blunted, it dulled public interest in helping him make the laws work. "Why don't people, especially young people," President Johnson once complained, "really jump into the poverty program, roll up their sleeves and get it roaring, like we did back in the New Deal?" None of the men in the room with the President had the heart to tell him.

In foreign policy, the pervasive suspicion meant that L.B.J. was given little benefit of the doubt. Worried citizens, facing World War I, World War II or the Korean War, had been inclined to hesitate before opposing the President. He was a good man doing his best, with greater knowledge of the situation than themselves; the odds were that he was right. Few worried citizens hesitated to oppose Lyndon Johnson's Vietnam policy, and once in opposition, their attacks came with special virulence.

There was President Lyndon Johnson, the human being, and then there was President Lyndon Johnson, the maker of and symbol of certain national policies.

Those policies were coming from a man of exceedingly high intelligence. Many times when I have remarked this, during and after my White House days, people have looked at me as if I were a sycophant of the President or as if, during my association with him, I had taken leave of my good sense. Of course, they were thinking of intelligence in terms of a well-educated mind or, I'm afraid, being stuffy and parochial and finding it impossible to associate brains with a man who looked like a polished cowboy and who drawled out so much buncombe and bawdiness. They were decidedly wrong. After years of meeting first-rate minds in and out of universities, I am sure I have never met a more intelligent person than Lyndon Johnson—intelligent in terms of sheer I.Q.—a clear, swift, penetrating mind, with an abundance of its own type of imagination and subtlety.

The point is that little had happened to fill or to stretch this mind. The high school Lyndon Johnson attended, Johnson City High School, was so bad it lacked accreditation even by the lax standards of its region. Southwest Texas State Teachers College taught a watery pedagogese. Almost nothing in such schooling suggested to Lyndon Johnson that, once out of college, he ought to read books, travel, seek out interesting people, try to keep up with new trends, shake himself out of Johnson City and into the later 20th century.

Uncomfortable in the bigger world, obsessed with his political career, he had no personal urge to do these things. The powerful mind was feeding on small fare. The grown man came to the White House with a grab-bag of facts and non-facts, conceptions and misconceptions, ways of thinking and ways to avoid thought which had been gathered largely from his early crabbed environment.

It was this mental matrix which explains why, in his basic policy attitudes, L.B.J. was a passé President all the while he crowded the daily television screens. A man out of a kind of boondocks liberalism that had marked one element in Texas politics, he was easily able to move into New Dealism and to take over much of the tone of the thirties, but for the most part he stopped there. The United States did not stop at all. Nations change not at a steady pace but in slow swings or in rampant rushes, and America had been rampaging between the thirties and the sixties. The alterations were so swift and so deep that the country was changing right out from under President Lyndon Johnson.

Like a good nineteen-thirties man, he expressed his authentic thinking during the campaign of 1964 when he would shout, "Remember Molly and the children," or "We Americans don't want much. We want decent food, housing and clothing." In the nineteen-sixties there were still plenty of Mollies with plenty of troubles. But the essential mass problem had shifted; it was less food, housing and clothing than how to live with a weirdly uneasy affluence, marked by maldistributions that a significant part of the population was no longer ready to accept and a mounting race problem that was only in part economic. Like F.D.R., President Johnson might think of domestic policy in terms of satisfying the economic and social urges of the grand political coalition which dominated the period before World War II—labor, the farmers, the cities, the minorities and the youthful voters. But now much of labor sounded like threatened burghers, and the farm vote was disappearing into technology. The uplifted white minorities had been lifted to a condition where their concern was less social legislation than assuaging their own status trauma. The cities meant more and more the Negroes; the Negroes were wondering how much they wanted to do with any white leadership. The youthful, whether moving left, right or careering down the middle, were inclined to think of bread-and-butter liberalism as quaint, if not downright camp.

Among all age groups, the idealism which had helped sweep

along the F.D.R. program, and which L.B.J. kept trying to touch, now sought not simply better pay for teachers and more school buildings but a drastically altered educational atmosphere and cur- riculum; not simply Medicare but aid for the aged fitted into a whole social welfare structure that found a way of asserting human dignity; not simply civil rights laws but a society in which civil rights laws would not be necessary. A new era, a new pattern of social and political forces, a new agenda—President Johnson, acting upon the kind of consensus domestic policy that would merely codify and expand the programs of the thirties, was about as con- temporary as padded shoulders, a night at the radio and Clark Gable.

Again in the mood of the thirties, President Johnson assumed that foreign policy was something you had, like measles, and got over with as quickly as possible. Suddenly forced to confront the world, he reached into the past and laid hold of an attic doctrine which included even apostrophes to the flag and international deeds of derring-do. At the farthest stretch of his modernity, he reached think- ing that was substantially of cold war vintage.

In the nineteen-sixties, a considerable and influential part of the public simply would not go along with such a foreign policy. They assumed that international affairs were a constant high-priority sub- ject. Contemptuous of talk of the flag and derring-do, they were alarmed by what they were sure were outmoded cold war attitudes of crusading against Communism and of joining with foreign regimes that sought to use military power to stop social change. Out of a sense of guilt over America's past role in world affairs, a sympathy with the aspirations of underdeveloped nations and fear of nuclear holocaust, they favored accommodation, compromise, political and economic rather than military moves.

Many of these critics were Metro-Americans, part of a group in the cities and even more in the suburbs which was steadily growing in numbers and in its influence in determining national opinion. Relative to the rest of the country, the Metro-American was youthful, well-educated, affluent, more likely to have some minority blood in his veins. His mind had been shaped by an environment which had been good to him. It was no less formed by an American scene of irritating big organizations, brassy media and grinding social dis- locations, and by a world situation of wars and threats of still worse wars. His thinking and his attitudes were a tangle of ambivalence. The Metro-American was avidly on the make, economically and socially, but he shied away from the appearance of sheer money-making or sheer caste and preferred the manner of public-spiritedness and cultivation. He had ideals but was skeptical of other people's —and even, a bit, of his own. He was liberal but without ideology; tolerant but intolerant of do-goodism; flexible, pragmatic and a devotee of the ironic edge.

Metro-America was increasingly the focal point of the abrasion between President Johnson and his public. There the uneasiness with him as a human being was greatest; the dissatisfaction with his domestic and foreign policies, the strongest. There, too, was the chief gathering place for a disaffection that joined the criticisms of the man and of his programs and added a third—that one concerning "style"—which really had little to do with the other two but increased the virulence of both.

The Metro-American—whether living in New York, Chicago, San Francisco or Houston—tended to take his style of life from the successful classes of the Northeast; to him, everything else was darkest boorishness. Over the years Texas and Texas mores had become a cherished subject for the gibes of Metro-American cocktail parties. Mention almost any of the personal habits of Lyndon Johnson— whether the sentimentalities or the big white Continental on a roar down a Texas highway—and you brought up something that made Metro-America snicker.

And always there were the Kennedys. After his sweeping victory in 1964, President Johnson may have eliminated virtually all references to President Kennedy in his public remarks. He could not eliminate the fact that his predecessor was legend and that the legend was a restive, bitter, yearning element in the whole life of the generation, especially in Metro-America. Not only did the urge to be different from J.F.K. affect what L.B.J. did and did not do day after day; every difficulty of President Johnson with public opinion was magnified by the Kennedy legend, which made John Kennedy precisely the opposite of all the things that Americans, and especially Metro-Americans, thought were wrong with Lyndon Johnson.

Eight times American Vice Presidents become Presidents have had to cope with the memory of the men they succeeded. Only once has the new Chief Executive been faced not only with a memory but with its living embodiment in a large, talented, energetic, abundantly endowed family, most of whom considered Lyndon Johnson a temporary and unfortunate interruption of the Kennedy years and one of whom thought so from a powerful political base. Senator Robert F. Kennedy was the looks, the voice, the long stabbing finger of the martyred President. He was youthfulness, celebritese, the Northeast, the new-mode family, canoeing into high rapids and then sitting quoting Aeschylus; the Metro-American's unabashed ambition and the Metro-American's delight in the throwaway manner. He was post-nineteen-thirties politics, talking the quality of American civilization, moving increasingly toward outright opposition to the Vietnam war, centering his domestic legislative program on the cities, probing for a voting coalition based not on the old economic lines but on the new sense of dislocation bringing together Negroes, young people, intellectuals and the suburbanites who had acquired money at the price of malaise.

Nine weeks after President Johnson's speech of withdrawal, more crazed bullets were fired in Los Angeles. An R.F.K. legend immediately started forming, an idealization of the younger brother that joined perfectly with the J.F.K. legend.

The Johnson years were clamped in grim parentheses of happenstance. Lyndon Johnson came into the White House to the caissons for John Kennedy and he was leaving it to the dirges for Robert Kennedy. He entered and he was departing with a Kennedy more central than he in the national thinking and emotions.

In the final months, President Johnson tried hard to appear, what did not come easily to him, philosophical and serene. Strange, complex man in strange, complex circumstances—the towering figure still stalking, endlessly stalking the Oval Office, too astute not to know how seriously things had gone wrong, too limited by background and by self to grasp what had really happened.

No one who worked in Lyndon Johnson's White House can fail to have been moved by the dedication, the abilities and the force he brought to the Presidency of the United States. It is equally difficult not to recall the lines from one of the copybook poems of his school days in Johnson City, John Greenleaf Whittier's "Maud Muller": "For of all sad words of tongue or pen,/The saddest are these: 'It might have been.' " The story of Lyndon Johnson's Presidency is a story of tragedy in the ancient haunting sense of the word, the strong man overwhelmed by forces from within and without.

Hurtled into the leadership of the United States and of the free world in the fiercely demanding nineteen-sixties, he was not ready for them. Seriously flawed in personal characteristics, his virtues could not transform him into an engaging public figure. Functioning in the shadow of a relentless legend, he was beset by a host of attitudes which that legend continuously fed.

Lyndon Johnson could win votes, enact laws, maneuver mountains. He could not acquire that something beyond, which cannot be won, enacted or maneuvered but must be freely given. He could not command that respect, affection and rapport which alone permit an American President genuinely to lead. In his periods of triumph and of downsweep, in peace as in war, he stood the tragic figure of an extraordinarily gifted President who was the wrong man from the wrong place at the wrong time in the wrong circumstances.

Part **5**

THE NEW NIXON

A Skeptical Democrat Looks at President Nixon

by Arthur M. Schlesinger, Jr.

ON JAN. 20 next, Richard M. Nixon will become President of the United States. What sort of a President is he likely to be? Pre-inaugural forecasts are notoriously risky. No one can predict the impact of ultimate responsibility: the chemistry of the Presidency can turn a routine politician into a purposeful leader, as in the case of Polk, or a confident bureaucrat into a gloomy loser, as in the case of Hoover. In addition, forecasters may be not only fallible but prejudiced. This one certainly had better declare an interest: my enthusiasm for Mr. Nixon has always been well under control, and I strongly opposed his election.

Nonetheless, here we are. The election is over. Mr. Nixon has won. He will be our President until at least Jan. 20, 1973, God willing (a prayer uttered with special fervency in view of Spiro T. Agnew). So again: what sort of a President is he likely to be? He is hardly an unfamiliar figure. His public career goes back 20 years; he has not been one of our more laconic politicians; and there should be enough evidence about the man to frame a series of guesses about his Presidency. Not all this evidence, of course, is necessarily relevant today. Politicians can quite genuinely change their minds through the years; in any case, they too are entitled to the statute of limitations. I really do not think it matters any longer what Mr. Nixon said about Helen Gahagan Douglas in 1950. The clues must first be

From the *New York Times Magazine*, November 17, 1968.

sought in what he has done in 1968. What light does the Nixon campaign throw on the shape of the Nixon Presidency?

As candidate, Mr. Nixon could, to a degree, indulge in fantasies agreeable to himself and, he hoped, to the voter. As President, he must face realities. The first reality is that he is a minority choice; no President since Wilson in 1912 has had so low a proportion of the popular vote. The second reality is that he confronts a Congress controlled in both houses by the opposition party; no President-elect has had this as a first-time problem since Zachary Taylor in 1848. A third reality is the collapse of his campaign in his most urgent and perilous area of domestic responsibility—the cities: he did not carry a major city in the country. A fourth reality goes back to the nature of Mr. Nixon's campaign; it results from his failure to establish a definite mandate and a wide basis of informed public support. By evident design Mr. Nixon ran a campaign of banality and evasion.

By so doing, he minimized the risk of saying anything which might offend anybody; and, in the end, his anti-campaign worked, if only barely. Yet he paid a serious price for the way he won. Our quadrennial Presidential contests are about the only time the nation as a whole is willing to listen to political discussion. They therefore offer a rare chance for political education and mobilization. Mr. Nixon squandered this chance.

Samuel Lubell, that most realistic of political observers, has generally tended to deprecate the role of issues in American politics; still, reflecting on the campaign in mid-October, he wrote, "No candidate can hope to create the image of a leader who inspires trust and confidence unless he discusses the critical issues in specific detail." Mr. Lubell went on to raise the question whether "Nixon's 'play-it-safe' campaigning may not cause him to muff a historic opportunity . . . to develop and articulate a program of action around which the quiet, moderate majority in the country can rally."

Ducking the issues was very likely a sensible, don't-rock-the-boat strategy for a front-runner. In addition, it may have expressed an understandable desire to keep Presidential options open. No doubt Mr. Nixon, like every other President-elect, really isn't sure what he intends to do in the White House. Yet the consequence of so meaningless a campaign was to deny himself what he most needs now to be an effective President: a large body of people who understand and are prepared to support specific Presidential policies.

In an administrative sense, the Nixon campaign was organized with great mechanical efficiency; and so, one imagines, will be the Nixon Presidency. The allocation of responsibility will be clear, the chain of command will be sacred, everything possible will be computerized. Commissions will lurk around every corner to study controversial issues. Yet, as Franklin Roosevelt said in 1932, "The Presidency is not merely an administrative office. That's the least of it." If one judges by his campaign discourse on the Presidency, Mr. Nixon would agree. The intellectual content in his campaign came in a series of radio talks and position papers on key issues; and, of these generally able documents, the most interesting was an address on "The Nature of the Presidency."

This impressive statement even sounds at times like a rewrite of the speech on the President which John F. Kennedy gave at the National Press Club in early 1960. Hear the echoes in such passages as the following: "The days of a passive Presidency belong to a simpler past. . . . The next President must take an activist view of his office. . . . Under a Nixon Administration, the Presidency will be deeply involved in the entire sweep of America's public concerns. . . . The Presidency is a place where priorities are set, and goals determined."

In adopting this Jackson-Roosevelt-Kennedy view of the Presidency, Mr. Nixon was evidently rejecting the quietist conception favored by President Eisenhower (and, oddly, by Senator Eugene McCarthy).

Mr. Nixon went on to promise "a Cabinet made up of the ablest men in America." Every President-elect promises something of this sort; none carries it out; and Mr. Nixon won't either. The first designation in his official circle was hardly reassuring on this point. He had consulted, he said, "more than a hundred leading Republicans whose judgment I respected. . . . My primary concern was to select a man who had the courage, the character and the intellect not only to be Vice President but also to be an effective President if the need arose." Having said this, he solemnly unveiled Spiro T. Agnew. "I know Ted Agnew well," Mr. Nixon said in further explanation. ". . . He has real depth . . . tremendous brain power, great courage and an unprejudiced legal mind. He has vigor and imagination. . . . He is the man who can best work with me. . . . He has attributes of a statesman of the first rank. . . . There can be a *mystique* [sic] about a man. You can look him in the eye and know he's got it. This guy has got it." During his campaign Mr. Nixon displayed far less concern over Governor Agnew than General Eisenhower had displayed over Nixon in 1952.

If Mr. Agnew is half what Mr. Nixon says he is, he will no doubt be the President's strong right arm. If he falls very far short of the Nixon encomium, he will further impede the already sufficiently complicated relations between Mr. Nixon and a Democratic Congress. In either case, the obvious thing for the President-elect to consider at this point is some simulacrum of coalition government. The coalition idea does not fit very tidily into our political system, but a case can be made for it, and Mr. Nixon in his speech on the Presidency forecast something of the sort. He wants a Government, he said, "drawn from the broadest possible base—an Administration made up of Republicans, Democrats and Independents, and drawn from politics, from career Government service, from universities, from business, from the professions—one including not only executives and administrators, but scholars and thinkers."

This is a benign declaration of intent. But whom does Mr. Nixon wish to coalesce with? Much depends on whether his quest for unity will lead him to propitiate the followers of George Wallace or those of Hubert Humphrey. And if he brings Democrats into his Administration, what kind will they be? John B. Connally or Joseph S. Clark, Jr.? Dean Rusk or J. K. Galbraith?

The answer to this question depends on the policies he plans to pursue, and this remains a good deal of a mystery. Of course, there is a handsome, 194-page volume, entitled "Nixon on the Issues," which the Nixon-Agnew Campaign Committee distributed in mid-October. But I defy anyone to read, say, pages 6 through 12 on Vietnam and extract from this section any clear idea of how Mr. Nixon proposed to bring the war to an end. In the past, he tells us, "We used our military power ineffectively . . . [But] the swift, overwhelming blow that would have been decisive two or three years ago is no longer possible today." Now we must have an honorable settlement; coalition government is out; beyond that, Mr. Nixon felt he couldn't express his own views lest he jeopardize the negotiations in Paris. "I do not believe a Presidential candidate now should say, 'This is what I will do in January.' I believe that if you really want peace, then you have to respect a man, look at him, look at his judgment and background, and base your decision on which man you would rather have sitting at that conference table. . . . Foreign policy is my strong suit."

During the primary campaign, Mr. Nixon said once or twice that he did have a plan to end the war, only he could not tell anyone what it was. However, he may have thrown some light on this plan when he told the Southern delegates at Miami, as transcribed by The Miami Herald:

"How do you bring a war to a conclusion? I'll tell you how Korea was ended. . . . Eisenhower let the word go out—let the word go out diplomatically—to the Chinese and the North [Koreans] that he would not tolerate this continual ground war of attrition. And within a matter of months they negotiated."

He repeated this statement publicly in Pittsburgh on Sept. 8, putting the Eisenhower message in these terms: "that unless they negotiated a complete truce in Korea, that the military consequences would be ones that would be unacceptable to them." Apart from the historical problem whether this was, indeed, the way the Korean war ended, would Mr. Nixon plan in February to send a similar message to the North Vietnamese in case the Paris talks have not yielded quick results? If so, what would his alternative be to the ground war? Does he really think that conventional bombing could do in 1969 what it failed to do in 1965, 1966, 1967 and 1968? Or is he thinking about something else? He denies any desire to use nuclear weapons in Vietnam. What does he have in mind?

Mr. Nixon's more cynical supporters see hope in his Vietnam mystifications. He is, they contend, unprincipled but intelligent; therefore, he will not permit past words to stop him from doing what the present requires; he will have more freedom of maneuver than a Democratic President (true); and the pressure of events will lead him to liquidate the war as quickly as possible. This may well be so. But what will he do if the Joint Chiefs of Staff assure him that the Vietcong are on the verge of collapse, that they are all 13-year-old kids and women, that prisoner-of-war interrogations and captured documents prove their despair; give us three months, 25,000 more men, the resumption of large-scale bombing, and we will win the war for you?

Mr. Nixon may say yes, or he may say no. One cannot be sure. One can be sure, however, of his admiration for generals as well as for Lewis Strauss and nuclear scientists of the Teller-Libby persuasion. "I intend," he said on Oct. 24, "to restore ready access of our top military professionals to the President"—a perplexing statement since it is hard to see how this access could be much readier than it has been in the Johnson years.

And one of the few concrete positions he took in the campaign was his repudiation of the McNamara doctrine of "nuclear parity." This is the doctrine that decisive nuclear superiority is unattainable; that neither America nor Russia can ever develop enough strength to destroy the other country without guaranteeing its own destruction in return; and that a condition of rough equality—not in numbers of weapons, but in capacity to destroy—is the best way to stabilize a wretched situation. Mr. Nixon condemns this view. "This 'parity' concept," he has strangely argued, "means superiority for potential enemies. We cannot accept this concept and survive as a free people." "Our objective" must be "clear-cut military superiority."

If Mr. Nixon means this, and the indication is that this is one of the few questions on which he has a fixed position, he plans a big increase in our nuclear weaponry at a time when the United States already has enough explosive power to blow up the planet. He also promises to "restore the goal of a Navy second to none," as if the United States did not at present have a Navy second to none; and he has promised to replace the draft by a professional army—a plan which, however sensible, may well cost an additional $8-billion a year.

Nor will military expansion be confined to offensive weapons. In applauding the Senate decision to go ahead with an antiballistic missile system, Mr. Nixon added, "For the first time, emphasis shifted from countering the potential Communist Chinese missile threat of the early nineteen-seventies, to meeting the clear and present danger to American security posed by the rapid buildup of the Soviet Union's missile forces. . . . The whole rationale for deploying ballistic missile defenses was warped by misplaced emphasis on the distinctly secondary threat which Peking may mount in the future." Instead of the thin Johnson A.B.M. system supposedly directed against China, Mr. Nixon plainly contemplates a major A.B.M. system to be explicitly directed against Russia—a program that would be both enormously expensive and, in its effect on the world's power balance, enormously de-stabilizing.

The insistence on "clear-cut military superiority," whatever that may mean, can only push the nuclear arms race into new and shuddering dimensions. But Mr. Nixon has never shown much concern about nuclear war—not that for one moment he would wish such a war, but rather that, unlike Kennedy, Macmillan and Khrushchev, he seems unable to conceive imaginatively how horrible a nuclear holocaust would be. Once we have achieved our position of strength, then Mr. Nixon proposes to "negotiate" with the Soviet Union through a series of summit conferences.

The Pentagon is already muttering about a defense budget of $102-billion for the next fiscal year. If Mr. Nixon goes down the road of massive increase in military spending, this will mean, of course, a curtailment of Government resources which might be available for other purposes. He has faced this problem with commendable candor. He has said that he intends to cut back even further on foreign aid. And he made clear in a series of speeches in the spring his view that we can afford no more public spending for the cities or for the war against poverty. "The economic crisis confronting America today," he said, "is so acute that it rules out a massive transfusion of Federal funds into the nation's cities. Rather than spending more, the Federal budget must be cut by some $8-billion if the fiscal crisis is to be averted and the dollar itself preserved. . . . It is gross irresponsibility to promise billions of new Federal dollars for the cities, or even for the poor."

What then will he do about the terrifying problems of our national community—the problems of racial injustice, urban decay, poverty, violence and crime? For the United States today is in a state of deep and angry internal division—division between affluent and poor America, between white and black America, between old and young America, between educated and uneducated America. One reason so many of us were so strongly for Robert Kennedy was that his identification with the victims and casualties of our society made him seem the only candidate capable of bridging these gaps and unifying the country.

Mr. Nixon enters this situation with grave handicaps. He is the hero of the possessing classes. He has shown no great concern for, interest in, or curiosity about the alienated classes. During the campaign newspapermen marveled at the absence of black faces in the well-scrubbed, well-dressed Nixon crowds. One doubts whether he understands the full bitterness of our internal divisions or the problems he must overcome before he can hope to pull the country together; one senses here a failure of imagination and sympathy comparable to his attitude toward nuclear war. In this respect, "Nixon on the Issues" is pathetic. It gives 12 urgent pages to a section entitled "Crime," four more urgent pages to "Order" and then two remarkably perfunctory pages to "Civil Rights" and two more to "Poverty." A study of these pages, along with another eight pages on "The Urban Crisis," suggests Mr. Nixon's estimate of our internal crises. He is excited and indignant about crime and violence, "realistic" about poverty and racial injustice.

"At home," he has said, "the top-priority problem is the restoration of law and order." The Supreme Court, he repeatedly charged in the campaign, had given the "green light" to "the criminal elements." (Mr. Nixon will make, it should be noted, four or five Supreme Court appointments in the next four years, probably including the Chief Justice; he has promised to choose "strict constructionists" thoroughly versed in the criminal law and sharing his own theory "of the role some of the decisions of the high Court have played in weakening the peace forces in our society.") Next to foreign policy, Mr. Nixon considers law enforcement his strongest suit. "I myself am going to take personal charge in this field," he has said; and he has even threatened to give law enforcement "the kind of attention" President Johnson "has given to the day-to-day operations of the war in Vietnam"—not perhaps, in view of what happened in Vietnam, an entirely heartening assurance.

More third degrees, more confessions, more wiretapping, more punishment, a tougher Attorney General, a conservative Supreme Court: these comprise the distinctive elements of the Nixon anti-crime program. Oddly enough, his passion for law and order has not led him to favor so elementary a measure as Federal gun registration.

As for the blacks and the cities, Mr. Nixon, having renounced the notion of Federal spending, argues that they can be saved by private enterprise through the use of tax incentives. Now tax incentives have a real, if limited, role to play as one element in an urban policy, though Chairman Wilbur Mills of the House Ways and Means Committee may need some persuasion on this point. But are they a means of relieving the strain on the Federal budget? Of course not: tax revenues transferred in advance to private business are just as clearly Government spending and increase the budget deficit just as much as tax revenues directly received and used by the Government. Evidently Mr. Nixon believes that public funds spent by corporations in their quest for profit will serve public purposes better than public funds spent by Congress and the President. At any rate, his theory is that "private enterprise built the cities of America and given the necessary incentives, private enterprise can rebuild them." He aims to relieve race tensions by promoting "black capitalism"; it will cost "little or no *Government* money," he has said, "to set in motion many of the programs that would start rebuilding a firm structure of Negro economic opportunity."

In addition, Governor Agnew claims that Mr. Nixon is going to give him special responsibilities in the cities. In preparation for this assignment, the future Vice President resolutely declined to waste much time visiting ghettos ("If you've seen one city slum, you've seen them all") or talking to poor people ("You don't learn from people suffering from poverty but from experts who have studied the problem"). He also opined that overcrowding was the cause of slums. Mr. Nixon must have been kidding.

Since the election, Mr. Nixon has wisely altered his emphasis. His top priority now would seem to be the sentiment expressed in the sign at Deshler, Ohio: "Bring Us Together." This approach would appear more productive. But it will obviously require a good many more things than pious exhortation, cops and tax incentives. Because it will take a long time for economic and educational programs to have effect, no President is likely to bring us together who cannot identify himself sufficiently with the alienated groups to make them believe that he is in some sense on their side. Only in this way can he win their forbearance while he defends the processes of peaceful change against disruption and violence and while they wait for the legal and social justice to which they are entitled. Can Mr. Nixon do this? Does he understand the problem?

On the general management of the economy, Mr. Nixon has staked out a position as a conservative Keynesian. "I'm an activist as far as the economy is concerned and the use of fiscal policy to keep it going. To that extent I'm a 'new economist.'" All exponents of the "new economics" believe in increasing Government spending to make up for decline in private spending; liberal Keynesians prefer to have the money spent in the public sector, conservative Keynesians wish to transfer it through tax reduction to the private sector. Mr. Nixon has made clear his rejection of his party's old fetish about an annual balancing of the budget: "What we need is not a mechanically balanced budget, but an intelligently balanced economy." Apparently he has not succumbed to Milton Friedman's faith in the omnipotence of the supply of money and instead would follow more moderate advisers like Arthur Burns and Paul McCracken in placing main emphasis on fiscal policy.

Mr. Nixon will thus be the first Republican President committed to the new economics. Where he diverges from previous Democratic Presidents, however, is in the balance he would strike between the claims of full employment and monetary stability. "The greatest difference between Nixon and Humphrey," as Nixon himself recently put it, ". . . is in our attitude toward inflation." Where Democrats would trade the reduction of unemployment for a limited price rise— say, 2 per cent of the second to bring the first down to 3 per cent— Mr. Nixon, it may be, would prefer to increase unemployment by a percentage point (say three-quarters of a million people) in the hope of holding prices down.

It all depends on whether one's clients are in the middle or working class. There are risks in the Republican approach. The burden of increased unemployment would fall disproportionately on the non-white population; and some might think that the thing least needed in the United States today is more Negro unemployment. Moreover, inducing unemployment can be a tricky operation; it might throw the whole economy into reverse and produce a recession by 1970. Should recession come, Mr. Nixon will undoubtedly try to combat it by tax reduction.

Beyond this, Mr. Nixon, as his secret communiqué to the stock-brokers made clear, intends to cut back on Government regulation of business practices. Also, though in theory opposed to trade barriers, he seems prepared to yield to textile, steel and cattle clamor for a measure of Government protection.

In carrying out economic policy, Mr. Nixon proposes an interesting exercise in the rehabilitation of the venerable Republican opposition to big government. He has invoked the authority of such Kennedy Democrats as Richard Goodwin and Daniel Patrick Moynihan to seek new legitimacy for old slogans about the virtues of decentralization. "We are going to reverse the flow of power to the Federal Government in Washington," he has said, "and channel more power back to the states and localities. Tax sharing, block grants, decentralization, local option, community participation; this is the direction I believe America is about to choose."

This is all heartening. But one fears that Mr. Nixon has missed Senator Robert Kennedy's central point. When Senator Kennedy talked about decentralization he was not talking about the devolution of power to state and local government; he was talking about the creation of "new community institutions that local residents control, and through which they can express their wishes." It is not clear that Mr. Nixon means anything more than transferring resources from a level of government relatively immune to the pressure of local business interests to levels of government dominated by local business interests.

Military spending, up; social spending, down; the national Government on the offensive in the world and in retreat at home: these would seem the indicated directions of the Nixon Presidency. But Presidencies do not always follow indicated directions. Campaign speeches are not covenants with the people. Problems which seem simple on the hustings often acquire new complexity in the oval office. Like every other man elected to the White House, Mr. Nixon will forget as President many things he promised as candidate. This may not be as it should be, but it is as it has been and will continue to be. A man who becomes President promises more than he can ever perform; and, as he comes to recognize this, he must choose among his various hopes and commitments. In 1932 Franklin Roosevelt pledged action and planning and a balanced budget; the first two soon rendered the third unattainable. Mr. Nixon, too, may discover a conflict in his purposes. His manner of dealing with this conflict depends in the end on his qualities as a man.

Some observers comfort themselves by citing Mr. Nixon's well-known flexibility on issues and concluding that it is therefore safe to assume he did not mean a word he said during the campaign. His Presidency, they argue, will be dominated above all by his desire for re-election. He is, if nothing else, an intelligent political animal; and he will therefore know that, if he gets the nation into more Vietnams or into an unlimited arms race or into a depression, he is finished. Accordingly, the argument runs, he will make sure that none of these things happens.

This argument assumes either that Mr. Nixon thinks that fighting Communism or seeking "clear-cut military superiority" or using deflation to keep prices down are politically unpopular objectives; or else that, if he embarked on any one of these policies, he could quickly and efficiently prevent it from going to extremes. Yet Mr. Nixon himself, judging from the emphasis he gave these goals in his campaign, would seem to consider them all rather popular; and, once set in motion, some of these policies might well develop lives of their own. It could therefore easily be that Mr. Nixon, in seeking a second term, might stumble into jingoism, war or depression. Whether or not this happens will depend in part on the galaxy of pressures which surrounds a President, in part on Mr. Nixon's intellectual and psychological responses to pressure. So we are back with the man himself.

Mr. Nixon has always been an elusive figure. Part of this elusiveness lies, I think, in an extraordinary fact about him: that is, his rootlessness. Nearly every other American President has had deep and sturdy roots geographically and socially—Johnson in Texas feudalism, Kennedy in the Eastern aristocracy, Eisenhower in the military world, Truman in the middle border and so on. In contrast, Mr. Nixon, born in California, trained to the law in North Carolina, elected to the Presidency from New York, seems sectionless and classless. His nearest equivalents are the British political leaders Harold Wilson and Edward Heath. Nixon, Wilson and Heath are all products of the mobility of the new technical society; and they carry a particular appeal to those other rootless, sectionless, classless, mobile "new" men who inhabit what J. K. Galbraith has called the "technostructure."

The technostructure has, of course, its hip wing, which in the main followed Senator McCarthy. But its square majority in their suburban foxholes saw themselves happily, if not quite ecstatically, in Mr. Nixon. The highly programmed character of the Nixon campaign faithfully expressed the technical virtuosity of the new men, as the campaign's intellectual emptiness reflected their conviction that technique matters more than substance. Mostly salaried employees, moving from one place to another at the company's behest, they are discouraged by taxes, mortgages, installment debt, social permissiveness and racial integration. Mr. Nixon has called them "the forgotten people . . . those who are not breaking the law, those who do pay taxes, those who do go to work, those who do support their churches and their schools." These "forgotten Americans," Mr. Nixon declared in the campaign, "finally have become angry . . . because they love America and don't like what has been happening to America for the last four years."

Now social mobility is a fine thing. But sometimes it exists at the cost of a sense of inner identity. Rootless people are often quick to feel angry and threatened. Mr. Nixon has never seemed very sure or secure in his conception of himself. He appears easily rattled and panicked. Where others would accept the fortuity of events, he prefers to detect the hand of conspiracy. When the American Communist party named its youth clubs after W. E. B. DuBois, the black historian, Mr. Nixon was sure that the name was chosen because it sounded like the Boys' Club of America, of which he was an official; this, he solemnly said only two years ago, was "an almost classic example of Communist deception and duplicity." Whether or not this is so, it is certainly an almost classic example of Nixon's style of thought.

In particular, Mr. Nixon seems obsessed with the problem of his own response to crisis. This is an odd concern. When crisis came, the Roosevelts and the Kennedys simply met it with patrician nonchalance; these were the expected tests of life, not worth the fuss of extended comment. Nor did crisis, as such, ever worry Harry Truman or Dwight D. Eisenhower. But Mr. Nixon has always worried; he even wrote a book called "Six Crises," as if to find out, or prove, something about himself. As therapy, the book failed, alas, to prepare him for his seventh crisis; a few months after its publication, he gave that famous "last press conference" in which, as he said with exquisite self-pity, "You won't have Nixon to kick around any more." (Mr. Nixon often speaks of himself in the third person, almost as if he had to testify to the fact of his own existence.)

This wavering sense of self no doubt accounts for the recurrent speculation about the emergence of New Nixons. Certainly the Nixon of 1968 seemed, at the start, at least, very different from the rocking, socking, unctuous bully-boy of the fifties. This time he took great care to come on as moderate, judicious, sober, bland. He did not try to visit every state in the union or give several speeches a day. Instead, he severely limited his campaigning, stuck most of the time to a single speech, avoided debates and other adversary situations (he declined all network Sunday interview programs from Nov. 6, 1966, to Oct. 27, 1968) and showed himself in public only in the most rigorously controlled and protected circumstances. In the early weeks he would rush back to Key Biscayne for rest and recuperation whenever pressure mounted. He actually spent the four days of the next to last weekend before the election in the seclusion of his New York apartment.

Republicans had been unhappy about the alleged indolence of Henry Cabot Lodge's Vice Presidential campaign eight years ago. Next to the Nixon of 1968, the Lodge of 1960 seems a whirlwind of activity. But the system of protection had an obvious point this year. Watching Mr. Nixon, or rather looking for him, in the 1968 election, one began to have the sense of a man extremely uptight under his blandness, desperately aware of his own vulnerability to tension and fatigue, desperately determined to conserve his poise and energy. Certainly, whenever he began to tire, the old pattern surged back; the compulsion to reduce issues to personalities; the conviction that he was the target of a conspiracy and that the answer was to identify and punish the individuals wicked enough to thwart his plans.

An early, and comic, example came in his acceptance speech at the G.O.P. convention. After deploring the spread of crime, he boldly said that, when *he* became President, "We are going to have a new Attorney General." Since no one in his senses could have supposed that he intended to keep on President Johnson's Cabinet, this preposterous pledge could only have expressed his passion to personalize issues. More serious perhaps was his promise in October to appoint a Secretary of State "that will join with me in cleaning house in the State Department. . . . It has never been done. . . . It wasn't even done during the Eisenhower Administration." He added, "There are some good men in the State Department, and *I know who they are.*" This last clause, which I have italicized, is good vintage Nixon. Presumably he meant men like Otto Otepka, the McCarthyite bureaucrat for whose plight he soon expressed warm sympathy to The Chicago Tribune. And then there was that odd moment at the end of the campaign when he spoke of unnamed persons in the White House engaged in the nefarious plot of trying to end the Vietnam war. The new blandness seems only skin-deep. Has it really conquered the old paranoia?

No doubt these were only flashes induced by campaign tensions and fatigue. Yet will the Presidency be less tense and fatiguing than the campaign? The question is bound to arise whether Mr. Nixon has the sheer physical and moral vitality to stay on top of his new job and of himself. It will not be so easy now to escape for three days a week to Key Biscayne.

In his speech on the Presidency Mr. Nixon well said, "In order to lead, a President today must listen." The inability to listen was one of the great weaknesses of his immediate predecessor, as the ability to listen was one of the great powers of his predecessor but one. Good listening requires both intelligence and a certain strength of character. Mr. Nixon is said to be intelligent, though one has the impression that his is the lawyer's intelligence which reads briefs and remembers arguments rather than the reflective intelligence which produces fresh personal judgments on hard questions. His mind seems conventional and stereotyped; rarely independent, never original.

Still, he might be able to listen, if he has acquired sufficient character to examine criticism on its merits instead of denouncing the critic as an enemy of the republic. The greatest strength of all lies in the capacity to admit error and change course. But in the past, Mr. Nixon, like many rootless men, has been more given to talking about humility than displaying it. A few weeks ago Mike Wallace of C.B.S. asked him, "Did you commit no political excesses on which you look back with regret?" No, Mr. Nixon said, "throughout my political career I have campaigned only on issues, never on personalities. . . . I have no apologies to make." One fears that a man who could say this will never dare admit he might be wrong.

Still, history remains inscrutable; and for four years Mr. Nixon will be the only President we have. Adam Smith used to say that there was a lot of ruin in a country. If Mr. Nixon tries to carry out his campaign promises, he may afford us ample opportunity to test that proposition. On the other hand, he may come to see that racial justice is not just a matter of law and order or even of making the blacks rich but an issue of supreme moral urgency; that crime may have some relationship to poverty; that, if unassisted private enterprise built the American city, it did a miserable job and must not be permitted to botch things again; that Federal funds must flow into the fight against urban disintegration, against ghettos, against poverty. He may discover, too, that generals are not infallible; that if you already have enough nuclear bombs to blow up the planet, it is not really essential to get enough to blow up the planet twice over; and that the most serious problems in the world require nonmilitary solutions.

If Mr. Nixon can really listen to the diversity of ideas, agonies and hopes in this great and turbulent land, he may yet achieve the capacity to move beyond himself and to serve the nation and the world.

Suggested Reading

Two general studies of the American electorate since the New Deal are Samuel Lubell, *The Future of American Politics,* New York, Harper and Row, 3rd ed. rev., 1965 (Harper paperback); and V. O. Key, Jr., *The Responsible Electorate: Rationality in Presidential Voting, 1936–1960,* Cambridge, Harvard University Press, 1966. Richard Neustadt, *Presidential Power: The Politics of Leadership,* New York, Wiley, 1960 (Signet paperback), examines how our recent Presidents have governed, the interrelation of power and politics, and the difference between "strong" and "weak" Presidents. James L. Sundquist, *Politics and Policy: The Eisenhower, Kennedy, and Johnson Years,* Washington, D.C., Brookings Institution, 1968, analyzes the responses of political and governmental institutions to major domestic issues from 1953 to 1966.

Harry S. Truman's *Memoirs,* 2 vols., New York, Doubleday, 1955 (Signet paperbacks), are useful for the insights they provide into the former President's mind and personality. The best work on Truman's early life remains Jonathan Daniels' *The Man of Independence,* Philadelphia, Lippincott, 1950, while Cabell Phillips, *The Truman Presidency,* New York, Macmillan, 1966, is the most comprehensive history of his administration available. Two necessary books for studying the Truman years are Richard S. Kirkendall, ed., *The Truman Period as a Research Field,* Columbia, University of Missouri Press, 1967; and Barton J. Bernstein and Allen J. Matusow, eds., *The Truman Administration: A Documentary History,* New York, Harper and Row, 1966 (Harper paperback).

President Eisenhower details the success of his two terms in office in *The White House Years: Mandate for Change, 1953–1956,* New York, Doubleday, 1963 (Signet paperback), and *Waging Peace, 1956–1961,* New York, Doubleday, 1965. For a critical view of the General as President, see Emmet J. Hughes, *The Ordeal of Power: A Political Memoir of the Eisenhower Years,* New York, Atheneum, 1963. Arthur Larson, *Eisenhower: The President Nobody Knew,* New York, Scribner's, 1968, provides a new defense of Eisenhower while admitting his shortcomings. Robert J. Donovan, *Eisenhower: The Inside Story,* New York, Harper, 1956, and Sherman Adams, *Firsthand Report: The Story of the Eisenhower Administration,* Harper, 1961 (Popular Library paperback), are also useful works.

Books on the Kennedy-Johnson years are numerous and increasing in number every day. The elections of 1960 and 1964 have been chronicled by Theodore H. White in *The Making of the President 1960,* New York, Atheneum, 1961 (Signet paperback), and *The Making of the President 1964,* New York, Atheneum, 1965 (Signet paperback). Theodore C. Sorensen, *Kennedy,* New York, Harper and Row, 1965 (Bantam paperback), is the best volume by one of the former President's close associates. Arthur M. Schlesinger, Jr., *A Thousand Days: John F. Kennedy in the White House,* Boston, Houghton Mifflin, 1965 (Fawcett paperback), is a well-written but uncritical account. A good anthology is Aida DiPace Donald, ed., *John F. Kennedy and the New Frontier,* New York, Hill and Wang, 1966 (Hill and Wang paperback). An interesting study of the last two Presidents is Tom Wicker, *JFK and LBJ: The Influence of Personality upon Politics,* New York, Morrow, 1968. William S. White, *The Professional: Lyndon B. Johnson,* Boston, Houghton Mifflin, 1964 (Fawcett paperback), is an uncritical portrait by an admiring journalist. Robert Novak and Rowland Evans, *Lyndon B. Johnson: The Exercise of Power,* New York, New American Library, 1966 (Signet paperback), is the fullest account of Johnson's political life. Marvin E. Gettleman and David Mermelstein, eds., *The Great Society Reader: The Failure of American Liberalism,* New York, Random House, 1967 (Vintage paperback), is an excellent, critical collection.

Index

A Note on the Editor

Richard M. Dalfiume is the author of the forthcoming *Fighting on Two Fronts,* a history of the desegregation of the armed forces. Born in San Antonio, Texas, he studied at Louisiana State University, San José State College, and the University of Missouri. He is now Assistant Professor of History at the State University of New York at Binghamton.